Palgrave Studies in Business, Arts and Humanities

Business has much to learn from the arts and humanities, and vice versa. Research on the links between the arts, humanities and business has been occurring for decades, but it is fragmented across various business topics, including: innovation, entrepreneurship, creative thinking, the creative industries, leadership and marketing.

A variety of different academic streams have explored the links between the arts, humanities and business, including: organizational aesthetics, arts-based methods, creative industries, and arts-based research etc. The field is now a mature one but it remains fragmented. This series is the first of its kind to bring these streams together and provides a "go-to" resource on arts, humanities and business for emerging scholars and established academics alike. This series will include original monographs and edited collections to further our knowledge of topics across the field.

Karen Messer

How to Work with Space

Spatial Knowledge in Organizations and Research Practice

palgrave
macmillan

Karen Messer
Concordia University
Montreal, QC, Canada

ISSN 2662-1266 ISSN 2662-1274 (electronic)
Palgrave Studies in Business, Arts and Humanities
ISBN 978-3-031-46540-6 ISBN 978-3-031-46541-3 (eBook)
https://doi.org/10.1007/978-3-031-46541-3

This Palgrave Macmillan imprint is published by the registered company Springer Nature Switzerland AG.
The registered company address is: Gewerbestrasse 11, 6330 Cham, Switzerland

to my loves
Mark and Charlie

Abstract

How to Work with Space draws on relational concepts of physical space as a way of understanding and framing organizational experience. Space is framed as something central and entangled, freeing it from objective, external binaries by positioning it alongside the social, inter-subjective sphere. This cultivates an emplaced, relational, and more-than-human understanding of the emotional, sensory, and atmospheric experiences that happen at work. By tapping into personal experience, spatial theories become intwined with everyday spaces at home and at the office. This subtly shifts the discussion towards what is possible when space is interwoven into day-to-day actions. The book culminates with a case study exploring the aesthetic, sensory, and embodied relationships between a not-for-profit, youth health organization and their office encounters during a significant relocation. By highlighting before and after moments between the staff and their offices, a rich picture of their experience emerges through spatial memory, sensory knowledge, and aesthetic understanding.

Keywords

Office space • Socio-material • Organizational aesthetics • Relational space • Office relocation • Entangled space • Emplaced

Acknowledgements

I am incredibly grateful for the support of Samantha Parsley, Steve Taylor, and Palgrave for transforming these ideas and words into material form and for giving the book a place in the *Palgrave Studies in Business, Arts and Humanities* series. Thanks to Samantha for her enthusiasm and encouragement and to Steve for his consistent guidance.

I owe David Howes distinct gratitude as he has supported this entire journey and generously provided me a home and community at Concordia University's *Centre for Sensory Studies*. Research for this book received funding from Canada's *Social Science and Humanities Research Council* through the Centre's *Exploration in Sensory Design* project (grant No 435-2020-1279).

Thanks to the staff of Head & Hands for allowing me to be a part of your experience and to the old and new offices that were thoughtfully entangled throughout the story.

Many people have sustained and uplifted me over the years in visible and invisible ways, and you are woven into the learning, reflection, spaces, and words. I cannot thank anyone more than my husband Mark; his enduring support, on every level, made this book possible. Thanks to my daughter Charlie for embodying the delight and wonder in our lives so beautifully; Mum and Dad for the foundation, inspiration, and endless love; Myra and Art for consistent support, regular check-ins and timely retreats; various editors: Edwin Janzen, Lori Messer, and Mark Slutsky; advisors Warren S. Linds, and Don de Guerre; and Margot Flores Torre for allowing me to include her photographs of Head & Hands.

Lastly, to our beautiful home, neighbourhood, and all the places in this book that inspired, held, and shaped my experience.

Contents

List of Figures

1

Introduction

I don't really love my office, although it is conveniently located in a decommissioned school directly across the street from my home. The office itself is shabby and shared with four other freelancers, including my husband. The floors are dirty linoleum and there are florescent lights that direct their monotonous glare at me. My studio mates are all nice, but the space is piled high with random boxes of who-knows-what and often feels more like a storage room than a place to work. To access the washroom, we must leave our "classroom" and use the bathroom in the hall. There is no main door, and for a few months last year it was being repaired, which meant there were construction workers everywhere and no privacy. During that time, I walked across the street to use the toilet.

My home on the other hand is a place I love. Architecturally it is beautiful, with large windows along the back and layers of interesting interior cut-outs that create unique shapes and flows. I have spent a lot of time tending the space. There are countless plants, including a large Ficus tree that dominates the living room. Its leaves and branches create constantly morphing shadows on the wall. Each area is filled with little tableaus that work together to create the space. I could fill all my time tinkering with the textures, scents, colours, and forms. Just like a garden, the space

K. Messer, *How to Work with Space*, Palgrave Studies in Business, Arts and Humanities,
https://doi.org/10.1007/978-3-031-46541-3_1

requires constant attention and care. I tend to it, and in return it holds me and my body.

But I cannot work there. Or not usually anyway. I am too drawn into its layers and folds. The fur blanket calls to my coldness, wanting to wrap itself around me as I lay my head on a soft pillow. The sun beams in and warms my face, its light hitting the little hanging crystal blasting dozens of rainbows around the room. They appear on the wall and the floor, subtly mimicking the path of the sun. I listen to the distant calls of the dirty dishes in the sink and let my eyes glaze over the scattered paper bits, coloured markers, a doll's body—her clothes out of sight but nearby—the weeks-old tulips whose petals lie crumpled on the tabletop.

My work ebbs and flows between home and the office across the street. While working on this book, I have thought a lot about these two spaces and how they influence how I write, think, behave, feel, and perceive myself in the world. I pay attention to the different moods I feel in the spaces. There are days when I avoid the office—my entire body pulling me away from the work it contains—only to push past the resistance, walk across the street, and enjoy the writing. Or the way I can dread the housework my home requires one day, and relish in it the next—savouring the scent of laundry, the delicate arranging of fresh flowers, the touch of flannel sheets against my palm—its resonance shifting and changing with the movement of my body.

Writing about space often begins with a thick, sensory description (as I have done in this introduction). Every detail is described at length in an attempt to bring readers into the space. When it is done right, the reader is transported to another world, feeling the light on their cheeks or hearing the birds outside. However, more often, the description fails at bringing the environment into the body. The author, so preoccupied with the space, forgets to include their presence. In these moments, the space remains external: described in detail, yet separate from the bodies that are helping to create it. In focusing on everyday moments *between* space and those who interact with it, the living exchange taking place is more likely to come through. For Kathleen Stewart, who devotes much of her work to *ordinary affects*, these moments are a "collection of trajectories and circuits … glimpsed unsteadily in the light of the present like the flickering light of a candle".[1] These more ephemeral and elusive qualities can be difficult to notice, let alone describe, document, and research, and yet they provide a rich portrait of our spatial nature. I think of them as the entanglements that connect our bodies and minds to its environment.

Setting the Scene

More than ever, researchers are studying every aspect of our physical space. There is detailed information on how lighting, air quality, window access, personalization, layout, colour, and sound can effect worker productivity well-being, stress, communication, innovation, and more. Through wearable technology, companies can track their employees' use of space to an alarming degree. In many ways, this is an exciting time. However, the way this information is collected, coded, and categorized can strip it of its less-quantifiable qualities. Rich and dynamic accounts of how space is experienced and felt lose their resonance, becoming fragments of themselves or removed all together as unwanted variables from the research.

This book is a collection of those unplaceable experiences, ephemeral moments, gut feelings, and spatial memories. It is a response to the increased need for exploration of an experiential, socio-material approach to organizational studies. Drawing on the work of organizational aesthetics[2] and sensory ethnography, *The Entangled Office* is an interdisciplinary look at what the material world offers researchers and organizations. The themes of this book, however, are by no means limited to these groups as they simultaneously exist in how we all attend day-to-day life through the body, memory, senses, imagination, and emotion. While organizations are the focus, the book provides reflective exploration on research and everyday spaces applicable to almost anyone wishing to engage with their surroundings. In fact, much of my own spatial exploration occurs not in the office but at home and in the streets of my community. Exploring

[1] Kathleen Stewart, *Ordinary Affects* (Duke University Press, 2007), 59.

[2] Antonio Strati, *Organization and Aesthetics* (Sage Publications, 1999).

how my perception, as a human and researcher, is entangled with my environment became an all-consuming practice.

One of the goals of this book was to stay open and explore the potential of a relational aesthetic lens without reducing and limiting the scope of the study. My hope was to surface as many nuanced moments and themes as I could so that I, as well as other researchers, academics, and organizations, could understand the breadth of meaning bound within spatial research. While much is written about the theoretical aspects of aesthetic research, there are fewer projects successfully applying the method to convey a "dynamic and performative dimension" of material space.[3] Is it possible to seduce you (the reader) with an evolving rhythm of aesthetic thoughts and moments, by delving into space as something full of possibility, curiosity, wonder, imagination? Can the office be transformed from its status as an exterior container—predicted and controlled—to something more sensuous, alive, and porous?

How to Work with Space is both small and large in breadth. It does not aim to develop new theoretical models or grand truths about the nature of organizational space. It is not about existential or philosophical debates regarding the minutiae of human spatial relations, although I touch on, and draw from, these concepts. Rather the book follows the whimsical explorations of a researcher being-in-the-world, as well as the tale of one organization in two office spaces who acted upon one another and evolved over time. Just as David Abram emphasized, this book attempts to surface the "unnoticed or overlooked presences" so that they may "engage our awareness" and inform our discussion.[4]

This exploration intends to further the practice of understanding physical space through an *emplaced*, *relational*, and *aesthetic* focus within organizational studies. These ontologies help shift our focus from the purely social (human) and the purely material (physical space) into something that is entangled and co-productive—something that is more than the sum of its parts.[5] An *emplaced* orientation situates embodiment—the

[3] Federica De Molli, "An Aesthetic Account of Space: A Report on Recent Developments in Organizational research", *Studi Organizzativi* no. 1 (2019): 18.

[4] David Abram, *The Spell of the Sensuous* (Vintage Books, 1996), 63.

[5] Ibid.

reflective joining of body and mind—through a "sensuous interrelationship of body-mind-environment".[6] David Howes offers *emplacement* as a way of "reposition[ing] ourselves in relationship to the sensuous materiality of the world".[7] Such wisdom, nestled at the intersection of the social and the material, or, more appropriately, the socio-material world, offers rich potential for understanding how spatial "context alters perception".[8] Seeing through an *emplaced* and *relational* perspective highlights this in-between experience,[9] while a *more-than-human* approach draws non-human, material, or ecological perspectives into view.[10] The exploration of employee experience before and after an office move offers insights into the staff's emplaced, sensory, and emotional journey through and alongside the changing and evolving space. As Abram so eloquently outlines, my intention is "not to explain it but simply to pay attention to its rhythms and textures, not to capture or control it but simply to become familiar with its diverse modes of appearance—and ultimately to give voice to its enigmatic and ever-shifting patterns".[11] In a sense, this book represents a momentary act of witness via observation and surfacing of emplaced relationships.

Influence and Evolution

This book began as an effort to grasp the influence and role(s) of office space in an organization's life. Architecture and design have always been of interest to me, particularly their role in how we feel and act. In university, I remember writing a feminist essay on my mother's empowering relationship with her kitchen and how she used a renovation to manifest a supportive space for herself. Through light, location, and materials, her

[6] David Howes, "Introduction", in *Empire of the Senses: The Sensory Culture Reader* (Routledge, 2005), 7.

[7] Ibid.

[8] David Howes, *The Sensory Studies Manifesto* (University of Toronto Press, 2022), 16.

[9] Hilary Bradbury and Benyamin M. B. Lichtenstein, "Relationality in Organizational Research: Exploring the Space Between", *Organization Science* 11, no. 5 (2000).

[10] Abram, *The Spell of the Sensuous.*

[11] Ibid. 35.

kitchen was transformed from a bleak, confining space, into a powerful and beautiful centre of the household. The kitchen became the main floor's focal point and connective tissue, with the entrance, living room, and dining room all radiating outward from it. A large, carved piece of wood encircled the rounded hand-cut countertops, removing any sharp edges. It was lit by windows on all sides (including from above), giving it—and Mum—a radiant quality. Rather than disparage her domestic side, Mum not only embraced it but found power in it, her kitchen.

Years later, after working with Santropol Roulant—a meals on wheels organization—during a major relocation, I began to think more about how space affects and impacts those working within it. In the weeks and months before the move, staff were deeply affected by their emotional attachments to the old building and anxieties around the new space. There was tension between those who were excited and those who felt the need to mourn the old space. Even though the new building had been in the works for many years, and with frequent design consultations, some staff understood the organization would never be the same. To acknowledge the change and loss, I facilitated a candlelit memorial service for staff to share their feelings, memories, and hopes without fear of repercussion. It is an experience I will never forget. After the move was complete, the new premises became even more influential, as decisions regarding future directions for the organization were closely linked to features offered in the new space, such as rooftop gardens, rentable office space, and kitchen workshops. At the time, I was fascinated by how the physical space was contributing to the organization's evolution through macro and micro decisions that were made in relation to the office layout and facilities. However, characterizing space in this way—as an active participant within the organization—was not something I had heard talked about in any organization. Nor was it a topic I had read about in articles in the field of organizational studies.

When space was discussed, it tended to emphasize environmental elements that can be quantified and controlled—such as temperature, window access, air quality, noise, and personalization—or framed objectively, such as employee satisfaction.[12] The focus on office space for knowledge work tends to be on the end state—a finished product that may be assessed and measured. These qualities are common in contemporary business models such as strategic planning, five-year plans, and SMART goals (Specific, Measurable, Achievable, Relevant, and Time-bound). Such approaches stem from the underlying belief that an organization is a "means of ordering, structuring and controlling the chaotic world outside".[13] In this paradigm, spatial research is used to design offices that will yield the best possible results in terms of productivity, production, and, more recently, well-being (inasmuch as it contributes to the former two qualities). Leftover principles from the production line and Frederick Taylor's efficiency-based management style "reflect, to this very day, the dominant values of machine-like organizations"[14] in contemporary office environments. Today's "creative" spaces, with their kombucha fridges and ping-pong tables, may be different aesthetically and culturally, but they ultimately reinforce the same demands: productivity and efficiency.[15] If we frame office space within this paradigm, we may miss some of the more dynamic, nuanced, emotional, or unseen ways in which organizations interact with their environments.

The workplace is more than a room in which to accomplish tasks. Seeing space as an active contributor to how we exist in the world elevates office space out of the realm of the *container* or *stage*—terms that situate physical space outside ourselves as a backdrop to, rather than a contributing element in, what happens. Considering the physical environment as a key component in shaping our existence in the world, with "its own materiality, its own nooks, crannies and folds, aesthetics and ugliness",[16]

---

[12] Guy Newsham et al. "Linking Indoor Environment Conditions to Job Satisfaction: A Field Study". *Building Research & Information 37* no. 2 (2009).

[13] Stewart R. Clegg, Martin Kornberger, & Carl Rhodes, "Learning/Becoming/Organizing", *Organization* 12, no. 2 (2016), 152.

[14] Francis Duffy, "Design and Facilities Management in a Time of Change", *Facilities* 18, no. 10/11/12, (2000): 371.

[15] Karen Dale & Gibson Burrell, "All Together, Altogether Better". In *Organizational Spaces*. ed. Alfons H. van Marrewijk & Dvora Yanow (Edward Elgar Publishing, 2010).

[16] Stewart Clegg and Martin Kornberger, "Organizing Space", In *Space, Organizations and Management Theory*, eds Stewart Clegg and Martin Kornberger (Liber & Copenhagen Business School Press, 2006), 144.

shifts how office space is treated, talked about and, potentially, funded, and researched. While these concepts are commonplace in philosophy, geography, anthropology, and architecture, the interwoven relationships between spatial structures and those who dwell within them are less common in the field of organizational studies.

In this book, no singular, dominant theory underpins the research. Instead, I draw from a combination of philosophies, theories, and concepts to inform the exploration of office space within organizational studies, my own lived experience, and, later, the specific experience of Head & Hands, a youth, not-for-profit, aid organization. In examining an organization's relationship to its physical, material office, there is a unique interdisciplinary opportunity for meaningful relational understanding that combines day-to-day spatial interaction with the office's structures over time. Rather than focus on the quantifiable impacts of physical space, concentrating on more nuanced and embodied interaction with socio-material space will produce a different kind of spatial and organizational knowledge. The value of this knowledge and its uses remains to be seen. As the boundaries blur between social and material dynamics, new questions emerge regarding the process: What is the role of designers in choreographing the social and embodied dimensions of an environment? To what extent is it possible to represent the "symbiotic relationship" between the social and the "environment within which it breathes and mutates"[17] in academic literature? Might a more attuned spatial awareness and recognition shift an environment's connection to, and influence upon, our minds and bodies?

Words, Meaning, and Flow

Before we go further, I will clarify some terms that appear in this book as well as my approach. I use the terms *physical space*, *material space*, and *physical environment* often and interchangeably to denote the tangible, material structures of physical space, as opposed to immaterial

[17] Gavin Turner & Jeremy Myerson, *New Workspace, New Culture: Office Design as a Catalyst for Change*, (Gower Publishing, 1998), 1.

conceptions of space as an invisible field of influence[18] as expressed in terms such as *safe space*, *creative space*, and *open space*, among others. The term *built environment* distinctly refers to a humanly constructed environment, while the *natural environment* indicates the opposite. In this book, I use the terms *space* and *place* interchangeably—since debating these distinctions does not advance the work of *this* investigation—even as others, especially in the field of geography, have stressed their differences[19] and varying meanings.[20] In these domains, *space* more or less becomes *place* after it has been imbued with meaning,[21] although the distinctions and discernments of this transformation are owed more attention than I give them here. On the other hand, a more relevant distinction exists between *objective* and *subjective* qualities of space. Rather than separate—as Ropo et al. have done—the "objective physically observed space (architecture, interior design … and other material aspects) and the subjectively perceived space, that is, how each person perceives the environment with their senses, emotions and cognition",[22] I consider their *intersubjective* state.[23] Drawing from Husserl's notion of intersubjectivity, Abram explains how the objective world exists not through a solid or a fixed state, but from multiple and intermingling perspectives to create a "collective field of experience lived through many different angles".[24] These interwoven subjective experiences, which include the presence of non-human beings and objects, manifest an "ever-shifting fabric, a single phenomenal world or 'reality'".[25] The objective world is discernable not through external reason, but from interwoven, collective perception. In this context, to borrow from Elizabeth Grosz, I "explore the constitutive and mutually defining

[18] Margaret Wheatley, *Leadership and the New Science* (Barrett-Koehler Publishers, 1994).

[19] Yi-Fu Tuan, *Space and Place: The Perspective of Experience* (University of Minnesota Press, 1977).

[20] Arja Ropo, Erika Sauer, & Perttu Salovaara, "Embodiment of Leadership through Material Place", *Leadership* 9, no. 3 (2013): 381.

[21] Tuan, *Space and Place.*

[22] Arja Ropo et al. "Why Does Space Need to be Taken Seriously in Leadership and Organization Studies and Practice" in *Leadership in Spaces and Places*. Eds. Arja Ropo et al. (Edward Elgar Publishing, 2015), 3.

[23] Abram, *The Spell of the Sensuous.*

[24] Ibid, 39.

[25] Ibid, 39.

relations"[26] existing between and within office spaces, organizations, their staff, and research.

In this spirit, I explore what and how the built environment communicates and how we communicate back. *Chapter 2, "Entangled Office Space"*, begins by situating office space research within the current socio-material trends taking place across the social sciences. Considering how space is positioned within organizational research, I explore what is needed to engage with the entangled nature of the socio-material office environment. As office space becomes part of our homes, in cafes, and on Zoom, understanding how we live with and are affected by these spaces becomes even more apparent. This ontological discussion presents space as living, porous, and embedded in day-to-day experience. Questions such as "What happens when we see space as a co-creator in an organization's evolution?" and "How can our perception of physical space contribute to how we move forward as organizational researchers—not simply in terms of office design but how we understand the relationship between people and space?" frame the discussion. With forays into the repercussions of technology on research and as well as recent advances in sensory, emplaced, and aesthetic research, this chapter grounds the ensuing exploration.

Chapter 3, "Writing the Invisible", offers an honest glimpse into my process as a researcher as I explored how to put into words my and others' aesthetic knowledge. Questioning the effectiveness of words to convey nuanced and ephemeral experience, this chapter dives into the ultimate power of words, not only to describe space but also to evoke and co-create it. Drawing from a variety of writers, artists, and academics to explore stories told through text and material spaces, we begin to see space as a contributing character and, in some cases, co-author of the plot. In this sense, the narrative framework becomes an important aspect of experiencing, creating, and documenting our environments. Words and conversations with space can surface qualities of the material world, becoming entwined with our experience of them. Listening to and speaking with space are part of how we perceive and notice our surroundings. This chapter also investigates the potential within the act of noticing as a

[26] Elizabeth Grosz, "Bodies-cities", In *Places Through the Body* (Psychology Press, 1998), 43.

way to attune and acknowledge the material world. This chapter is aimed at reflexive researchers, and practitioners looking at the nuanced ways in which space takes shape in their writing and research. As space is explored on the page, readers (and writers) can simultaneously connect with their own surroundings. Reflecting on how space shows up will transform writing and speaking into spatial practices in and of themselves.

Chapter 4, "Spatial Attunement", shifts the discussion to a more personal and experiential realm. Part autoethnography, part spatial attunement, and part design, this chapter plays with the presence of possibility. Pushing past the notion of organizational space as "controlled, defined and predictable"[27] into more interactive, embodied, and whimsical territory, I explore themes of health, well-being, and support, as well as qualities like potential, hope, and curiosity. Accompanied by spatial reflections of my experiences at home, the discussion shifts into how spaces engage the body, through aspects such as memory, the senses, emotion, and atmosphere. Drawing on my experience with material landscape provides moments of reflection that explore details such as how a cotton nightie transforms the atmosphere into something magical, how a fireplace on a television creates an unexpected warmth, and how the noticing of light and shadow added a depth of presence and awareness. Over time, these explorations in spatial awareness fostered greater attunement and sensitivity to my environments, which ultimately became part of and benefited my research into office space. Throughout this chapter, moments of how we engage and design space offer possible practices and ideas for application and experimentation.

Chapter 5, "Emplaced Research", explores the ontological and methodological implications of including aesthetic and spatial qualities in research. How do we position and attune ourselves to see the world as more-than-human? Building on the conversational aspects of space through emplaced interviews, complementary research methods such as sensory ethnography and photography offer a rich basis for spatial research. In addition to spatial inquiry, this chapter emphasizes the importance of maintaining a socio-material and participatory approach

[27] Stewart R Clegg, Martin Kornberger, & Carl Rhodes, "Learning/Becoming/Organizing", *Organization* 12, no. 2 (2016), 152.

for data analysis. Looking at how spatial moments, emotions, and encounters are presented, the chapter concludes with tangible examples of research studies that manage to keep space at the forefront.

Chapter 6, "Head & Hands Relocation", presents a case study that follows the organization through their office relocation over a period of three years. After a brief introduction to the participants and the research process, this extended chapter presents two parallel narratives. One is the turbulent yet remarkable journey of the staff as they dislocated—physically removing themselves and their departments from a rundown, yet beloved house—and relocated into a newly renovated, intelligently designed space. The other story follows the transition of Head & Hands through a period of disruption and potential, as the organization adapted and reformed itself with and within the new space. Here memories, feelings, and lived experience take centre stage as staff members describe their day-to-day encounters with two unique office spaces. Their experiences were materialized through memories and ghosts, emotions, embodied displacement, well-being and light, sterile coldness, echoes, transition, and camaraderie, as well as feelings of support, pride, and hope. These stories do not represent the experiences of Head & Hands as a singular unit, lived and shared equally by all staff; rather, they offer glimpses from those who participated in entering a myriad of possible relationships and ways of being in the organization's two very different spaces. Drawing from themes explored earlier, this chapter reveals how moments of change and disruption can highlight organizational insight and disrupt patterns through increased aesthetic awareness. Through the staff's diverse "constellation of social [and spatial] relationships", their office is "brought to life".[28]

The case study emphasizes the entangled relationships between organizations and their environments as they shift and evolve over time. As the world grapples with a morphing landscape and the uncertainty of a future office to inhabit, looking at the minutiae of spatial experience offers a rich opportunity to reflect on the collaborative and reciprocal nature of our work environments. This narrative sets out to answer the question posed

[28] Alberto Coursin Jiménez, "On Space as a Capacity", *Journal of the Royal Anthropological Institute* 9 (2003): 139.

in the first chapter: What happens when we see space as a co-creator in an organization's evolution? Head & Hands' emplaced and embodied experiences offered valuable insight into their socio-material relationships. We see how office walls, lighting, and atmospheres permeated bodies, emotions, and behaviour, which ultimately lead to shifts in the perception of current and future programmes. When the physical office is treated as a participant, there is better potential and possibility for actively shifting and shaping experience *in concert with* the material world.

Implications of this shift are considered as they apply to future office work, design strategies, and group processes. This experiential approach to socio-materiality assigns greater value to our surroundings and accords organizations, workers, and researchers' greater agency to engage with it—whether that be at a dining room table, a community hot desk, or traditional office. If the physical world is seen with greater respect, consideration, and influence, what shifts between organizations and offices? Emphasizing the relationship—the stuff in-between—we get a different picture than when space is valued as an end result or finished design. Seeing the material as an unknown part of us makes room for possibilities.

References

Abram, David. *The Spell of the Sensuous.* New York: Vintage Books, 1996.

Bradbury, Hilary and Benyamin M. B. Lichtenstein. "Relationality in Organizational Research: Exploring the Space Between." *Organization Science* 11, no. 5 (2000): 551–564. https://doi.org/10.1287/orsc.11.5.551.15203

Clegg, Stewart R., and Martin Kornberger, "Organizing Space." In *Space, Organizations and Management Theory*, edited by Stewart R. Clegg & Martin Kornberger, 143–162. Liber & Copenhagen Business School Press, 2006.

Clegg, Stewart R., Martin Kornberger, & Carl Rhodes. "Learning/Becoming/Organizing." *Organization* 12, no. 2 (2016): 147–167. https://doi.org/10.1177/1350508405051186

Dale, Karen and Gibson Burrell. "All Together, Altogether Better." In *Organizational Spaces,* edited by Alfons H. van Marrewijk and Dvora Yanow, 19–40. Edward Elgar Publishing, 2010.

De Molli, Federica. “An Aesthetic Account of Space: A Report on Recent Developments in Organizational research,” *Studi Organizzativi* no. 1 (2019): 36–63. https://doi.org/10.3280/SO2019-001002

Duffy, Francis. “Design and Facilities Management in a Time of Change,” *Facilities* 18, no. 10/11/12, (2000): 371–375. https://doi.org/10.1108/02632770010349592

Grosz, Elizabeth. “Bodies-cities,” In *Places Through the Body*, edited by Heidi Nast and Steve Pile, 42–51. Psychology Press, 1998.

Howes, David. “Introduction,” in *Empire of the Senses: The Sensory Culture Reader*, edited by David Howes, 1–17. Routledge, 2005.

Howes, David. *The Sensory Studies Manifesto*. University of Toronto Press, 2022.

Jiménez, Alberto Corsin. “On Space as a Capacity.” *Journal of the Royal Anthropological Institute* 9, no. 1 (2003): 137–153. https://doi.org/https://doi.org/10.1111/1467-9655.t01-1-00008

Newsham, Guy, Jay Brand, Cara Donnelly, Jennifer Veitch, Myriam Aries, and Kate Charles. "Linking Indoor Environment Conditions to Job Satisfaction: A Field Study." *Building Research & Information* 37, no. 2 (2009): 129–147. https://doi.org/10.1080/09613210802710298

Ropo, Arja, Erika Sauer, and Perttu Salovaara. “Embodiment of Leadership Through Material Place.” *Leadership 9,* no.3 (2013): 378–395. https://doi.org/10.1177/1742715013485858

Ropo, Arja, D De Paoli, Peruttu Salovaara, and Erika Sauer. “Why Does Space Need to be Taken Seriously in Leadership and Organization Studies and Practice.” In *Leadership in spaces and places*, 1–24. Edward Elgar Publishing, 2015.

Stewart, Kathleen. *Ordinary Affects.* Duke University Press, 2007.

Strati, Antonio. *Organization and Aesthetics.* Sage Publications, 1999.

Tuan, Yi-Fu. *Space and Place: The Perspective of Experience*. University of Minnesota Press, 1977.

Turner, Gavin and Jeremy Myerson. *New Workspace, New Culture: Office Design as a Catalyst for Change*. Gower Publishing, 1998.

Wheatley, Margaret. *Leadership and the New Science.* Barrett-Koehler Publishers, 1994.

2

Entangled Office Space

Dear Bubble App Team Members,

Good news! In response to your "concerns" about our current open-plan creative campus, we are pleased to announce our new building: a towering panopticon à la Jeremy Bentham's eighteenth-century vision of utilitarian corporate efficiency!

Right now you're probably saying, "Whoa, awesome sauce!" or "Jeremy who?" Let us explain.

In our new office, all team members will work in isolated, transparent rooms called "Cells" on the periphery of a circular tower called "Synergon." At the center of Synergon, management will reside in "Nest," a glowing, elevated sphere of omniscience. …

—Alex Baia (for McSweeney's (2017)).[1]

For many years, efficiency, productivity, and cost dominated the rationale and motivation for office space research and amendments. As a result, these considerations seeped into the design, construction, and use of the office. Over the past few decades, how healthy organizations are

[1] Alex Baia, "Our Open-Plan Office Failed, so We're Moving to a Towering Panopticon", *McSweeney's*, September 27, 2017: https://www.mcsweeneys.net/articles/our-open-plan-office-failed-so-were-moving-to-a-towering-panopticon

K. Messer, *How to Work with Space*, Palgrave Studies in Business, Arts and Humanities,
https://doi.org/10.1007/978-3-031-46541-3_2

described and characterized in management literature has shifted. The metaphors used metamorphosized from tightly controlled machines (predict and control) to large families (leadership over management) to evolving organisms (resiliency and adaptation).[2] These are new definitions that, in practice, should shift how organizations operate, evolve, and interact with their physical space. However, the fundamental shifts taking place in organizational management are not always accompanied by shifts in office space. Or rather, the spatial shifts taking place are not in alignment with systemic or cultural trends. The rise of independent co-working spaces, cafes-as-office, work-from-home mandates, and the advance of online workspaces has generated an adaptable atmosphere that companies are desperate to integrate, but not sure how. With the rise of wearable technology and computer monitoring services, new data is emerging that gives companies precise information on the way employees are using their space and time. In fact, there has never been more data on our daily interaction and bodily responses to our surroundings. However, how this information is translated, understood, and applied remains uncertain. *Is the picture it paints the correct one?*

Sensory, emotional, and cultural qualities of the material world have often been neglected by organizational scholars until more recently, with Pascale Gagliardi[3] making the claim in 1990 and Clegg and Kornberger in 2006[4]—however, office space itself has never been completely disregarded. Interest in workspace has existed since offices in their modern form were first established in the late 1800s, with Taylor and Ford studying industrial efficiency and architects like Frank Lloyd Wright and Mies van der Rohe cementing the contemporary design in the early to mid-1900s. Movements like the Bürolandschaft (German for "open office") emerged in the 1950s; these were followed about twenty years later by the rise of cubicles and modular walls.[5] While this evolution is fascinating, these trends do not always reveal the way space is researched,

[2] Frederic Laloux, *Reinventing Organizations,* (Nelson Parker, 2014).

[3] Pasquale Gagliardi, *Symbols and Artifacts,* (Routledge, 1990).

[4] Stewart Clegg & Martin Kornberger, "Organizing Space", In *Space, Organizations and Management Theory,* (Liber & Copenhagen Business School Press, 2006).

[5] See Gideon Haigh's *The Office: A Hardworking History* for a comprehensive look on the history of office space culture and design.

portrayed, and given meaning within organizational studies. For that we need to look at how space is conceptualized and understood from a relational and ontological perspective.

For many years, space was considered a fixed container—a box or a stage within which things happen. This paradigm places space as external to those working within it, a mere backdrop to the work being done. The environment is considered separate from the people and their social interactions, which remain distinct and isolated from the material realm. As more and more organizations noticed the impact space can have on employee well-being and productivity, space moved out of the shadows to become more integrated with "specific organizational goals".[6] The physical office itself became connected to organizational values and goals such as creativity,[7,8,9] organizational change,[10,11,12] and productivity,[13] among others. New knowledge that office layout can impact human interaction[14,15] led companies to completely redesign their work environment to create more spontaneous contact between employees.

---

[6] Frederica De Molli, "An Aesthetic Account of Space: A Report on Recent Developments in Organizational Research", *Studi Organizzativi* 1, (2019): 40.

[7] Yuri Martins, "Creative Workplace: Instrumental and Symbolic Support for Creativity", *Facilities* 29 no. 1/2 (2011).

[8] Graham Drake, "'This Place Gives Me Space': Place and Creativity in the Creative Industries", *Geoforum* 34, no. 4 (2003).

[9] James Moultrie et al., "Innovation Spaces: Towards a Framework for Understanding the Role of the Physical Environment in Innovation", *Creativity and Innovation Management* 16, no. 1 (2007).

[10] George Cairns, "Seeking a Facilities Management Philosophy for the Changing Workplace", *Facilities* 21, no. 5/6 (2003).

[11] Francis Duffy, "Design and Facilities Management in a Time of Change", *Facilities* 18 no. 10/11/12 (2000).

[12] van Marreqijk, "Corporate Headquarters as Physical Embodiments of Organisational Change", *Journal of Organizational Change Management* 22, no 3 (2009).

[13] Derek Clements-Croome Ed. *Creating the Productive Workplace,* 2nd ed. (Taylor & Francis, 2006).

[14] Bill Hillier & Alan Penn, "Visible Colleges: Structure and Randomness in the Place of Discovery", *Science in Context* 1 (1991).

[15] Bill Hillier, "Space and Spatiality: What the Built Environment Needs from Social Theory", *Building Research & Information* 36, no. 3 (2008).

While the excessive implementation of open-concept offices has led to ongoing loathing and criticism,[16] nothing has rattled the office more than the global Covid-19 pandemic. While millions of workers were abruptly forced to set up an office at home (for months, if not years), the return to work outside the home has been slow to materialize. This lack of enthusiasm to repopulate the office has been labelled, by some, as the death of the office,[17] foretelling a new era of online work environments.

The pandemic highlighted how shifts in location can drastically change our experience of work. Regular tasks became less exact, less predictable, more fluid, and more embodied as the pandemic landscape transformed work conditions. Working from home can be extremely convenient, offering more flexibility to incorporate downtime and other demands. It can also be exceptionally difficult (as it was for me), when the rooms of a home are shared with kids or roommates and the kitchen table cannot become a temporary office. In addition to new location and decor, the home office brought laundry, home-cooked meals, errands, kids, or pets into work, or rather it brought work into them. These evolving variables and variations change what is smelled, tasted, heard, and touched, which in turn shifts how we interact with work and the space. Space is not just a place *where* work happens, but a key ingredient in shaping and experiencing that work.

Many people have not, nor do they wish to return to the office. Some people have no choice but to return. For others, coming into an empty office to sit in Zoom meetings all day because the rest of your team is at home does not benefit anyone. Taking the time to understand why workers come to the office and when they need to be there will go a long way in utilizing and shaping the space.[18] While most knowledge work

[16] Lindsey Kaufman, "Google got it Wrong. The Open-Office Trend is Destroying the Workplace", *The Washington Post* (December 4, 2014).

[17] Catherine Nixey, "The Death of the Office", *The Economist,* April 29, 2020: https://www.economist.com/1843/2020/04/29/death-of-the-office

[18] If you want an in-depth look at hybrid work trends, Charlie Warzel and Anne Helen Petersen explore the benefits and pitfalls of where we work in their book *Out of Office: The Big Problem and Bigger Promise of Working from Home* (2021).

can be done from just about anywhere, what is significant in this context is how the organization and the workers and their space impacts these decisions.

Controlling Design

A few years ago, as I scanned headlines for interesting offices, I came across a slick, black website promoting 444 South Flower, a recently renovated forty-year-old high-rise in downtown Los Angeles. The main page fades in with the slogan "defining the art of workplace" before transitioning to a slideshow featuring pictures of sleek facades, green roofs, and shiny interiors. The website aims to sell more than a new office space; the story it presents provides onlookers with a vision of what is possible.

This vision can be seen and felt on the sixth floor, which is home to the Workspace Innovation Lab. Grab a beer, flop into a hammock or atop an oversized bean bag, and feel the warm breeze on your neck as you listen to a babbling brook. Walk through the space and you will encounter a variety of scenarios—office layouts and workstations meant to lure young, prospective businesses to the building. The lab features soundproof pods, a massive outdoor common space, responsive ambient speakers that use algorithms to listen to and modify sound production, video screens showcasing numerous nature scenes, and an ocean scent wafting through the space.[19] The art of the workplace, it seems, is a carefully orchestrated *mise en scène* designed to dazzle the senses.

Meanwhile, billion-dollar technology companies have built Disneyland-like compounds with flamboyant services catering to their employees' every want and need. While most of us do not work at these types of extravagant offices, they nonetheless play an important role in our conception of the office. At Invention Land, a product development company self-described as an "invention factory", the office space seems like a choose-your-own-adventure story, offering employees their choice

[19] Amoreen Armetta "Workplace Innovation Lab Hacks Aging LA Building to Attract Young Companies", *Dornob*, November 21, 2018: https://dornob.com/workplace-innovation-lab-hacks-aging-la-building-to-attract-young-companies/

of workspace in a pirate ship, a treehouse, or a cottage in the woods. The symbolism of fun and play loom large in pictures of the office. It seems more like a place I would take my daughter to play than go to work. Similarly, Google's office in Tel Aviv, designed by Camenzind Evolution, provides employees with dozens of unique spaces catering to different moods or work demands. There are what look like forested rooms with trees that create dappled light on the picnic tables; another room has a beach vibe with underwater blues and surfboards on the wall, entrance into which can be gained from the floor above through a tubular slide. This detailed attention to the needs of their employees could be admired, or perhaps these expensive and playful trends are nothing more than corporate signaling. While these spaces may symbolize fun, their colourful and diverse settings do not necessarily equate to a positive work environment. As employees' initial delight—at the novelty of office bars, sleep pods, pool tables, and free breakfast, lunch, and dinner—cools down, questions may surface around the true motivation for these perks. In one study of these work environments, Karen Dale and Gibson Burrell speak of several consistent themes in corporate makeovers and new design, such as "play or fun at work … the employee as consumer, the workplace as home, and the workplace as community",[20] that act to manifest specific work habits, interaction, and behaviour.

In addition to the desire for employees to be more devoted and work more flexible hours, Dale and Burrell explore ways in which "materiality is incorporated in social control" and how these are "enacted and embodied" repeatedly from day to day.[21] This faux-horizontal community, rooted in spaces referred to as villages, towns, or neighbourhoods, is simultaneously "linked with other forms of control" used to benefit the corporation.[22] However, the material nature of this type of influence makes the power behind it trickier to identify. With each colourful theme and quirky layout discretely reinforcing the bureaucratic hierarchy embedded within, there must be caution against letting these signs go

[20] Karen Dale and George Burrell, "All Together, Altogether Better", In *Organizational Spaces,* eds. Alfons H. van Marrewijk and Dvora Yanow (Edward Elgar Publishing, 2010), 20.

[21] Karen Dale, "Building a social materiality: spatial and embodied politics in organizational control", *Organization* 12 no. 5 (2016), 651.

[22] Dale and Burrell, "All Together" (2010), 26.

unnoticed. In their exploration on *fun* workplaces, Samantha Warren and Stephen Fineman equate these developments to "wider social expectations about warm, friendly, conditions of work and the importance of 'all things fun' in everyday life".[23] As more offices begin to morph into highly designed and structured spaces with nuanced symbolism and embedded values, it is important to understand the relationships with and within these spaces.

Optimal Space

Well-designed buildings are considered an investment as they are connected to reduced absenteeism, healthier and happier employees, and—bottom line—increased productivity.[24] This stark bottom-line thinking has driven many studies on office space in organizational studies. While different types of research are necessary to examine the various ways in which an office's environmental factors affect those working within it, the correlative model of *perfect space equals perfect workers* is flawed. For one thing, much of the information being collected to create optimal spaces comes from measurable and quantifiable environmental factors: temperature, lighting, air circulation, noise levels, required distance to a window. While understanding how hot a large office might get in the summer is a significant factor for architects and engineers when designing a building, to solely frame our interaction with space in such terms can reduce or simplify what optimal space entails. We can see it in the mystery of a new space that is expertly designed and executed but does not feel right. We have all walked into rooms that should, by all measures, be wonderful but are not.

Part of that problem might be missing knowledge. Instead of being valued and explored, outlying experiences (or bodies) in research are often considered an unwanted nuisance. In a study comparing participants' evaluation of their office's thermal environment to that of another

[23] Samantha Warren and Stephen Fineman, "Don't get me Wrong, it's fun here, but…". In *Humour, Work and Organization*, eds. Robert Westwood & Carl Rhodes (Routledge, 2007), 93.

[24] Clements-Croome, *Creating the Productive Workplace*, (2006).

building, alongside a record of both spaces' actual temperatures, researchers presented participants' lived experiences as untrustworthy, exaggerated complaints in regard to a building deemed to be—according to *objective* analysis—perfectly adequate and comfortable. Their conclusion suggested that "the occupants, rather than the building, may be the problem".[25] While obtaining accurate measures of a building's thermal environment to achieve a comfortable temperature is important—especially as comfort standards historically have been based on men dressed in full suits[26]—dismissing the lived experiences of those working within it as little more than "lengthy" and "emotional" responses from participants "predisposed to complain" is unhelpful and disrespectful.[27]

A more interesting conclusion, perhaps, would discern possible correlation between an employee's state of mind and their embodied assessment of the workspace's thermal environment. How fascinating that perceived temperatures can change or feel different depending on mood and environmental qualities such as lighting, glare, and noise (all of which were mentioned in participant response notes). The temptation to clean confusing, emotional, and subjective experience because the participants' perceptions differ from the study's standardized metrics leads research on human subjects into unhelpful and potentially unethical territory. While it is understandable that not all research can detail the human experience with a sensitivity and diversity, the straightforward expression of the office environment in management literature may well contribute to its reputation as insignificant.

Surveys and questionnaires that require people to objectively assess environmental factors deemed to be quantifiable, such as lighting, temperature, acoustics, or air quality, impose an unstated condition that the body's internal systems of measurement and assessment be immune to emotional variance. The very assumption that a person would experience

---

[25] Max P Deuble & Richard J de Dear, Is it Hot in Here or is it Just Me? Validating the Post-Occupancy Evaluation. *Intelligent Buildings International* 6, no. 2 (2014): 128.

[26] See Boris Kingma & Wouter van Marken Lichtenbelt, Energy consumption in buildings and female thermal demand. *Nature Climate Change* 5, no. 12 (2015).

[27] Deuble, Max Paul, and Richard John de Dear, "Is it Hot in Here or is it Just Me? Validating the post-occupancy evaluation", *Intelligent Buildings International* 6, no. 2 (2014): 127.

the same space repeatedly, in exactly the same way, completely strips their way of being of its emotional and evolving nature. To then discredit individuals' evaluations as subjective or affected—as though their inability to monitor environmental levels correctly and effectively is an inherent malfunction—is a failure to appreciate the complex relationships between people and their environments.

Working with Technology

Data, whether collected by a person or a computer, is neither impartial nor separate from the culture-specific scientific paradigm within which it exists.[28] A smartphone application capable of tracking one's every movement, or a watch that synchronizes with one's heartbeat and body temperature, provides a wealth of user data heretofore incomprehensible. As research is supported and perhaps driven by recent technological advances, it is relevant to understand how the process is impacting meaning, results, and our bodies.

These developments are simultaneously exciting and terrifying. Being able to base decisions on current data is crucial, especially when it comes to our health. However, our contemporary obsession with numbers has led businesses to become increasingly reliant on data by "utilizing analytics to guide strategic decision-making and automate coordination".[29] These processes shift the culture as decision-making and value signifiers change over time. It is important to understand how data is being used, and how it is shaping organizational life through our encounters with it.[30] Having too much data can have a similar "debilitating effect on organizational decision-making" as not enough information.[31] As data sets pile on top of more data sets, it can be hard to see the meaning in the numbers. Incorporating research and analysis into organizational operations can

[28] David Howes, Ed. *Empire of the Senses: The Sensory Culture Reader* (Routledge, 2005).

[29] Adam Saifer & M. Tina Dacin, "Data and Organization Studies: Aesthetics, Emotions, Discourse and our Everyday Encounters with Data", *Organization Studies 43* no. 4 (2022), 624.

[30] Ibid.

[31] Stefan Schwarzkopf, "Sacred Excess: Organizational Ignorance in an Age of Toxic Data", *Organizational Studies* 41, no. 2 (2020): 198.

aid groups in gaining a deeper understanding of their processes and results; however, when the data collector is fitted around your wrist, tracking your body, your heartbeat, and every link you click, it becomes personal. As these devices deliver unprecedented insight to management, it becomes increasingly important to build our knowledge around how data is being used and collected.

Wearable sensors are now available to collect information about employees' movements and interactions in the workplace. Microphones embedded in ID cards record how often each employee speaks during meetings or with colleagues. One such method, developed by Boston-based company Humanyze, collects information that is intended to help improve organizational effectiveness by "understanding their people".[32] These devices, known as Sociometric® Badges, can capture face-to-face interactions, extract social signals from speech and body movements, and measure users' proximity and location. Problematizing human observation and surveys as "subjective, inaccurate, and time consuming", Humanyze touts its products' exactness of measurement and feedback regarding real-time social behaviour.[33] Confronted with such intimate numbers, underperforming employees may take steps to boost the level or quality of their interactions. Overtime this type of tracking and reporting may "foster a paradigm of habitual performance self-management"[34] as part of the organizational culture.

In a research paper published by two of the company's founders, the message is clear: for organizations to be truly *sensible*, they must "start deploying hundreds or thousands of wireless environmental and wearable sensors capable of monitoring human behavior".[35] Having access to this information means that changes to the workplace can be understood and utilized almost immediately. Based on information gathered using Humanyze sensors, one consulting firm in St John's, Newfoundland,

---

[32] www.humanyze.com

[33] Daniel O Olguin et al. "Sensible Organizations: Technology and Methodology for Automatically Measuring Organizational Behavior", *IEEE Transactions on Systems, Man, and Cybernetics, Part B (Cybernetics) 39,* no. 1 (2009): 46.

[34] Bjorn Nansen, "Step-Counting: The Anatom- and Chrono-Politics of Pedometrics", Continuum: Journal of Media & Cultural Studies 22, no. 6 (2008): 799.

[35] Olguin et al. "Sensible Organizations", 43.

discovered that its workers took less breaks when working in brightly lit cubicles.[36] At a Bank of America call centre, after Humanyze recommended that employees take their breaks at the same time rather than intersperse them, productivity rose by 20%, while stress levels decreased by 19%.[37] Monitoring factors such as employee conversation rates, email efficiency, Internet usage, and number of breaks taken all form part of an effort to make companies become more productive. While some interventions may have positive outcomes, this invasive means of observation, intended to perfect efficiency and production, echoes surveillance techniques of industries past (just no longer on the factory floor). Indeed, it is not a stretch to suggest that while "factory organization enabled certain kinds of surveillance, digital technology enables others".[38] As these devices become entangled in our behaviour, control and scrutiny are embedded in the body's movement, speech, and interaction. Overtime, organizational "experience and rhythms" are increasingly formed by these data-feedback technologies.[39]

As Humanyze implies on its website, technologically based research is portrayed as superior to human data collection. This sentiment is directed both towards the researchers, in regard to their inherent bias and the limits of their ability, and the participants, in regard to their awareness of their own behaviour. In many cases, data that is technologically gleaned is collected without a research participant's full awareness—through skin temperature, eye movement, and unconscious behaviours—which may yield very different results than verbal responses to questions on the same subjects. This type of information has many applications and real value; however, it can also easily place the researcher in an imbalanced position relative to the participant. When the gleaning of data depends on one's unconscious choices or actions, the participant's conscious views may be considered less trustworthy or even

[36] Tara Kimura, "How New Data-Collection Technology might Change Office Culture," *CBC News,* September14, 2015: http://www.cbc.ca/news/technology/how-new-data-collection-technology-might-change-office-culture-1.3196065

[37] Ibid.

[38] Calle Rosengren and Mikael Ottosson, "Employee Monitoring in a Digital Context", in *Digital sociologies,* eds J. Daniels, K. Gregory, & T. M. Cottom (Policy Press, 2017), 182.

[39] Nansen "Step-Counting", 799.

invalid. This becomes problematic if research participants lose their agency and are thereby downgraded to a level of research subject. Placing the researcher in such a position of authority harkens back to the kind of research that is practiced *on* humans rather than *with* them.[40] In today's technologically advanced research environment, the technology itself is taking the seat of authority.

As more employees enter hybrid models of work, either moving between the office and home or fully away from the office, such methods of digital tracking and observation will no doubt accompany them. With homes and cafes becoming offices, tracking programmes and wearable devices easily slide into "Orwellian" spyware territory to erode privacy.[41] Employees now are tracked in almost every industry. In addition to the problematic ethics underpinning big data collection is that how we behave when being monitored changes.[42] When given unmonitored time and space, workers "do more trial-and-error learning, they're more willing to make mistakes in private".[43] Happy accidents have long been touted as one of the key ingredients in innovation and creativity, but it is not the same when every minute of your time is being documented and reviewed. Knowing that every website you click on, or every time you leave your computer, is tracked can have a considerable impact on how you work, while simultaneously "warping the foundations of time and trust" at work.[44] What do we lose when untracked offline work—face-to-face conversations, idle thoughts or brainstorms, bathroom breaks, creative problem-solving—forces employees to choose only the most visibly productive ways of working?

---

[40] John Heron and Peter Reason, "The Practice of Co-operative Inquiry: Research 'with' rather than 'on' people", in *Handbook of Action Research: Participative Inquiry and Practice*, (London: SAGE Publications, 2001).

[41] Tara Kimura, "Too Orwellian? Companies monitoring personal time, for 'self-improvement,'" *CBC News,* September 15, 2015: http://www.cbc.ca/news/technology/too-orwellian-companies-monitoring-personal-time-for-self-improvement-1.3196321

[42] Jodi Kantor and Arya Sundaram, "The Rise of the Worker Productivity Score", *New York Times*, August 14, 2022: https://www.nytimes.com/interactive/2022/08/14/business/worker-productivity-tracking.html

[43] Kimura, "Too Orwellian?" para. 8.

[44] Kantor & Sundaram, "Worker Productivity", para. 17.

When considering data collection at this scale, we must ask: *Who is doing the tracking?* It has been argued, for example, that big data must be evaluated through a lens of colonialism as it mimics the "predatory extractive practices" of the historical reality.[45] As those forces that can harness these resources as a commodity gain power and wealth, the remaining population navigates a society and workplace increasingly influenced and shaped by (their own) data and technology (think Facebook or Amazon). Increasingly, employers are choosing to have employees work entirely from home to capitalize on the cost savings of less real estate and increased efficiency that is ultimately "shouldered by you".[46] While working from home is considered a coveted perk by many knowledge workers, the reality can be less noble. Remote work often comes with the promise of flexibility, "but in practice it capitalizes on the total collapse of work-life balance".[47] As work moves into your home, it slowly creeps into every aspect of your life. Rather than have more time for laundry, kids, and errands, those tasks are done under the looming umbrella of work.

Embodied Technology

Since it is hard to escape technology's growing influence and availability, let's consider its role in producing data and how that information is relied on. With the proliferation of technology at work and in the home, many everyday tasks and knowledge are being filtered through digital platforms. In *A Sensory Education*, Anna Harris draws our attention to the intimate entanglement of home life, sensory knowledge, and technology. She uses new parents as an example of the ways in which technology has infiltrated parenting to create "a digital-sensory kind of noticing … embedded with the digital infrastructures".[48] As a parent, this was something I related to immediately. In the days after our daughter was born,

[45] Nick Couldry and Ulises A Mejias, "Data Colonialism: Rethinking Big Data's Relation to the Contemporary Subject", *Television New Media* 20, no. 4, (2019), 337.

[46] Charlie Warzel & Helen A Peterson, "Out of Office: Unlocking the Power and Potential of Hybrid Work" (New York: Alfred A. Knopf, 2021), 4.

[47] Ibid.

[48] Anna Harris, *A Sensory Education* (New York: Routledge, 2021), 90.

we were asked to log feeding times, diaper changes, and naps to create a record and an eventual schedule. At first, it seemed unnecessary and too calculating, but when a nurse stopped in to ask specific questions about how often the baby fed and which breast, I (and my sleep-deprived brain) quickly realized the benefit of keeping track. Soon I was able to view my daughter's days on a colourful graph that showed her tendencies and rhythms. My delusional exhaustion seemed justified after seeing the number of times she (and I) was up at night.

Baby monitors with night-vision cameras allow parents to see in the dark, while simultaneously tracking the baby's breathing rate and body temperature. These devices as well as online social platforms dictate how and when parents interact with their babies. Harris argues that these technologies "can never be separated from sensing" as they are now "embedded in the socio-material landscape".[49] As digital data entwines itself with our body's system of sensing and knowledge formation, it has the potential to enhance our understanding of the world, but at the same time it could "hinder or subvert" our capacities.[50] While a baby monitor that detects breathing is attractive to new parents concerned with the unimaginable consequences of Sudden Infant Death Syndrome (SIDS), there is in fact little scientific evidence to support the effectiveness of such monitoring. In this case, the technology may in fact distract from building tacit knowledge over time through a misplaced trust in assistive devices. With less hands-on learning, will parents know how to detect a fever on the back of their hand?

Deborah Lupton and Sarah Maslen believe that technology's presence on human bodies, which works to "datafy sensory perceptions and experiences", has the potential to create "unprecedented" forms of personal knowledge through self-monitoring.[51] In other words, rather than displace sensory knowledge, the "recursive engagements" between embodied, sensory experience *and* technology offer enhanced learning and awareness.[52] In this scenario, the parent's hand on the fevered child's

[49] Ibid.

[50] Ibid.

[51] Deborah Lupton and Sarah Maslen, "The More-than-Human Sensorium: Sensory engagements with digital self-tracking technologies", *The Senses and Society* 13, no. 2, (2018), 190.

[52] Ibid. p. 191.

forehead not only feels a fever but, in combination with a digital temperature, aids their ability over time to differentiate between 38 and 40 degrees Celsius (101–104 Fahrenheit). What seems essential with the adoption of a self-tracking device is the engagement with it, not as a replacement of our own sensory monitoring, but as an interesting contrast or comparison. As people make sense of the data they are given, it is up to them to "decide how valid or valuable it is" which depends on the knowledge already stored in our bodies.[53] This "sensemaking" is interactive and iterative—"an ever-emergent enactment of human-non-human relations".[54] For women in particular, tracking apps and devices can provide great insight into bodies' rhythms and cycles traditionally left out of the male medical gaze. From this angle, there is possibility and enhancement to fend off a future of technology's domination and erasure of our tacit, sensory knowledge. As organizations and organizational research no doubt continues to incorporate and rely on technological advances, we must advocate for individual participants to engage and work in tandem with the data to co-produce new knowledge.

Situating Work

Whether people are working at home, in a car, at a hot-desk, or online in digital environments, the emergent and routine connection between mind–body, technology and environment are entangled in their work, behaviour and emotion. With the rise of Zoom and other online meeting platforms, participants are faced with multiple layers of screens and space.

Despite being referred to as placeless, perhaps due to a lack of common in-person space, working virtually is anything but. In fact, perhaps it is the multiplicity of spaces—vis-à-vis multiple screens and reflections—that can feel disorienting. While the body is situated *in-place*, that place may be hidden to those on the other end of the screen or modified to project an alternative image. If that is the case, there are now two (if not more) places engaging with the mind–body. There is the room I am

[53] Ibid. p. 192.

[54] Ibid. p. 198.

currently sitting in, as well as the place I can see my digital body inhabiting, which may be a replica or simulation; I can be sitting in a small windowless basement, while meeting others in a glorious sunroom, dappled with light and draped with vines. Which space contributes to how I am feeling and speaking? Both? What about the places my meeting participants are streaming in from? How do those places influence our call?

During a recent Zoom meeting, I commented on the beautiful home of the person I was speaking with only to discover it was not his home at all but a background picture. He took down the image to reveal his real location, his home during a renovation, and I will admit to feeling a little deceived and unsettled. I was meeting this person for the first time, and while their environment does not necessarily reveal *essential* information, it does affect them and our interaction—even through a screen. If we had been on a phone call, where no faces, bodies, or surroundings are visible, our imagination fills in the gaps—in some contexts, we might describe our surroundings. Working from home has thrust our private surroundings into an observable domain. Whether someone is forced to work from home or requests it, finding a place to set up your computer is not as simple as settling into the most comfortable spot in your house. The space you choose to work surrounds you physically and energetically and projects a sort of spatial communication.

The atmosphere of a Zoom call or meeting becomes the merging of multiple projected spaces, facial expressions, tone, and language—many of which are constantly changing. As more and more meetings and conversations are being held virtually, we are becoming more aware of our projected image, which often includes our home. The words of an expert may seem less reliable if they are sitting in a dirty chair or surrounded by mess. Our environment can affect the perception of ourselves too, and how we feel in and about a certain space can impact our work and our ability to perform tasks. That does not mean my environment determines my success or outcome, but it does become part of it.

Even before Zoom provided infinite worlds to inhabit with their endless options of background slides, efforts to control or contort our image were in play; think of a person who wears a dress shirt and jacket all the while covertly hiding their pyjama bottoms below the sight line; or a highly decorated wall of a room that is not congruent with of the rest of the house. During Canada's latest federal election, I sat in my living room and watched a panel of political pundits all of whom were at home sitting in front of bookshelves, in which every book was sorted by colour. Scrolling through the popular Twitter account Room Rater, you can find hundreds of screenshots featuring people and their backdrops along with the site author's critique of the aesthetic and a 1–10 rating. While this is a comic commentary on real-life Zoom backgrounds, it succeeds in pointing out the aesthetic importance of these spaces. In a recent *New York Times* article, Ronda Kaysen speaks to the struggle of maintaining this open window into our private lives.[55] She writes: "Sure, great lighting can make your complexion sparkle, but at some point you might want to shut the camera off because you can't control all that your co-workers witness, or how they interpret what they see". This sentiment morphs into additional energy required to maintain a certain neutral or professional image. Kaysen spoke with Roshni Raveendhran, an assistant professor in Virgina, who "pointed out that video is data—data about you that other people are assessing, whether or not they intend to". All encounters can be understood as information exchanges, as we work consciously and unconsciously to interpret various symbolic, non-verbal, cultural, or spatial cues. If your co-worker has a chaotic home, could that be a quality of their work too? If your co-worker had time to colour code their books, why didn't they finish the report?

For those who don't have access to the perfect space, a quick google search for Zoom backgrounds pulls up dozens of pristine office backdrops. After clicking on a few pictures, I quickly find myself on a website of luxury real estate imagery designed to provide the professional charm and demeanour I may have lost with a kid running around and the dirty dishes in the sink. I can choose between a swanky, modern apartment with a floating staircase and floor-to-ceiling windows; a cozy library office, complete with a leather armchair and fireplace; or a work–vacation vibe, with a Tuscan villa, sunken pool, and palm tree. But even with a fake backdrop, a message is being sent.

[55] Ronda Kaysen, "For Weary Workers, Video Backdrops Are Becoming Too Close and Personal", *New York Times* Online, April 22, 2022.

Entangled in the Material

The recent focus on virtual spaces doesn't mean that the "actual" places we surround ourselves with don't merit consideration—indeed, both categories do. As we move forward, organizational studies requires a new way of negotiating materiality that sees the material world as "*constitutively entangled* in everyday life".[56] This requires a paradigm shift that fuses the material and social beyond a relational dynamic—such that without one, the other cannot exist. Organizational theorist Wanda Orlikowski believes this will bring the discussion away from "interacting entities" into a more circular relationship wherein "humans are constituted through relations of materiality—bodies, clothes, food, devices, tools, which in turn are produced through human practices".[57] The difference between this approach and an ontology that views human and non-human subjects as operating in a mutually influencing relationship is that the former alludes to distinct (potentially separable) subjects. Here, the material world becomes more than a physical by-product or reflection of ourselves; rather, it is a "fundamental dimension of society, inseparable of the overall process of social organization".[58] More than a tool or device, these objects and technological landscapes become entangled in our day-to-day rhythms and cadence over time. The important consideration with such views is the inseparable nature and co-evolutionary trajectory existing through these relationships.

In her book *For Space*, Doreen Massey outlines three overarching qualities of space that together form a foundation of experience and help situate this exploration: first, that space is considered a "product of interrelations", meaning it only exists inasmuch as it's "constituted" through its relationship with other human and nonhuman forms. Second, that space is understood as a "sphere of the possibility" and, within it, a coexistence of "district trajectories". She connects this openness to latent or possible futures—a stance which differs from the predicted and closed

[56] Wanda Orlikowski, "Sociomaterial Practices: Exploring Technology at Work", *Organization Studies* 28, no. 9, (2016), 1437 (emphasis in original).

[57] Ibid. 1438.

[58] Manuel Castells, "Space of Flows, Space of Places", in *The City Reader* 6th Ed. (London: Routledge, 2016), 231.

system that accompanies much modern development. And third, that space is recognized as "always under construction", a result of being the "product of relations-between", whereby space, rather than a static construction, is in a continuous process of unfolding.[59] This conceptualization draws space into us, rather than seeing it as an external, solitary form. Though walls and tables do not have agency—they cannot move or make choices on their own—their presence and form shift and change according to whom they interact with or upon.

To represent space as static, objective, and autonomous is "problematized by the recognition of objects as powerful actors-in-space".[60] Understanding the dynamic relationship between the human and the spatial places material objects into a "spatial context within which they themselves help to produce".[61] There is a communication, which, over time, shapes both the material and those who interact with it. These ideas are explored in Latour's *actor network theory (ANT)*, which describes the "momentary association"[62] with objects that renders them social through their ability to act upon a situation. He uses hand tools as an example: hammers that *hit*, knives that *cut*, baskets that *hold*.[63] These verbs describe these objects' actions and, thus, their role in altering a situation. Latour does not suggest that these objects "do things" of their own accord, but that they need to be considered as being part of the social action taking place.[64] As we explored with technology, for those utilizing the information gleaned from wearable monitoring devices, "a reciprocal entanglement emerges, whereby the object in turn works on the body".[65] Over time, the body is shaped by the technology and objects it is using.

Elizabeth Grosz frames this process as one of mutual production, drawing on simulation and the hyperreal as "introjections and

[59] Doreen Massey, *For Space* (London: Sage Publications Ltd., 2005), 8.

[60] Bawaka Country et al. "Co-becoming Bawaka: Towards a Relational Understanding of Place/Space", *Progress in Human Geography* 40, no. 4 (2016), 5.

[61] Ibid. 5.

[62] Bruno Latour *Reassembling the Social: An introduction to actor-network-theory* (Oxford University Press, 2005), 65.

[63] Ibid. 71.

[64] Ibid. 72.

[65] Nansen "Step-Counting", 799.

projections [in] a complex feedback" loop.[66] What is significant about how Grosz draws upon simulacra and constructed realities is her grounding in the body. A tangible, pliable substance is being touched here, which extends beyond a purely symbolic reading of space. Similar to Latour, Grosz extends this thinking to how tools, instruments, and other objects extend or reshape the body when in use. From hammers and iPhones to cars and planes, these objects temporarily become "part of the body image".[67] When driving, for example, the car, "its perils and breakdowns, chasing another car … are all experienced in the body image of the driver".[68] This new bodily form, a co-creation of machine and body, shifts and alters the corporeal experience of the road and the city. These extensions and transformations illuminate the body's elasticity.[69] To see space and bodies as "flexible and ambiguous" challenges how they may be experienced and perceived, and changes the attention given to both space and body.[70] Shifting how we perceive and characterize these sensations and experiences can highlight their relational and interwoven qualities. As the body's physical and social limits dissolve, isolating discrete elements—material or social—becomes difficult.

Possible Futures

Just as the car transforms its driver's body into something more powerful and mechanical, can the building transform the organization? Frederick Taylor's[71] notion of the workplace as a well-oiled machine designed to achieve "maximum efficiency" literally and physically shaped our concept of work. Open-plan offices with long tables or desks that are either shared or labelled as *hot desks* enable anyone can sit down to work anywhere. In other arrangements, spaces are designed in-line with the type of work

[66] Elizabeth Grosz, "Bodies-Cities", In *Places through the Body* (Psychology Press,1998), 43.

[67] Elizabeth Grosz, *Volatile Bodies*. (Indiana University Press, 1994), 80.

[68] Ibid.

[69] Patricia Pringle, "Spatial Pleasures", *Space and Culture* 8, no. 2, (2005).

[70] Ibid. 144.

[71] Frederick W. Taylor, *The Principles of Scientific Management.* (Easton Hive Publishing, 1911/1985).

activity: quiet or loud, individual or collective. Some designs, seeking to calm swelling hatred of the open-office concept, are bringing back the cubicle, but modernized and marketed as a flexible, modular office to aid individual work.

Lefebvre reminds us that to conceive of a space without considering what inhabits it, or to think of a moment separate from the place in which it occurred, renders them "empty abstractions" of themselves.[72] For the "substance" of which they are made—"energy, space and time—can neither be conflated nor separated from one another".[73] How the material and the immaterial are entwined and co-produced is not necessarily easy to comprehend and perhaps impossible to fully understand or communicate, despite the fact, as Lefebvre notes, that "its existence stares us in the face".[74] The shift comes from within by breaking down the barriers between this and that, human and non-human, mind and body, material and immaterial, inside and outside, and so on. When this happens, the office, as an affective space, becomes implicated in how the organization functions and evolves. Such affects, often quite subtle, emerge through our encounters and embodied experiences with the space. Shifts in perception can become shifts in behaviour, which result in new or different actions within the organization. Here, the spatial experiences of individuals are intrinsically linked to the porousness of the organization: desk surfaces, scents, closed doors, light beams, dead plants, and whispers are embodied by workers like threads tugging at the organization. The space hums with life and becomes an active participant in the organization. With creative work, it is understood that an artist and therefore their artwork could be influenced by the place where it is made but is seems harder to extend that influence to an office (or home) where reports, brainstorms, or conversations take shape.

Our material surroundings are simultaneously a reflection of experience and the experience in itself. Atmospheres, emotions, and relationships are the connective tissue—forever entwined with what they are

---

[72] Henry Lefebvre, *The Production of Space*, trans. D. Nicholson-Smith (Blackwell Publishing, 1991), 12.

[73] Ibid.

[74] Ibid.

producing. Taking time to observe and document these scenes offers a spatial portrait of life, one that may not fit easily within the boundaries of research categories, disciplines, or objective pursuits. These accounts offer texture—the surface of things—to a social history we may not have noticed before. Such a perspective emerges over time out of conversations, memories, language, and the body, as well as the material space itself. Rather than focus solely on the material or the social, it is the material *in use*—its affective and emotional grip on the people who interact with it—that forms the story.

References

Armetta, Amoreen. "Workplace Innovation Lab Hacks Aging LA Building to Attract Young Companies," *Dornob*, November 21, 2018: https://dornob.com/workplace-innovation-lab-hacks-aging-la-building-to-attract-young-companies/

Baia, Alex. "Our Open-Plan Office Failed, so We're Moving to a Towering Panopticon." *McSweeney's,* September 27, 2017: https://www.mcsweeneys.net/articles/our-open-plan-office-failed-so-were-moving-to-a-towering-panopticon

Cairns, George."Seeking a Facilities Management Philosophy for the Changing Workplace." *Facilities* 21, no. 5/6 (2003): 95–105. doi:https://doi.org/10.1108/02632770310476705.

Castells, Manuel. "Space of Flows, Space of Places." In *The City Reader* 6th Ed, 240–251. Routledge, 2016.

Clegg, Stewart R. and Martin Kornberger. "Organizing Space." In *Space, Organizations and Management Theory*. Edited by Stewart R. Clegg and Martin Kornberger, 143–162. Liber & Copenhagen Business School Press, 2006.

Clements-Croome, Derek. *Creating the Productive Workplace*. Taylor & Francis, 2006.

Couldry, Nick and Ulises A Mejias. "Data Colonialism: Rethinking Big Data's Relation to the Contemporary Subject." *Television New Media* 20, no.4, (2019): 336–349. doi:https://doi.org/10.1177/1527476418796632.

Country, Bawaka, Sarah Wright, Sandie Suchet-Pearson, Kate Lloyd, Laklak Burarrwanga, Ritjilili Ganambarr, Merrkiyawuy Ganambarr-Stubbs, Banbapuy Ganambarr, Djawundil Maymuru, and Jill Sweeney. "Co-becoming

Bawaka: Towards a relational understanding of place/space." *Progress in human geography* 40, no. 4 (2016): 455–475. doi:https://doi.org/10.1177/0309132515589437.

Dale, Karen and George Burrell. "All Together, Altogether Better." In *Organizational Spaces*. Edited by Alfons H. van Marrewijk and Dvora Yanow. Edward Elgar Publishing, 2010.

Dale, Karen. "Building a social materiality: spatial and embodied politics in organizational control." *Organization* 12 no.5 (2016): 649–678. doi:https://doi.org/10.4324/9780203260241.

De Molli, Frederica. "An Aesthetic Account of Space: A Report on Recent Developments in Organizational Research." *Studi Organizzativi* 1, (2019): 36–63. doi:https://doi.org/10.3280/SO2019-001002.

Deuble, Max Paul, and Richard John de Dear, "Is it Hot in Here or is it Just Me? Validating the post-occupancy evaluation," *Intelligent Buildings International* 6, no. 2 (2014): 112–134. doi:https://doi.org/10.1080/17508975.2014.883299.

Drake, Graham. "'This Place Gives Me Space': Place and Creativity in the Creative Industries." *Geoforum* 34, no. 4 (2003): 511–524. doi:https://doi.org/10.1016/S0016-7185(03)00029-0.

Duffy, Francis. "Design and Facilities Management in a Time of Change," *Facilities* 18, no. 10/11/12, (2000): 371–375. doi:https://doi.org/10.1108/02632770010349592.

Gagliardi, Pasquale. *Symbols and Artifacts.* Routledge, 1990.

Grosz, Elizabeth. *Volatile Bodies*. Indiana University Press, 1994.

Grosz, Elizabeth. "Bodies-cities." In *Places Through the Body.* Edited by Heidi Nast and Steve Pile, 42–51. Psychology Press, 1998.

Haigh, Gideon. *The Office: A Hardworking History*. Miegunyah Press, 2012.

Harris, Anna. *A Sensory Education.* New York: Routledge, 2021.

Heron John and Peter Reason. "The Practice of Co-operative Inquiry: Research 'with' rather than 'on' people." In *Handbook of Action Research: Participative Inquiry and Practice,* 144–154. London: Sage Publications, 2001.

Hillier, Bill. "Space and Spatiality: What the Built Environment Needs from Social Theory." *Building Research & Information* 36, no. 3 (2008): 216–230. doi:https://doi.org/10.1080/09613210801928073.

Hillier, Bill and Alan Penn. "Visible Colleges: Structure and Randomness in the Place of Discovery." *Science in Context* 1 (1991): 23–49.

Howes, David, ed. *Empire of the Senses: The Sensory Culture Reader*, Routledge, 2005.

Kantor, Jodi and Arya Sundaram, "The rise of the Worker Productivity Score." *New York Times*, August 14, 2022. https://www.nytimes.com/interactive/2022/08/14/business/worker-productivity-tracking.html
Kaufman, Lindsey. "Google got it wrong. The open-office trend is destroying the workplace." *The Washington Post,* December 30, 2014. https://www.washingtonpost.com/posteverything/wp/2014/12/30/google-got-it-wrong-the-open-office-trend-is-destroying-the-workplace/
Kaysen, Ronda. "For Weary Workers, Video Backdrops Are Becoming Too Close and Personal." *New York Times* April, 22, 2022. https://www.nytimes.com/2022/04/22/realestate/video-backdrops-work-from-home.html
Kimura, Tara. "How new data-collection technology might change office culture." *CBC News*, (September 14, 2015a).http://www.cbc.ca/news/technology/how-new-data-collection-technology-might-change-office-culture-1.3196065
Kimura, Tara. "Too Orwellian? Companies monitoring personal time, for 'self-improvement'." *CBC News,* September 15, 2015b. http://www.cbc.ca/news/technology/too-orwellian-companies-monitoring-personal-time-for-self-improvement-1.3196321
Kingma, B., & van Marken Lichtenbelt, W. (2015). Energy consumption in buildings and female thermal demand. *Nature Climate Change*, 5(12), 1054–1056. doi:https://doi.org/10.1038/nclimate2741.
Laloux, Frederic. *Reinventing Organizations.* Nelson Parker, 2014.
Latour, Bruno. *Reassembling the Social: An introduction to actor-network-theory.* Oxford University Press, 2005.
Lefebvre, Henri. *The Production of Space*. Translated by D. Nicholson-Smith. Blackwell Publishing, 1991.
Lupton, Debora and Sarah Maslen. "The More-Than-Human Sensorium: Sensory Engagements with Digital-Self Tracking Technologies." *The Senses and Society* 13, no. 2 (2018):190–202. doi:https://doi.org/10.1080/17458927.2018.1480177.
Nansen, Bjorn. "Step-counting: The anatom- and chrono-politics of pedometrics," Continuum: Jounal of Media & Cultural Studies 22, no.6 (2008): 799.
Martens, Yuri. "Creative Workplace: Instrumental and Symbolic Support for Creativity." *Facilities* 29 no.1/2 (2011). doi:https://doi.org/10.1108/02632771111101331.
Massey, Doreen. *For Space*. London: Sage Publications Ltd, 2005.
Moultrie, James, Mikael Nilsson, Marcel Dissel, Udo-Ernst Haner, Sebastiaan Janssen, and Remko Van der Lugt. "Innovation Spaces: Towards a Framework for Understanding the Role of the Physical Environment in Innovation."

Creativity and Innovation Management 16, no. 1 (2007): 53–65. doi:https://doi.org/10.1111/j.1467-8691.2007.00419.x.

Nixey, Catherine. "The Death of the Office," *The Economist,* April 29, 2020: https://www.economist.com/1843/2020/04/29/death-of-the-office

Olguín, Daniel, Benjamin N. Waber, Taemie Kim, Akshay Mohan, Koji Ara, and Alex Pentland. "Sensible Organizations: Technology and Methodology for Automatically Measuring Organizational Behavior," *IEEE Transactions on Systems, Man, and Cybernetics, Part B (Cybernetics)* 39, no.1 (2009): 43–55. doi:https://doi.org/10.1109/TSMCB.2008.2006638.

Orlikowski, Wanda. "Sociomaterial Practices: Exploring Technology at Work," *Organization Studies* 28, no.9 (2016): 1435–1448. doi:https://doi.org/10.1177/0170840607081138.

Rosengren, Calle and Mikael Ottosson. "Employee Monitoring in a Digital Context." In *Digital sociologies*. Edited by Tressie McMillan Cottom, Karen Gregory and, Jessie Daniels, 181–194. Policy Press, 2017.

Saifer, Adam and M. Tina M Dacin. "Data and Organization Studies: Aesthetics, Emotions, Discourse and our Everyday Encounters with Data." *Organization Studies* 43 no.4 (2022): 623–636. doi:https://doi.org/10.1177/01708406211006250.

Schwarzkopf, Stefan. "Sacred Excess: Organizational Ignorance in an Age of Toxic Data." *Organization Studies* 41, no.2 (2020): 197–217. doi:https://doi.org/10.1177/0170840618815527.

Taylor, Frederick W. *The Principles of Scientific Management*. Easton Hive Publishing, 1911/1985.

van Marreqijk, Alfons. "Corporate Headquarters as Physical Embodiments of Organisational Change." *Journal of Organizational Change Management* 22, no 3 (2009): 290–306. doi:https://doi.org/10.1111/j.1541-0072.1995.tb00520.x.

Warren, Samantha and Stephen Fineman. "Don't get me Wrong, it's fun here, but… ." In *Humour, Work and Organization*. Edited by Robert Westwood & Carl Rhodes, 92–112. Routledge, 2007.

Warzel, Charlie and Helen A Peterson. *Out of Office: Unlocking the Power and Potential of Hybrid Work*. New York: Alfred A. Knopf, 2021.

3

Writing the Invisible

> As we reacquaint ourselves with our breathing bodies, then the perceived world itself begins to shift and transform. When we begin to consciously frequent the wordless dimension of our sensory participations, certain phenomena that have habitually commanded our focus begin to lose their distinctive fascination and to slip toward the background, while hitherto unnoticed or overlooked presences begin to stand forth from the periphery and to engage our awareness.
>
> —David Abram[1]

To be aware of our surroundings demands a certain mindfulness and awareness of qualities not immediately audible, visible, or long-lasting. As Abram states, our perception of the world is shaped by our body's actions, emotions, memories, and senses. Reacquainting ourselves with how we move through and interact with space provides "unnoticed or overlooked presences" and knowledge. There are historical resonances embedded in material objects and natural landscapes that pulse with meaning and value; we can engage with these (and other) forces or flows that surround our thoughts, movement, communication, and behaviour.

[1] David Abram, *The Spell of the Sensuous* (New York: Vintage Books, 1996), 63.

K. Messer, *How to Work with Space*, Palgrave Studies in Business, Arts and Humanities,
https://doi.org/10.1007/978-3-031-46541-3_3

All these ways of knowing and of connecting bring space into an evolving conversation. But is it possible for the spoken or written word to do justice to these aesthetic encounters? Can language, by itself, translate nuanced moments that we experience (not necessarily with other people) but with our surroundings?

The inherent power of words to shape and infuse meaning is as compelling as it is daunting. Not only is it difficult to convey meaningful moments in life, how they are described may shift their essence. Experience can twist and morph as it is outlined in ink or communicated as a whisper to the trees. As more ephemeral or heretofore hidden qualities of space begin to emerge in academia and organizational studies, it is worthwhile to consider what we can learn from other kinds of practitioners, such as artists, writers, and philosophers who explore space through their work. How does the material world show up and contribute to experience, meaning, and knowledge? Is writing and researching space for academic pursuits different (or the same) as describing space in creative literary works? What happens when, as Lefebvre points out, "communication brings the non-communicated into the realm of the communicated"?[2]

Andrew Juniper navigates a similar conundrum in the introduction to his book on *wabi-sabi*, the Japanese art of impermanence, which represents the sacred aesthetic qualities of life. It is considered unwise to try to describe *wabi-sabi*, for language cannot capture its complete essence. Therefore, it is preferable to "leave the unexplainable unexplained".[3] In fact, Juniper describes how words are considered the "fundamental obstacle to clear understanding",[4] as though their very utterance forever taints the thing being described—an accidental droplet of opaque ink into a crystal-clear pond. If necessary, only the most poetic language can be considered worthy of such a task. It is true that a poor description of *wabi-sabi* may end up birthing an entirely different, yet related, way of appreciating art, and yet, perhaps, that imperfect version may lead to something unique.

[2] Henry Lefebvre, *The Production of Space,* trans. D. Nicholson-Smith (Blackwell Publishing, 1991), 28.

[3] Andrew Juniper, *Wabi Sabi* (Clarendon, VT: Tuttle Publishing, 2003), ix.

[4] Ibid.

The abilities given to writing and words seem, in themselves, transformative. Sheila Heti, a contemporary writer, speaks to the intimate repercussions of portraying our life—what she refers to as "one's insides".[5] In a personal essay, Heti explains how writing can transform "objects and people", who inevitably "take on the qualities of how you portrayed them".[6] As if by magic, our words and descriptions shift the way we see and engage with the world so that "a friend drawn ugly becomes ugly. A life drawn sweet becomes more sweet".[7] It is both a thrilling and a terrifying prospect to describe a person, situation, or space. Just as a designer—through paint, materials, and lights—can transform a room from something drab and rundown into a brightly coloured and well-lit space, writers have the ability to create whole worlds with their words.

~~Academic~~ Writing

Within the academic paradigm, the use of words to share work and communicate findings is relied upon and has become a marker of legitimacy.[8] Too often, words are framed as "the instruments of reason", whereas theatre and the arts represent "aesthetic communications".[9] Words, in-and-of-themselves, can trigger a comparison to objective thinking and the rational mind. However, rather than perpetuate the dichotomy between rational language and art aesthetics, the question becomes: How can words, written or spoken, be used to communicate aesthetic experience? Especially when it seems that even the most rhythmical words can have consequences. The challenge, then, is how best to achieve "the translation of aesthetic experience to intellectual knowledge of that experience".[10]

[5] Sheila Heti, "A Common Seagull", *Yale Review* 107, no. 4 (2019): https://yalereview.yale.edu/common-seagull

[6] Ibid.

[7] Ibid.

[8] Steven S Taylor, "Overcoming Aesthetic Muteness: Researching organizational members' aesthetic experience", *Human Relations* 55, no. 7 (2002).

[9] Augusto Boal, *The Aesthetics of the Oppressed* (New York: Routledge, 2006), 24.

[10] Taylor, "Overcoming Aesthetic Muteness", 823.

How do we write about that which transcends words? Even Augusto Boal, who claimed that words are the language of reason, understands that "reason and feeling, idea and form" cannot be separated, "even when at loggerheads, even when they come to blows".[11] Suggesting that words may only convey a rational form of experience strips writing of its creative potential and power. It also strips it of its material connection. Keeping words in the rational domain undermines the material influence over thought.[12]

Changing how we write the story could mean investigating beyond academic writing to more descriptively convey and connect with the ineffable. Qualitative research methods that use poetry and other creative art forms are becoming more popular for those wishing to push the boundaries of academic writing. Arts-based research can include photography, drawing, poetry, performance, theatre, and other research–creation modalities.[13] While creative techniques do not necessarily simplify the process, nor do they completely circumvent the role of language, they do connect participants and researchers to various materials, tools, and their surroundings. This embodied and emplaced process actively draws space and material into the knowledge being created. Arts-based methods are more than stylized presentation techniques and indeed actively conjure embodied, sensory, or emotional experiences, in which the exploratory process of their creation unlocks hidden or unconscious insights. The final performance or art piece in-and-of itself may or may not be the end goal; it can also include the active process of making it, which can "elicit deeper, more emotional, more reflective accounts".[14] Creative research methods often generate a more embodied wisdom, through its "capacity to engage with tensions and ambiguities", that enriches our understanding about a particular topic or issue.[15] In connecting to the material

[11] Boal, *Aesthetics of the Oppressed*, 24.

[12] Christopher Bardt, *Material and Mind* (MIT Press, 2019).

[13] (See Patricia Leavy (2011, 2015); and Jenna Ward and Harriet Shortt (2020) for detailed creative approaches).

[14] Jenna Ward and Harriet Shortt, "Using Arts-Based Methods of Research" In *Using Arts-Based Research Methods: Creative approaches for researching business, organisation and humanities*, Palgrave Macmillan: 2020: 2.

[15] Ibid.

world, these processes help participants and researchers surpass habitual ways of thinking and seeing that are bound up in routine ways of being and thinking.

Bringing aesthetic and ephemeral spatial elements into qualitative research can become tricky. It can be time consuming to sift through the shadows, textures, and sounds of aesthetic research. Many researchers attempt to shift language-based research towards objective certainty through discourse analysis with "interviews that can be recorded, transcribed, and formally coded", often using computer software or online tools.[16] This methodological habit towards standardization and generalizability—to endow research with a particular value and legitimacy—comes at a cost. In his article "Confessions of an Organizational Space Writer", Fabio James Petani laments the current state of academic writing. "Why", he asks, "do journal reviewers and editors so often flatten out all gentle irony, suggestive humour and evocative hesitancy"?[17] In a conversational tone, Petani pleads with his readers (who he assumes are organizational scholars) "to act up" and imbue their writing with simple, honest, and emotional attributes.[18] This call to arms challenges academics to expand their audience and write from the heart, so that research may motivate people and create positive change instead of seeking legitimacy in dull language and standardized expression.

The use of dedicated and specialized language has its place and can create a "highly selective lexicon of terms and phrases" to describe the nonrepresentational aspects of life.[19] Creating a familiar, well-trodden set of words to foster understanding and kinship among academics and authors certainly has its benefits. However, there is an irony when the approved terms and descriptions "comes up short of the manifold of affective events and textures [they seek] to speak up for".[20] This structure

[16] Dvora Yanow, "Giving Voice to Space", In *Organizational Spaces,* eds. Afons H. van Marrewijk & Dvora Yanow (Edward Elgar Publishing, 2010), 140.

[17] Fabio James Petani, "Confessions of an Organizational Space Writer", *Organization* 35, no. 4 (2019): 2

[18] Ibid.

[19] Hayden Lorimer, "Cultural Geography: Non-Representational Conditions and Concerns", *Progress in Human Geography* 32, no. 4 (2008): 7.

[20] Ibid.

places writers at a loss when attempting, and failing, to describe the intangible. The combination of standardized language and rigid style guides guts academic writing of any flounce and whimsy. What places are lost when writers are forced to format their words so strictly and precisely that they lose all resemblance?

Over the last decade, there has been a steady rise of spatial, aesthetic, sensory research. However, these strides have prompted Cnossen and Bencherki to question the degree to which spatial research is "overemphasizing sensemaking".[21] Spaces are broken down, rated, coded, and analysed to derive specific meaning from layout, colour, temperature, or natural light. Cnossen and Bencherki remind us of the "very tangible character" of our daily interactions and practices with spaces that "cannot be reduced to talking about it or understanding it in one way or another".[22] Rather, it is the sum of complex and dynamic relationships in which value can be recognized. Trying to interpret significance from spatial data bound up in every aesthetic encounter reduces space to something "'out there', waiting to be made sense of by human beings".[23] Instead, the goal is to develop new methods of attention and interaction that can entwine spatial qualities into the thoughts onto the page. Through attending and inclusion, aesthetic dimensions become part of the research process and outcome in a multiplicity of ways.

Spatial Language

Describing how the moon light flows into a room, the texture of carpet imprinted on the skin of your leg, the soft murmur of someone speaking in the next room, the swell of memories in your chest, and the rush of air

[21] Boukje Cnossen and Nicolas Bencherki, "The Role of Space in the Emergence and Endurance of Organizing: How Independent Workers and Material Assemblages Constitute Organizations", *Human Relations* 72, no 6 (The citation "Cnossen and Bencherki 2019" has been changed to "Cnossen and Bencherki 2018" to match the author name/date in the reference list. Please check if the change is fine in this occurrence and modify the subsequent occurrences, if necessary.Cnossen and Bencherki 2018): 1073.

[22] Ibid.

[23] Ibid.

on your face as you push through the door "carries a pivotal magic"[24] that connects us to the natural world and buildings we inhabit. In *The Spell of the Sensuous*, David Abram makes a case for how the potency of language can and should be harnessed:

> For those of us who care for an earth not encompassed by machines, a world of textures, tastes and sounds other than those that we have engineered, there can be no question of simply abandoning literacy, of turning away from all writing. Our task, rather, is that of taking up the written word, with all of its potency, and patiently, carefully, writing language back into the land. Our craft is that of releasing the budded, earthly intelligence of our words, freeing them to respond to the speech of the things themselves.[25]

Throughout the book, Abram successfully achieves this assignment with elegant, descriptive writing, which pulls the reader into the words themselves. Forgetting the air—"the loss of the invisible richness of the present"—is one of the ways in which Abram suggests we have lost touch with a "palpable realm" of sensuous magic.[26] The dance that once existed between the seen and unseen has largely shifted to what is visible, static, and solid. This includes the way we interact with language and the written word. Rather than consider writing as fixed, it must interact, call forth, and become, through the relationships with our surroundings.

For architecture and design, Alberto Pérez-Gómez suggests that language is a necessary function to convey the atmospheres and moods of rooms, which he deems the "harmonic potential" of architecture. For without such descriptive words, architects would become too reliant on measurements and blueprints and other technological systems of design. Pérez-Gómez draws on the work of Nicolas Le Camus de Mézières, an architectural philosopher of the mid-eighteenth century, to explore the "production of meaningful architecture".[27] Le Camus saw "metaphorical language" as necessary for "describing rooms' aspects—textures, smells,

[24] Abram, *The Spell of the Sensuous* (1996), 273.
[25] Ibid.
[26] Ibid. 254–255.
[27] Alberto Pérez-Gómez, *Attunement* (MIT Press, 2016), 83.

decoration, and colors, among others".[28] Similarly, Carl Leggo, a poet and educator, suggests that poetic language "works to open up possibilities for constructing understanding" about the world.[29] While imagery is often considered one of the most powerful forms of expression, with its ability to convey nuanced and ephemeral qualities of atmosphere,[30,31] words have their own role to play.

Pérez-Gómez cautions against a world built without these emotional and aesthetic words should they be replaced with more "fashionable innovations" such as those driven by technological advances—a kind of innovation which, he believes, "hides [place] from our experience".[32] Thus, part of the value of language in articulating the less-visible, less-quantitative, less-stable nuances of spatial atmospheres is to serve as a form of prevention against spaces devoid of emotional connection. Through descriptive language, "deep emotional and narrative aspects that articulate places" become reality.[33] How we speak about space influences how buildings are perceived and built; words "and their meaning bind concepts and material, transforming both".[34] These are not ornamental aesthetic and sensory attributes, but a relational and connective tissue of atmospheric qualities forged between the social and the material.

We are often drawn to a space through its atmosphere, which is in a constant state of becoming and transforming. Certain qualities and times may resonate and conspire with our body's rhythm. As different emotions surface or shift within a space, they are "taken up and reworked" into the atmosphere, producing a constantly evolving environment and experience.[35] Kathleen Stewart describes atmosphere as a "force field".[36] She

[28] Ibid. 84.

[29] Carl Leggo, "Astonishing silence", In *Handbook of the Arts in Qualitative Research*, eds. Gary J. Knowles & Arda L. Cole (Sage, 2008), 165.

[30] Samantha Warren, "Having an Eye for it: Aesthetics, Ethnography and the Senses", *Journal of Organizational Ethnography* 1, no. 1 (2012).

[31] Sarah Pink, *Doing Visual Ethnography* (Sage Publications, 2013).

[32] Pérez-Gómez, *Attunement* (2016), 108–109.

[33] Ibid. 108.

[34] Bardt, *Material and mind* (2019), 6.

[35] Ben Anderson, "Affective Atmospheres", *Emotion, Space and Society* 2, no. 2 (2009): 79.

[36] Kathleen Stewart, "Atmospheric Attunements", *Environment and Planning D: Society and Space* 29, no. 3 (2011), 452.

explores how this “lived affect” creates “an attunement of the senses, of labors, and imaginaries to potential ways of living in or living through things”.[37] For Stewart, engaging in atmospheric understanding requires writing that does the same; she writes: “things hanging in the air are worth describing”.[38] In calling upon theory to become a “descriptive method awkwardly approaching the thing that is happening by attuning to it”, Stewart offers an approach to spatial, atmospheric research that draws the researcher, and their words, into the event itself. Paying attention to and writing about everyday “rhythms” gives voice to their affective “tempos, sensory knowledges, orientations, transmutations, habits, [and] rogue force fields”.[39] Through such accounts, aesthetic vocabularies go beyond describing experience; they are both born of the experience and become co-creators of the event itself.

A few years ago, while trying to make sense of this, I decided to describe a picture that my then three-year-old daughter had given me to hang in my office. After experiencing that process, my thoughts on the drawing began to change:

> At first, I look at the drawing as a finished product, but when I look deeply, at the quality of the marks, I begin to see more. I see her hand moving across the page quickly and then slowly, back and forth, up and down. Something static becomes animated, partly through my imagination and partly through the marks on the paper. The scribbles become a manifestation of her energy and emotion onto paper through colour, rhythm, and ink.

Taking the time to look and describe this image on my wall brought something faded into view and transformed it from a static image into a series of dynamic movements, relationships, emotions, and materials. Now, years later a different drawing hangs in its place on my wall, and yet this earlier process remains effective at evoking my daughter’s presence. That descriptive practice has forever changed how I interact with these drawings. It made it easier for me to connect with the compelling energy my daughter felt during its creation and the life it brought to the drawing.

---

[37] Ibid.

[38] Ibid. 447.

[39] Ibid. 446.

Private Murmurs

The act of writing is itself a process of becoming and transforming thoughts, experiences, stories into something else. Fabio Petani suggests that "writing is 'an embodied space', suspended between pain and pleasure, body and mind, self and other".[40] The "other" that Petani refers to could be the natural and/or the built environment—the physical world where the writing is occurring, the location where the writing is being read and consumed, or the place that is written about. The placement of these words and their interaction with the reader summons language into a sensorial and physical realm that shifts and transforms with their surroundings. Nathalie Cochoy describes how Annie Dillard's nature writing—specifically *Pilgrim at Tinker Creek*—becomes part of the natural world:

> Annie Dillard situates her writing on nature on the threshold where the meditative ramblings of the mind ephemerally crystallize into the ever-changing substance of nature—where the metatextual or metaphoric "waves" of discourse skillfully coincide with the "heaving" materiality of the world in order to weave the throbbing texture of the book.[41]

What Cochoy describes is the ebb and flow of writing and perceiving, wherein words—alive with potential and materiality—become part of new ways of seeing and understanding how we are in the world. Dillard has stated that for her, "seeing is of course very much a matter of verbalization" through its role as a mediator of perception.[42] Words, like thoughts, are co-created with the place they are situated within. How they enter and are received by the environment can enhance or diminish them. Places give sounds context and meaning by embracing their vibration or rejecting them as out of place or unwelcome. Words may bounce off walls or be absorbed into them; they may be hardly audible or be carried afar. Libraries, theatres, restaurants, churches, and offices all create

---

[40] Petani, "Confessions" (2019): 7.

[41] Nathalie Cochoy "The Imprint of the 'Now' on the Skin of Discourse: Annie Dillard's *Pilgrim at Tinker Creek*", *Revue Française D'études Américaines* 4, (2005): 35.

[42] Ibid. 34.

particular settings that frame sounds and our voice.[43] Using our words to engage with particular aspects of our surroundings changes what we sense and how we perceive them. But what happens when we stop communicating?

I think about the countless times I used to drive home from university and, upon arrival, have no recollection of the journey. What happened to the rain forests and ocean side I must have observed along the way? The trip—so familiar as to almost become invisible—filled instead with rotating thoughts of the day's events. In his book *Seeking Awareness in American Nature Writing*, Scott Slovic details a similar account of biking tirelessly along shoulderless roads to the university, most of which he hardly notices.[44] He contrasts those hasty trips with much rarer ones, which he describes as "scheduleless"; during these rides, Slovic says, "I barely pedal, talking to myself about the distant hills, the scrubby bushes and moss-distorted trees, and the dead animals—snakes, raccoons, armadillos—on the road".[45] The passing countryside is no longer invisible, as words act to manifest insects, animals, bushes, and trees. Through internal, dialogical observations, the landscape emerges as a companion and becomes an essential component of the journey. Perhaps when there is nothing to say about the spaces we inhabit, it is not because there was nothing there but because we forgot to participate in the conversation. Slovic suggests that much of writing about nature is "a kind of private murmuring" that strives towards an understanding of our experience and, I would assume, our relationship to it.[46]

Reading these private murmurings shifts writing about the environment from absolute accounts to a more whimsical repartee. The meaning of the word murmur conveys something quiet and blurred as though it is not fully formed, but in a process of becoming. Rather than depend on spatial research for concrete proof and answers to office space conundrums, having conversations with space can deepen our understanding of the relationships at play. Like other creative art forms that engage

[43] Barry Blesser and Linda-Ruth Salter, *Spaces Speak, are you Listening?* (MIT Press, 2007).

[44] Scott Slovic, *Seeking Awareness in American Nature Writing* (University of Utah Press, 1992), 172.

[45] Ibid.

[46] Ibid.

aesthetic and emotion communication, writing can be a subversive act from within the system, in which the material author collaborates in the story being told.

Material Author

Stories are not only found in words and writing. Dvora Yanow writes about how "built spaces are at once storytellers and part of the story being told".[47] These built narratives become a fundamental component of how space is lived and experienced by communicating "values, beliefs and feelings" through their material vocabulary.[48] Annie Ernaux, the French writer and novelist, well known for her observational descriptions of her life, offers everyday tableaus that exude depth and substance. In one well-known description, she offers an imaginary painting to symbolize a moment in her life. She writes: "it would be a small table with a Formica top pushed up against a wall and an enamel basin with a probe glowing on the surface. Slightly to the right – a hairbrush".[49] The painting, entitled "The Abortionist's Studio", which hangs in no art gallery, calls upon these objects to "give voice to the silences of many women" of her generation.[50] Here, a still life comprised of a Formica table, an enamel basin, a probe, and a hairbrush brims with emotion and knowledge of what took place. These material remnants are entwined with women's experience of that room, and they are important storytellers.

Tricia Austin, author and director of the Narrative Environments master's programme in London,[51] suggests that conceptualizing space through narrative can lead to overlooked questions: "who is the audience, who is the author? What is the story? What is its underlying message? How is it

[47] Dvora Yanow, "Space Stories", *Journal of Management Inquiry* 7, no. 3 (1998): 215.

[48] Ibid.

[49] Annie Ernaux, *Happening* (Seven Stories Press, The citation "Ernaux 2001" has been changed to "Ernaux 2000" to match the author name/date in the reference list. Please check if the change is fine in this occurrence and modify the subsequent occurrences, if necessary.Ernaux 2000), 67.

[50] Rhiannon Lucy Cosslett, "We are Made of Words: the Radically Intimate Writing of Annie Ernaux", *The Guardian* (Oct, 7, 2022): https://www.theguardian.com/books/2022/oct/07/we-are-made-of-words-the-radically-intimate-writing-of-annie-ernaux

[51] Central Saint Martins College of Arts and Design, London.

told? How is it framed by its context? What transformation does it bring?"[52] These questions immediately take us beyond the design- and ocular-centric dimension into the experiences and meanings bound up within a spatial encounter. A story can reveal a space's embedded agency, its "power to change the world".[53] This is especially important in considering how people can experience space in different ways: as powerful, oppressive, celebratory, confining, beautiful, or banal.

Take the example of riots and protests that occur across the world. Space has co-authored these movements in the parks and streets where protesters have been celebrated, threatened, attacked, and killed; in the vandalized storefronts; and in the historical statues toppled for embodying racist or oppressive legacies. The stories of these places highlight "the openness of objects, people and spaces as they act upon each other producing constant flux of events and the dramatic conflicts that arise … through arcs of interaction".[54] In this sense, space becomes a co-author of the story, changing not only the plot but also the actors. Applying a narrative perspective to space broadens our understanding of the various roles that space can play and how these roles become embedded in the social interactions taking place. Questions of context, author, and audience also remind us of the ways in which forms and atmosphere can shift and morph depending on who is occupying them and how we move through them.

In *Wanderlust: A History of Walking*, Rebecca Solnit writes of the uniqueness of roads, trails, and paths in their inability to be captured in a single moment. As built structures, they "cannot be perceived as a whole all at once"; rather, they "unfold in time as one travels along them".[55] This journey through time and space becomes its own story, in which "a hairpin turn is like a plot twist, a steep ascent a building of suspense to the view of the summit [and] a fork in the road an introduction of a new

[52] Tricia Austin, "*Culture-led City Regeneration: Design Methodologies*", [Unpublished essay] (2011): 4.

[53] Ibid. 6.

[54] Ibid. 7.

[55] Rebecca Solnit, *Wanderlust: A History of Walking* (Penguin Books, 2001), 72.

storyline".[56] As the wanderer takes in new vistas, subtle details or unexpected places may emerge: sunlight passing through branches, a red door, a spilled coffee on the sidewalk, a spider weaving her web, a single lost glove.

A Call to ~~Action~~Attention

Artists have long been part of a movement to cultivate greater attention and awareness through their practice, performance, and work. Art often serves as an opportunity for pause and reflection, for shifting perspectives and seeing daily life anew. Nicolas Bourriaud writes in *Relational Aesthetics* about how, "even when inert forms are involved, there is a possibility of immediate discussion".[57] It is through this conversation and participation, he says, that "I see and perceive, I comment, and I evolve in a unique space and time".[58] Bourriaud touches on the situated and reciprocal nature between the art and audience/participant. The very act of encountering art becomes transactional and alive, transforming gallery visitors into an extension of the art itself. This atmosphere of engagement differs from the increasingly automated and mechanical nature of daily life, which, says Bourriaud, "restricts the possibilities of inter-human relations".[59] As technology and machines enable a much greater volume of communication, a less present, less attentive, less relational way of being becomes the norm.

Artist Janet Cardiff creates immersive installations that destabilize viewers and pull them out of their daily routines. While some of her work combines elaborately constructed sets with detailed narrative soundtracks, other pieces subtly subvert an existing environment. Her site-specific audio walks, for instance, guide participants through cities all around the world with perfectly timed accompanying soundtracks. *Were those chirping birds coming from the tree or my headphones? Did someone just call out*

[56] Ibid.

[57] Nicolas Bourriaud, *Relational Aesthetics*. trans. Simon Pleasance & Fronza Woods (Les presses du reel, 2002), 16.

[58] Ibid.

[59] Ibid.

to me? These walks, purposefully unsettling, challenge and distort our reality, resulting in a magical reinterpretation of the city street. All of a sudden, everything becomes something to question and examine. Everything—and nothing—is ordinary. Jenny Odell aptly notes that "nothing is so simultaneously familiar and alien as that which has been present all along".[60] Cardiff's art calls attention to how the senses can be deceptive when we have certain expectations about what constitutes reality. In creating an audio walk for London's East End, with its history of bombings—the Brick Lane bombing, IRA-related bombings, and the German Blitz during the Second World War—she wove sounds from those events together with the present day. In 2006, I interviewed Cardiff for a magazine article about how her work plays with the perception of reality. Describing her London audio walk, she said, "as you're walking down one street you hear bombs go off, sirens from the Blitz, helicopters, machine guns and people running past you", an effect that feels remarkably real.[61] The result is a blurring of past and present, certainty and illusion, which manifests an entirely unique and embodied experience. By simply questioning what reality is, it inevitably shifts and transforms.

History and experience are embedded in the pavement, along the façade, and in the trees. In her work on walking, Solnit comments on how roads "are a record of those who have gone before, and to follow them is to follow people who are no longer there".[62] As such, perhaps Cardiff's audio walks emphasize what is *already* there—the combined experience of person, history, and space—through a heightened sensory paradigm. As with most other living things, humans are affected and influenced by the places they inhabit through a myriad of conscious, unconscious, and embodied ways, many of which we do not fully understand. Because familiar details can fade into the background, it is easy to feel indifferent to their existence. Cardiff sees people with greater openness and awareness as "talented viewers" who are able to "create more synchronicity than others".[63] While everyone moves through the world in

60 Jenny Odell, *How to do Nothing* (Melville House, 2019), 125.

61 Karen Messer, "Creating Worlds", *Ascent magazine* (July 2006): 44.

62 Solnit, *Wanderlust* (2001), 72.

63 Messer, "Creating Worlds" (2006), 45.

their own way, some people seem to have a more attuned way of sensing and attending that increases their ability to notice and respond. Details, muted for others, appear clearer and more vibrant. Is it possible to learn this almost-enhanced and detailed sensuous way of perceiving the world?

The Discipline of Noticing

Noticing our surroundings and connecting to our senses—feeling our body in the world—can require practice and discipline. Honing these skills involves shifting our definition of productivity and production to include slowing down and occasionally doing nothing[64]—sort of. The advantage of viewing the world at a snail's pace is in the depth of texture and resonance that can be felt. In *Researching Your Own Practice*, John Mason connects possibility and openness with sensitivity and presence. Mason explores the potential of what he calls *the discipline of noticing*. In order to notice, he says, we must "be awake to possibilities"[65] and willing to adjust or change course as a result. In this example, Mason is referring to classroom teachers who, upon sensing their students' needs, may require an adjustment to their lesson. Noticing is like gathering data about our situation and, as we begin to notice, more data unfolds—be it personal observation about our emotions and bodily sensations, the reactions and behaviour of others, or details about the places inhabited or passed through. "As multi-sensate beings", Mason writes, "we are inundated with sense impressions all the time, but only some of them ever register in our conscious awareness".[66] Noticing more, or different, qualities requires deepening our sensitivity and attentiveness.

In a similar line of thinking, Davis et al.[67] write about what they call *occasioning*. The word *occasion*—when used as a verb—describes moments of possibility that arise through deliberate or "incidental" interactions.[68]

---

[64] Odell, *How to do Nothing* (2019).

[65] John Mason, *Researching your Own Practice*. (Routledge, 2002), 7.

[66] Ibid. 31.

[67] Brent Davis et al., *Engaging Minds: Changing Teaching in Complex Times* (Routledge, 2008).

[68] Elinor Vettraino and Warren Linds, "Living the Experience of Learning: Embodied Reflexivity as Pedagogical Process", *South African Theatre Journal* 31, no. 1 (2018): 21.

Shifting and "changing the conditions of interaction" can lead to different ways of seeing and relating to a situation.[69] All around us, these "rich and diverse possibilities are always present" if we observe and respond to them.[70] What makes spaces unique is not necessarily the place itself but "our notice of them and their effect on us".[71] The places we remember are those that have influenced us in some way. This shifts the discussion from the impact of particular spatial qualities to our personal relationship with those qualities. Here inter-subjectivity and personal connection become a strength rather than a weakness. If we begin, collectively, to notice the physical landscape more intimately, what will emerge?

Massey's third principle of space highlights exactly this: the stories unfinished and untold. Conceptualizing spaces as "always under construction" keeps them open to different possible futures.[72] Therefore, a space as it currently stands is neither an end nor a conclusion, but a "simultaneity of stories-so-far".[73] Becoming more aware of our environment and more conscious of how we are looking and feeling will not, most likely, radically transform the future, but it will increase the possible futures available to us. With increased attention to our surroundings, details previously muted can begin to emerge. The more you listen, the more you hear. Pausing to notice surrounding sounds can ignite a magical transformation from muffled din to orchestra of life—kids playing, cars passing, birds chirping, computers humming, coffee brewing. When these details are given space to emerge on paper or in the air, they can lead to unexpected and overlooked moments of possibility and ways of being in the world.

Attunement

Noticing more, through deeper levels of awareness, is only part of the journey. Ultimately, our goal is the emergence of a deeper connection and synchronicity with the material and atmospheric world. Geoffrey Mead

[69] Ibid.

[70] Ibid.

[71] David M. Friedman, *A Place in Mind* (Véhicule Press, 2010), 10.

[72] Doreen Massey, *Of Space* (Sage Publications, 2005), 8.

[73] Ibid.

suggests that our interactions "do not represent arbitrary designations … but a profound attunement to a reality".[74] This notion of attunement calls to mind balance, harmony, resonance, and deep awareness—terms well established in the mindfulness movement—but what does being attuned to our environment look like? In his aptly titled book, *Attunement*, Alberto Pérez-Gómez reminds us, while reflecting on Greek and Roman design, that the role of architecture "was to mediate between man and nature, the living cosmos, and thereby contribute fundamentally to the maintaining of such balance".[75] Here, the built environment itself acts as a connecting bridge—a dance between humans and nature.

This dance is evident in the Japanese word *shizen*, which is commonly considered to mean nature or natural, but has a variety of nuances; the word contains two characters found in ancient Chinese: the first references "one's self" and the second "the cycle of the sun, water, and living things".[76] In this sense, shizen encompasses the natural world of which humans are a part. In architecture, the traditional Japanese house is meant to encapsulate this "connection between humanity and nature" through its materials, design, and use of light and shadow.[77] Framing the built environment as a connective tissue with the natural world shifts its role from the destroyer of greenspace to something more aligned and co-productive. Can the same be said of language? Can the spoken or written word help attune us to the socio-material world? I believe it can. Taking the time to see and describe my daughter's scribbled drawing forever changed my relationship to it. Through a deepened act of seeing and writing, I brought something I was disconnected to—something from the background—and transformed my relationship with it into something vibrant.

Returning to the art of *wabi-sabi*, viewers are called to leave behind their preconceived notions of aesthetic value to "rediscover the intimate

[74] Geoffrey Mead, "Bourdieu and Conscious Deliberation", *European Journal of Social Theory* 19, no. 1 (2016): 61.

[75] Pérez-Gómez, *Attunement* (2016), 3.

[76] Clare Farrow, "Interview: Kengo Kuma—Sharing the same shadows", *Designcurial* (November 11, 2013): http://www.designcurial.com/news/kengo-kuma-sharing-the-same-shadows-by-clare-farrow/

[77] Ibid.

beauty" of what otherwise might be dismissed as imperfection.[78] A kind of unlearning is accompanied by new modes of attention, presence, and form. *Wabi-sabi* embodies the process of life and death in certain forms; it is "both the joy and melancholy" of what it means to be alive.[79] This fusion of contradiction in emotions and aesthetics rests beneath the surface and is available to those who are open to the exploration. In this regard, *wabi-sabi* emerges as an outcome of this process—a deeply felt beauty and appreciation for the world. Rather than praise "permanence, grandeur, symmetry, and perfection", *wabi-sabi* illuminates the opposite: imperfection, asymmetry, and impermanence.[80] When entrenched aesthetic values lose their dominance, the material and non-material worlds are transformed into something different. Finding ways to describe unexpected or overlooked beauty feels like a kinder, more attuned way of seeing and experiencing that which is unique to the beholder.

Writing Space

Over the course of this exploration, it has become clear that words constitute more than simple communication and do, in fact, act to construct and to shape the atmospheric and sensuous world that we inhabit and research. The act of describing and the description itself can become an important participant. Words can animate an unseen, scentless, flat, or quiet state, and infuse it with life. The more we describe these spaces (to ourselves and others), the richer and more enhanced our language and connection to them will become. The inclusion of material and immaterial forces acts as a "descriptive detour" that can inject prose with spatial "qualities, rhythms, forces, relations, and movements".[81] But more than a whimsical representation, words can become actors themselves that manifest the invisible spaces surrounding us. In articulating aesthetic qualities, those words in turn shape and create new resonance and relationships

[78] Juniper, *Wabi Sabi* (2003), ix.

[79] Ibid. 1.

[80] Ibid. 2.

[81] Stewart "Atmospheric Attunements", (2011): 445.

(on and off the paper). This may take place through a spontaneous murmur, or a more focused and formal expression; either way, the words entangle themselves in our perception until they are embedded parts of the landscape.

These moments may be phenomenal, or ordinary, occurring every day. In her writing on *Ordinary Affects*, Kathleen Stewart calls out the "objects [that] settle into scenes of life and stand as traces of a past still resonant in things".[82] When these resonances appear, it can be a shocking flutter, a pleasurable swell, or a peaceful daze—caused by a "momentary suspension of narrative, or a glitch"[83] in our daily programme. Stewart documents these day-to-day pulses in her life in a disconnected layering of flow and interaction. The stories she tells are of a time and place; they resonate with banality and intimacy, where nothing exists as something significant.

Like the role played by the seen and unseen, the ordinary is charged by patterns of "flow and arrest".[84] The significance of both these concepts lays in their temporary quality. We cannot be in awe, witnessing the immensity of the world around us, 100% of the time or our minds and bodies would overflow. Rather, it is the interplay between these states that becomes essential. For Stewart, these flashes of attention and emotion are vital to recognize and document. Times when the life brims with meaning and resonance: costumes strewn on the floor after Halloween, a forgotten red balloon tucked behind a chair from the last birthday, "the collection of sticks and rocks resting on the dashboard after a hike in the mountains, the old love letters stuffed in a box in the closet".[85] This is a list of companions on the journey, material or otherwise,– that are forever bound within the story. Capturing those sparks of energy draw us into moments where our sensations are vivid and our perception is heightened.

Writing and reading these accounts lures the material into our lives. As witnesses and contributors of experience, they are "charged" and

[82] Kathleen Stewart, *Ordinary Affects* (Duke University Press, 2007), 56.

[83] Ibid. 19.

[84] Ibid.

[85] Ibid.

"electric",[86] flooding our text with a richness of materials. Hans Ulrich Gumbrecht, author of *Atmosphere, Mood, Stimmung*, writes that his book is a product of many moods and atmospheres. He suggests literary works, when laced with a resonance of atmosphere, call "forth a vanished world" that can "affect us 'like a touch from the inside.'"[87] The visceral connection to writing and space is one that goes beyond the page. It touches us, effecting how we think about the world around us. Maggie Maclure sees these relational moments as "wonder".[88] They seem to originate both "out there" and "in" a person as a sort of "mutual affection".[89] "Wonder", she writes, "shades into curiosity, horror, fascination, disgust, and monstrosity".[90] These emotive and affective states become part of the experience and need to be part of the inquiry and presentation. Maclure suggests that the way we write and engage with research data needs to echo these "experiments with order and disorder" so that new sparks of wonder continue to ignite curiosity.[91]

At the beginning of this chapter, I struggled with how to research and convey invisible, ephemeral aspects of our day-to-day life. Moments that seem both extraordinary and yet inconsequential. They seemed out of reach—my ability to describe them lacking. Through this exploration, I have realized that including aspects of our surroundings in our words and our writing can be as simple as having a conversation. We can slow down[92] to engage with the spaces we inhabit, listen to the murmuring, play in the flows, and converse with them through our words and writing. But first, we must notice moments of wonder when the continual motion of the world pauses and becomes visible.

[86] Hans Ulrich Gumbrecht, *Atmosphere, Mood, Stimmung*, trans. Erik Butler (Stanford University Press, 2012), 19.

[87] Ibid. 39–40.

[88] Maggie MacLure, "The Wonder of Data", Cultural Studies—Critical Methodologies 13, no. 2 (2013): 229.

[89] Ibid.

[90] Ibid.

[91] Ibid.

[92] Suvi Satama, "Researching through Experiencing Aesthetic Moments: 'Sensory Slowness' as my Methodological Strength", in *Writing differently*, vol. 4. 209–230. Emerald Publishing Limited, 2020.

References

Abram, David. *The Spell of the Sensuous.* New York: Vintage Books, 1996.

Anderson, Ben, "Affective Atmospheres," *Emotion, Space and Society* 2, no. 2 (2009): 77–81. https://doi.org/10.1016/j.emospa.2009.08.005.

Austin, Tricia. "*Culture-led City Regeneration: Design Methodologies.*" [Unpublished essay] (2011): 4.

Bardt, Christopher. *Material and Mind.* MIT Press, 2019.

Blesser, Barry and Linda-Ruth Salter. *Spaces Speak, are you Listening?* MIT Press, 2007.

Boal, Augusto. *The Aesthetics of the Oppressed.* New York: Routledge, 2006.

Bourriaud, Nicolas. *Relational Aesthetics.* trans. Simon Pleasance & Fronza Woods. Les presses du reel, 2002.

Cnossen, Boukje and Nicolas Bencherki. The role of space in the emergence and endurance of organizing: How independent workers and material assemblages constitute organizations. *Human Relations* 72, no. 6 (2018): 1057–1080. doi:https://doi.org/10.1177/0018726718794265.

Cochoy, Nathalie. "The Imprint of the "Now" on the Skin of Discourse: Annie Dillard's *Pilgrim at Tinker Creek,*" *Revue Française D'études Américaines* 4, (2005): 33–49. doi:https://doi.org/10.3917/rfea.106.49.

Cosslett, Rhiannon Lucy. "We are Made of Words: the Radically Intimate Writing of Annie Ernaux," *The Guardian* (Oct, 7, 2022): https://www.theguardian.com/books/2022/oct/07/we-are-made-of-words-the-radically-intimate-writing-of-annie-ernaux

Davis, Brent., Dennis J. Sumara, and Rebecca Luce-Kapler. *Engaging Minds: Changing Teaching in Complex Times.* Routledge, 2008.

Ernaux, Annie. *Happening.* Seven Stories Press, 2000.

Farrow, Clare. "Interview: Kengo Kuma—Sharing the same shadows." *Designcurial.* November 11, 2013: http://www.designcurial.com/news/kengo-kuma-sharing-the-same-shadows-by-clare-farrow/

Friedman, Avi. *A place in mind.* Véhicule Press, 2010.

Gumbrecht, Hans Ulrich. *Atmosphere, Mood, Stimmung.* Trans E. Butler. Stanford University Press, 2012.

Heti, Sheila. A Common Seagull. *Yale Review* 107, no. 4. (2019): 24–35. https://yalereview.yale.edu/common-seagull

Juniper, Andrew. *Wabi Sabi.* Clarendon, VT: Tuttle Publishing, 2003.

Leavy, Patricia. *Handbook of Arts-Based Research.* Guilford Press, 2011.

Leavy, Patricia. *Method meets art: arts-based research practice.* Guilford Press, 2015.

Lefebvre, Henri. *The Production of Space*. Trans. D. Nicholson-Smith. Blackwell Publishing, 1991.
Leggo, Carl. "Astonishing silence." In *Handbook of the Arts in Qualitative Research*. Eds. Gary J. Knowles and Arda L. Cole. Sage, 2008: 165–174.
Lorimer, Hayden. "Cultural Geography: Non-Representational Conditions and Concerns." *Progress in Human Geography* 32, no.4 (2008): 1–9. https://doi.org/10.1177/0309132507086882.
MacLure, Maggie. "The Wonder of Data," *Cultural Studies - Critical Methodologies* 13, no. 2 (2013): 228–232.
Mason, John. *Researching your own practice*. Routledge, 2002.
Massey, Doreen. *For space*. London: Sage Publications, 2005.
Mead, Geoffrey. "Bourdieu and Conscious Deliberation." *European Journal of Social Theory* 19, no.1 (2016): 57–73. doi:https://doi.org/10.1177/1368431015590730.
Messer, Karen. Creating Worlds. *Ascent Magazine*. (2006, July).
Odell, Jenny. *How to Do Nothing*. Melville House, 2019.
Pérez-Gómez, Alberto. *Attunement*. MIT Press, 2016.
Petani, Fabio James. "Confessions of an Organizational Space Writer." *Organization* 35, no.4 (2019): 961–671. doi:https://doi.org/10.1177/1350508418821010.
Pink, Sarah. *Doing Visual Ethnography*. London: Sage Publications, 2013.
Satama, Suvi. "Researching through Experiencing Aesthetic Moments: 'Sensory Slowness' as my Methodological Strength." In *Writing differently*, vol. 4. 209–230. Emerald Publishing Limited, 2020.
Slovic, Scott. *Seeking Awareness in American Nature Writing*. University of Utah Press, 1992.
Solnit, Rebecca. *Wanderlust: A History of Walking*. Penguin Books, 2001.
Stewart, Kathleen. "Atmospheric Attunements." *Environment and Planning D: Society and Space* 29, no. 3 (2011): 445–453. doi:https://doi.org/10.1068/d9109.
Stewart, Kathleen. *Ordinary Affects*. Duke University Press, 2007.
Taylor, Steven S. "Overcoming Aesthetic Muteness: Researching organizational members' aesthetic experience." *Human Relations* 55, no.7 (2002): 821–840. https://doi.org/10.1177/0018726702055007542.
Vettraino, Elinor and Warren Linds. "Living the Experience of Learning: Embodied Reflexivity as Pedagogical Process." *South African Theatre Journal* 31, no. 1 (2018): 15–35. https://doi.org/10.1080/10137548.2017.1414630.

Ward, J., & Shortt, H. (Eds.). (2020). *Using arts-based research methods: creative approaches for researching business, organisation and humanities* (Ser. Palgrave studies in business, arts and humanities). Palgrave Macmillan.

Warren, Samantha Warren, "Having an Eye for it: Aesthetics, Ethnography and the Senses," *Journal of Organizational Ethnography* 1, no.1 (2012): 107–118.

Yanow, D. (1998). Space stories. *Journal of Management Inquiry*, *7*(3), 215–239. https://doi.org/10.1177/105649269873004.

Yanow, Dvora. "Giving Voice to Space." In *Organizational Spaces*. Eds. Afons H. van Marrewijk & Dvora Yanow. Edward Elgar Publishing, 2010: 139–158.

4

Spatial Attunement

> Human consciousness, one that is not merely in the brain but is fully embodied, needs an external environment pregnant with meanings and emotions for its self-awareness. It is futile to try to hypothesize what might happen if the environment was simply "smooth" and opposed no resistance, like a perfectly "comfortable" place or a drug-induced hallucination.
>
> —Pérez-Gómez[1]

While researching this book, as I explored the ways our surroundings interact, influence, and affect those in contact with them, my own space became more present in my life. As Pérez-Gómez eloquently suggests in the quote above, my consciousness was embodied in an environment briming with life. The more I read theories and research on space, the more I consciously and somewhat unconsciously began noticing its "resistance" and texture in my day-to-day. Over time this became a quasi-autoethnographic experiment, which existed in parallel to my writing. There was an intimacy involved in delicately and purposefully occupying

[1] Alberto Pérez-Gómez, *Attunement* (MIT Press, 2016), 8.

K. Messer, *How to Work with Space*, Palgrave Studies in Business, Arts and Humanities,
https://doi.org/10.1007/978-3-031-46541-3_4

my material world that was unexpected. Becoming attuned to my surroundings felt like an essential component of this work—one that took me beyond the words on this screen, beyond my stated research aims, and into my day-to-day. Being able to engage in an experimental process of awareness, contemplation, and play brought me closer to my research—not through a linear process of analytic understanding but an empathic and embodied knowledge. As I weave elements of this whimsical journey into in the subsequent pages, my goal in this exploration is not to conclude but to consider, be open and tune in to the potential and possibility embedded in our surroundings.

Bringing the research into my body and home in this way, was not intentional at first—or at least I did not think it was. In her own exploration on aesthetic and sensory research, Suvi Satama recently wrote that because of the "emergent, unfinished, and relational process" of aesthetic research, it is "not meaningful to distinguish between" the fieldwork, sense-making, or writing.[2] Instead, it all melds together, moving forwards and backwards, deep and shallow. My research on organizational space included building a tactile and tacit knowledge of space that manifested through doing and engaging with *my* material environment. Working creatively with the research became a sort of antidote to "the exercise of reason through interpretation, classification, and representation".[3] With so much literature detailing various philosophical relationships with space, I craved a tangible and malleable manifestation of them. I wanted to hold them, smell them, feel them in myself. For Satama, this type of embodied research becomes an "holistic experience which reaches beyond our academic selves in profound ways".[4] It also slowed things down as I meandered my way through the literature, unconsciously bringing the practices home and engaging with their material edges over time.

[2] Suvi Satama "Researching through Experiencing Aesthetic Moments: 'Sensory Slowness' as my Methodological Strength", In *Writing differently*, vol. 4 (Emerald Publishing Limited, 2020), 212.

[3] Maggie MacLure, "The Wonder of Data", *Cultural Studies – Critical Methodologies* 13, no. 2 (2013): 228.

[4] Satma, "Researching through Experiencing …" (2020): 212.

An Invitation

As I did, I invite you to experiment with your aesthetic awareness as an active participant. As George Cairns and Tamar Jeffers once wrote to their readers: "You are observer and observed. You interrogate and seek meaning from this text. The text interrogates you, and seeks meaning within you".[5] Just as I have been exploring, inquiring, and reflecting on my written, spatial, and aesthetic relationships, I invite you to do the same. You may wish to pause, attune to your body, engage with your surroundings, and notice. Through this engagement you become part of the text and shift its meaning.

Let's begin.

The themes of this chapter range from emotion, and connection, to shadow, and potential; they are meant to be an offering—an explorative and whimsical touchstone for reflection and contemplation—not an exhaustive compilation or conclusive framework. Together these fragmented moments begin to form an alternative paradigm for the active role physical space plays in our day-to-day lives. This could be at work, at home or while we walk down the street. Over time, the fibres that surround our skin, the wood that supports limbs or objects, and the air (or plastic) we ingest become part of us. As we investigate the various ways our surroundings affect our moods, behaviour, decisions, healing, and work, it is important to remain open and curious.

Emplacement

Natural materials generally feel best. We are told they breathe. I imagine my cotton T-shirt taking a deep breath, letting the air fill the space between each thread. In response to *my* inhalation, the shirt I am wearing spreads to accommodate the expansion of my lungs. If I were wearing a tighter, stiffer shirt, my breathing might adjust to become shallower,

---

[5] George Cairns and Tamar Jeffers, "Looking into/out of* Organizations Through the Rear Window" *In Art and Aesthetics at Work*, eds. Adrian Carr and Philip Hancock (Palgrave Macmillan, 2003), 38.

more restricted. The thought of a living and breathing shirt may be absurd; however, it demonstrates quite well how the environment can act upon our minds and bodies. In one scenario, my shirt expands to accommodate me; in the other, I adapt my body to the shirt. People shift and adapt to their work and home environments all the time; however, these modifications are often unconscious or considered unimportant—little more than a nuisance or whimsy.

When I moved into my now husband's apartment, I had given a lot of thought to the move in terms of our relationship, but I hadn't necessarily thought about how the house would affect my mind–body. How would its small office off the back of the kitchen support my work habits? Would I feel at home—at ease? When I first started sleeping in the new apartment, I would frequently wake up in the middle of the night, groping at the wall for the door handle. Disoriented, I would realize that the door was on the other side of the room. In the dark of the night, my sleeping self was still in my old apartment. Luckily there were no disastrous consequences. But it did take a while for my body to repattern itself in the new physical layout.

Being and working in new places can create unexpected reactions and take time to adjust, both physically and mentally. Sheila Heti, a contemporary writer, once described her attempt to work in an unfamiliar rented studio. She wrote: "I quickly found that the room was too empty of feelings and emotions and objects for me to work deeply. The space didn't belong to me the way my home belonged to me; my home was my insides".[6] Although working from home is equally loved and hated by many people, Heti draws our attention to what it felt like to be inside these spaces. Her own space—one that was familiar and full of history—and the rented studio—one so empty of objects that it made creating new connections on paper difficult. When we see space as something that can envelop us, it feels more intimate and almost frightening.

Space orients us. Our embedded relationship to the physical world is key to grounding the body. Through our bodies, this orientation informs our perception and understanding of others, the environment, and

[6] Sheila Heti, "A common seagull", *Yale Review* 107 no. 4 (2019), 24–35. https://yalereview.yale.edu/common-seagull

ourselves. While the term "embodiment" has become an established part of our lexicon, David Howes, an anthropologist of the senses, suggests we adopt the "emergent paradigm of emplacement" with its "sensuous interrelationship of body-mind-environment".[7] This configuration adds a rich dimension to how space and the mind–body are conceptualized and perceived. Emplacement sees people as "parts of places" rather than isolated subjects.[8] To take it even further, we could say that "perception is embedded" in its surroundings to which it is "bound together in a reciprocal" relationship.[9] This entangled and inseparable connection between our senses, our thoughts, and the environment shapes our daily interactions and experience. As Howes states in his most recent work, to continue this exploration we "must make space for the agency of the senses in rendering the built environment sensible".[10] This beckons the relational and atmospheric in-between into our bodies—the "fabric into which all objects are woven"[11]—to co-create our experience, perception, and knowledge.

Recently, my mother made my daughter the softest white, cotton nightie (see Fig. 4.1). I got one too. Perhaps due to the romantic or nostalgic memories of times past, or the love sewn into every stich by my mother, wearing the nighties made everything feel more magical. Their long, flowy shapes moved and transformed into different combinations of foldings, over-layerings of material that occasionally caught the breeze to dance with our bodies. Wearing the nightie shifted how my body moved, its cotton rhythms influencing how I walked and moved through the house. My daughter's nightie seemed to transform her way of being and moving in the space too. Through the nightie, she became an extension of its threads.

In an exploration on boundaries, Nijs and Daems draw our attention to William James' suggestion "that in 'pure experience', it is not clear yet

---

[7] David Howes, "Introduction", in *Empire of the Senses: The sensory culture reader*, ed. David Howes (Bloomsbury, 2005), 7.

[8] Sarah Pink, *Doing Visual Ethnography*. (Sage Publications, 2013), 347.

[9] Francisco Varela, Evan Thompson, and Eleanor Rosch, *The Embodied Mind* (MIT Press, 1991), 174.

[10] David Howes, *The Sensory Studies Manifesto* (University of Toronto Press, 2022), 152.

[11] Maurice Merleau-Ponty, *Phenomenology of Perception* (Routledge, 1962), 273.

Fig. 4.1 Magic nightie

what is body and what is world".[12] Asking how a nightie or building can shift the way we relate to ourselves—our perception of reality—draws the material world into an active construction of the day-to-day. In these examples, both cloth and walls dress our thoughts, actions, and emotions as we work and move through them. Henri Lefebvre[13] says that from the moment we wake up our body exists within the context of our bed, bedroom, house, city, and so on, and therefore its day-to-day habits, emotions, and sense of self are consciously and unconsciously co-determined by these spatial relationships. Bringing these affective qualities to how we research and write about space adds a much-needed sensuous and aesthetic dimension to our work. What happens if we see space as a sculptor rather than a container?

[12] William James quoted in Greg Nijs and Amélie Daems "And What if the Tangible Were Not, and Vice Versa? On Boundary Works in Everyday Mobility Experience of People Moving into Old Age: For Daisy (1909–2011)", *Space and Culture* 15, no. 3 (2012): 187.

[13] Henri Lefebvre, *The Production of Space*, trans. D. Nicholson-Smith (Blackwell Publishing, 1991).

Spatial Noticing 1. Dancing Fabrics

Spatial Noticing

Can you think of an article of clothing or a particular space that affects how you experience yourself? Does your body move differently? In what ways does it alter how you act or feel?

What spaces (in your life) impact how you behave in them (e.g. a church, library, café)? Think about the qualities of these spaces and how or why they affect you?

Have you ever moved your home or office and felt the changes in your body's habits and patterns? How long did it take to feel at ease or less aware?

Did you find the moving experience uncomfortable, confusing, exciting, refreshing, or stressful?

Emotional Materials

More than a century ago, Swiss art historian Heinrich Wölfflin wrestled with the mind–body's empathic connection to place. Astonished by architecture's ability to "express emotion or a mood"[14]—such as "serious", "somber", "cheerful", or "friendly"—Wölfflin drew a link between building and body, suggesting that "physical forms possess a character only because we ourselves possess a body".[15] This material connection, he argues, is also an empathic one. Therefore, as we encounter the non-human world, we read in it elements of ourselves and our own experience. Wölffin's descriptions of embodied reactions to our surroundings include painful asymmetries, powerful energetic columns, and expansive hallways that change the rhythm of our breath.[16] It is easy to see why, in

[14] Heinrich Wölfflin, "Prolegomena to a Psychology of Architecture", In *Empathy, Form, and Space: Problems in German Aesthetics, 1873–1893* (Getty Center for the History of Art and the Humanities, 1994), 149.

[15] Ibid. 151.

[16] Ibid. 155.

evolutionary terms, humans might have an innate fear of sharp, jagged rocks, but it also illustrates the unconscious connections at play.[17]

Interactions and encounters with our surroundings produce experiences that are co-created. In a similar vein to Wölffin, French philosopher Merleau-Ponty suggests that sounds and tactile data have particular moods and that colours may evoke the "equivalent of a particular sound or temperature".[18] This interplay between colour, emotion, and the senses is always taking place, though it may produce stronger affiliations in some. These metaphors elevate emotion from an untrustworthy or inappropriate quality to an essential component of our experience of being in the world. Describing our empathic and embodied bonds to things, Merleau-Ponty writes:

> The objects which haunt our dreams are meaningful in the same way. Our relationship with things is not a distant one: each speaks to our body and to the way we live. They are clothed in human characteristics (whether docile, soft, hostile or resistant) and conversely they dwell within us as emblems of forms of life we either love or hate.[19]

This eloquent, emotional depiction of haunting objects dwelling within us blurs the boundaries between our interior and exterior realms as it speaks to the strong emotional pull of the material. This emotional and sensorial connection to the landscape is more than a favourable quality; it is essential to our well-being. While modern design and décor of late has opted for white walls and minimalist styling, there is a dull, coldness about seeing the world clean and empty of clutter and ornament. Recently, sensory deprivation tanks have been lauded in spa-like atmospheres for their disconnect from a technologically driven and fast-paced world, but Ingrid Fetell Lee reminds us that rooms with little to no

---

[17] Recent studies in neuroscience have confirmed some of Wölffin's claims. According to neuroscientists Moshe Bar and Maital Neta (2007), angular or sharp edges trigger the amygdala, a brain structure involved in processing fear. This is mostly likely tied to an evolutionary caution from potential sources of danger, jagged rocks, for example.

[18] Merleau-Ponty, *The World of Perception* (1962), 46.

[19] Ibid. 49.

adornment are akin to torture.[20] In her book *Joyful*, she describes a study[21] in which participants chose to "give themselves electric shocks" over sitting alone in an empty room, while another study[22] revealed how even short amounts of sensory deprivation can lead to "hallucinations, paranoid thoughts and negative moods".[23] In thinking about the agony of emptiness, we are reminded just how essential sensory and environmental stimulation are for our well-being.[24]

These tacit and emotional connections to the socio-material world are something to take seriously, especially, as Davidson and Milligan remind us, "there is little we do with our bodies that we can *think apart* from feeling".[25] This includes "the most basic bodily tasks of resting, eating, working out or just getting around [which] can be 'fraught' with fear, guilt and shame, or infused with adrenaline thrills, cravings or dreamt-up desires".[26] Our minds and bodies experience so much in a day, and, depending on our physical location or emotional state, these experiences can feel entirely different from one day to the next.

Emotionally tinted perspectives do not produce realities that are entirely socially constructed, built solely from internal social experience, but instead are joint creations in which feelings and emotions are *located*—each "bound to a particular place with its specific temporality and qualitative character".[27] Bridging the bodily and material worlds underlines the role of environments in shaping our lived experience. As Pallasma writes: "the geometry of thought echoes the geometry of the

---

20 Ingrid Fetell Lee, *Joyful* (Little Brown Spark, 2018), 53.

21 Timothy D Wilson et al. "Just Think: The Challenges of the Disengaged Mind", *Science 345* no. 6192 (2014).

22 Oliver J. Mason & Francesca Brady "The Psychotomimetic Effects of Short-Term Sensory Deprivation", *Journal of Nervous and Mental Disease* 197, no. 10 (2009).

23 Fetell Lee, *Joyful* (2018), 53.

24 Fetell Lee continues in her book to discuss how sensory stimulation is useful to reduce stress, improve mood, and enhance attentiveness. Multi-sensory environments and techniques are also being used as treatments and therapies for developmental disabilities, brain injury, and dementia, among others.

25 Joyce Davidson and Christine Milligan, "Embodying emotion sensing space: Introducing emotional geographies", *Social & Cultural Geography* 5, no. 4 (2004) 523.

26 Ibid.

27 Pérez-Gómez, *Attunement* (2016), 1.

room".[28] Just as Sheila Heti could not write in her empty, unfamiliar studio, we behave differently, make different decisions, and "think different thoughts in different places".[29] Though subtle, these actions reinforce nonetheless the deeply *affective* nature of physical space. Our surroundings act upon us, just as we act upon them—hanging paintings, moving chairs, covering floors—transforming and creating spaces, "dressed with our memories and hopes".[30] Whether we are cognizant of it or not, the emotions that accompany our experience of space at the office, on the street, or at home offer glimpses into the deeper connections at play.

Spatial Noticing 2. Reorientation

Spatial Noticing

Which spaces do you feel most in your body? Do you feel in awe of expansive spaces or feel claustrophobic in tight ones?

What emotions do you connect to the material world? Do certain buildings or objects feel more than others?

What sensory stimuli do you notice the most? How would it feel without it?

Sensory Deception

As we've seen, sensory stimuli—what we hear, see, taste, smell, and feel—give shape to a room's energy or atmosphere. Purely functional spaces, as offices are sometimes considered to be, often lack qualities beyond the basic human comforts. Consider walking into a restaurant, a concert hall, or even a retail shop, where all the layers of materiality come together to produce an almost emotive affect. Such spaces can be described as *experiential* and therefore more likely to move beyond pure function and beyond comfort to the level of pleasure.[31] The sensory experience of an

[28] Juhani Pallasma, *The eyes of the skin: Architecture and the Senses.* (John Wiley & Sons, 2012), 48.

[29] Pérez-Gómez, *Attunement* (2016), 109.

[30] Ibid. 3.

[31] Trevor Keeling et al., "How the Sensory Experience of Buildings can Contribute to Wellbeing and Productivity", In *Proceedings of the 7th Windsor Conference: The changing context of comfort in an unpredictable world* (London: Network for Comfort and Energy Use in Buildings, 2012).

office space needs to be considered as more than a group of isolated components, but as a set of sensations to be delighted in rather than shut out.[32] However, it is one thing to design and build an environment rich in sensuous quality and another to incorporate our experiential relationship to those sounds, textures, or smells.

As more and more designers tap into the power within these qualities, it is interesting to think about how they are received. For many years, Judith Heerwagen has explored our evolutionary predisposition to natural environments, suggesting that "our ties to nature are deep and enduring; [so much so that] when we sever these ties we create conditions that are contrary to basic human needs".[33] While it has become common knowledge that access to natural environments is beneficial to our well-being, Heerwagen goes beyond nature prescriptions to advocate for buildings as habitats for people. These living spaces benefit from mimicking qualities of the natural environment such as sensory variability, which "enables people to actively select conditions that fit their current needs and desires".[34] When outside, people can access the shade of a tree if they are too hot or find a sunny spot to warm up; however, "building interiors seldom offer such personal adaptive possibilities".[35] Rather than simply adding plants to your desk, reflecting on how bodies react, adjust, and move through the natural environment offers a different wisdom about office space. Buildings with naturalistic features bring aspects of "patterned complexity and sensory variability"[36] indoors, which can elevate the space by allowing users to interact and engage according to their own needs and preferences. In these types of spaces, our material relationships become more involved and varied.

Recently, while walking through the Montreal airport, I was pleasantly surprised to see the addition of plants, trees, and living walls. The usually drab space was converted into something more organic and adaptable. Coupled with a recorded sound of birds projected from the intercom, the

---

[32] Ibid.

[33] Judith Heerwagen, "Design, Productivity and Wellbeing: What are the Links?", In *AIA Conference on Highly Effective Facilities* (Cincinnati, OH, 1998), 5.

[34] Ibid. 4.

[35] Ibid. 4–5.

[36] Ibid. 4.

Fig. 4.2 Montreal airport trees

traditional frenzied airport atmosphere, while not completely transformed, managed to shift into something a little more soothing and pleasant (see Fig. 4.2).

At home, I am sensitive to how the atmosphere shifts and changes with the addition of candlelight or loud air-conditioning—which I am constantly in trouble for turning off. One winter, as a joke, my husband put a video of a fire—a burning yule log—on the living room TV. We laughed at the tackiness of it. A real fire is so rich with sensory affect: the heat it projects; the crackling of wood and damp sizzling as the log burns; the light itself, first bright with flame and then glowing embers.

I grew up with a fireplace in the house. Winters were spent gathering in front of its warmth, pushing my heat-seeking dad out of the way so my legs could soak in the heat too. I did not have much expectation that this flat, filmed fire would add much value to our home, but I was wrong. Not all the fireplace videos, but some, allowed the fire's natural soundtrack to crackle in the background. When sitting in an adjacent room—with the TV out of sight—the sound of the fire filled the space. Despite knowing it wasn't real, the audible warmth shifted the atmosphere. I even caught my dad standing in front of it one visit, waiting—for some sort of magic—to warm up. It was glorious.

Spatial Noticing 3. Sensory Deceit

Spatial Noticing

What sounds, smells, or textures have the ability to transport you elsewhere?

Does it matter if sensory stimulus is fake or not?

Have you ever been tricked by a sensory cue that wasn't real?

What control do you have over your workspace? Can you open a window, turn off the lights, or add decoration or bird calls?

Stimulation

While sensory diversity and stimulation is a vital component to thriving in the world, a common complaint from people working in open-office spaces is the constant noise and distraction. Large open-office spaces can feel chaotic, with too much visual and aural stimulus, and few or no barriers allowing noise to accumulate and rebound. The consequence is often a room packed with workers wearing noise-cancelling headphones—an attempt to quell the turbulence raging around them. Instantly, the sea of people side by side are muted, each in their own little world. No music playing, no clicking of keyboards, no murmurs, no hums.

Researchers Rachel Kaplan and Stephen Kaplan have investigated stimulation in offices[37] and in nature[38] and developed an attention restoration theory (ART) from examining different types of environmental stimulation and the quality of attention they demand (Kaplan and Kaplan, 1989). Unlike the kinaesthetic stimulation provided by Japanese

[37] Rachel Kaplan, "The Role of Nature in the Context of the Workplace", *Landscape and Urban Planning* 26 no. 1–4 (1993).

[38] Rachel Kaplan & Stephen Kaplan, "The Experience of Nature: A Psychological Perspective" (Cambridge University Press, 1989).

gardens, mental fatigue has been linked to too much environmental stimulation. Urban environments tend to expose people to this type of relentless stimulation, which the authors say requires *hard fascination*. In these environments, people are "forced to use their attention to overcome the effects" of persistent distraction.[39] In contrast, natural environments are filled with visual qualities that are considered *soft fascinations*, such as leaves, branches, shadows, flowers, clouds, and patterns of dappled sunlight.[40] These abundant, sensory-rich features call for the kind of attention that feels unencumbered. Rather than monopolize focus or dampen the senses, they allow the mind–body to contemplate other things.[41] Such traits found in nature have been linked to cognitive restoration and reduced stress.[42,43] Becoming momentarily distracted by the multicoloured fall leaves allows the mind–body space for subconscious thought. Like insights that appear while in the shower or just before falling asleep, the presence of *soft fascination* seems to provide the conditions for unfettered, subconscious reflection—a push-and-pull between absence and presence, seen and unseen, and ambiguity and certainty.

In a study similar to that of Kaplan and Kaplan's[44] work on soft fascination, Kevin Nute and Zhuo Job Chen have been investigating the psychological benefits of what they refer to as "wind-generated movement" in traditionally static environments—such as the office.[45] Natural movement is defined as flickering sunlight or the animated shadows of tree leaves or branches. Nute and Chen found that the presence of these naturally mobile phenomena fostered a sense of presence and timelessness like

[39] David G. Pearson, and Tony Craig, "The Great Outdoors? Exploring the Mental Health Benefits of Natural Environments", *Frontiers in Psychology* 5 (2014): 1178.

[40] Stephen Kaplan, "The Restorative Benefits of Nature: Toward an Integrative Framework", *Journal of Environmental Psychology* 15 (1995).

[41] Kaplan, "The Restorative Benefits of Nature" (1995): 174.

[42] Kaplan & Kaplan, "The Experience of Nature" (1989).

[43] Catherine Ward Thompson et al., "More Green Space is Linked to Less Stress in Deprived Communities: Evidence from Salivary Cortisol Patterns", *Landscape and Urban Planning* 105, no. 3 (2012).

[44] Kaplan & Kaplan, "The Experience of Nature" (1989).

[45] Kevin Nute and Zhuo Job Chen, "Wind-Generated Movement as a Potential means to Psychological Presence in Indoor Work Environments", *International Journal of Design in Society* 1–9 (2020).

the results of meditation and mindfulness. Whether the room was large or small or the movement was found inside or outside the room did not have an impact on the participants level of presence and connection. Being aware of natural movement through space was effective at "reducing stress and improving attention" by drawing attention to the dynamic changes of the participants' surroundings.[46] While lighting strategies and natural light access are ordinary conversations for designers or those using the space, considering how shadows dance in room is a less-common consideration.

Last week, I travelled to another part of town for a dermatology appointment. The entrance was inside an underground mall; after walking through the corridor lined with various shops, low ceilings, and florescent lights, I took an elevator to the fifth floor.

The reception was windowless and modern. It had the usual polished surfaces with fake plants, faux leather chairs, and slick marble-esque countertops. After a moment or two of waiting I was escorted to one of the exam rooms. To my surprise and delight, the room was filled with dappled sunlight, a large Ficus tree, plants, and shadows. The leaf prints on the exam table were beautiful as they flickered from light to dark (see Fig. 4.3). The room existed in such contrast to the reception with its living textures and natural light that I audibly gasped as I walked in and almost immediately felt calmer.

Spatial Noticing 4. Living Office

Spatial Noticing

What elements of traditional workspaces (medical or otherwise) have surprised and delighted you?

Are there certain qualities of a room that make you feel calmer and more grounded?

Are there any shadows where you work?

What is the soundscape of your workspace?

Do you find your office to be over- or under-stimulating?

[46] Nute and Chen, "Wind-Generated Movement" (2020): 7.

Fig. 4.3 Dermatology office, Montreal

disConnection

As current technologies and building materials manifest an environment "increasingly devoid of qualities, reduced to a set of coordinates in a global positioning device", Pérez Gómez, an architectural historian and theorist, suggests that human beings today face not just boredom and fatigue, but a "sense of despair in view of the 'meaningless of existence'".[47] In his latest book, *Attunement*, Pérez-Gómez focuses on technology's role in distancing people from their surroundings and observes that despite the fact that humans actively perceive space through "our senses and our

[47] Pérez Gómez, *Attunement*, (2016), 108.

emotional consciousness, the technological world tends to deny the cognitive value of such perception".[48] Viewing and conceptualizing space through a screen, and actively accessing it through various technological instruments and devices, ultimately "impacts our perceptions, so that place effectively hides from our experience".[49] Perceiving through a phone limits the multi-sensory reality of the world by transforming space from something porous and all-encompassing into something flat and impenetrable (until the screen cracks).

In *The Urban Village*, Alberto Magnaghi blames the standardization of building materials such as "concrete, aluminum, plastic [and] steel" for the bleak portrait of contemporary city life. These materials manifest sameness throughout the cityscape by "dissociating architecture and the city from" the nuances of place.[50] Abstract spaces created by recent advances in technology abandon site-specificity in favour of the "virtual factory".[51] This detachment from our banal physical surroundings has a destabilizing impact, a dismemberment from material culture, and what Magnaghi refers to as relating in an *aspatial domain*.[52] At the same time, the bombardment of mass-produced imagery, plastered across the city, and streamed through screens produces a "mesmerizing flow without focus or participation".[53] Recipients are simultaneously over- and under-stimulated.

After years of living in the city, I realize I am used to walking on flat cement sidewalks. Straight lines and sharp corners take me to my destination. But in the winter, Montreal gets a lot of snow, most of which is plowed, piled, and picked up by giant snow removal trucks. Before that happens, while the city works, there's a moment where the sidewalk is transformed from a straight, cement grid, to a fluffy, winding pathway. This usually happens because plow drivers swerve down the sidewalk to avoid forgotten bicycles, telephone poles, and other miscellaneous street debris (see Fig. 4.4). The result is enchanting.

---

[48] Ibid.

[49] Ibid.

[50] Alberto Magnaghi, *The Urban Village*. (Zed Books, 2005), 13.

[51] Ibid. 18.

[52] Ibid.

[53] Pallasmaa, *The Eyes of the Skin* (2012), 25.

Fig. 4.4 Snow paths

The white coat lightens the shadows and quiets the hum. The city becomes softer as many of its edges and grit momentarily vanish. It smells cold and wet. Every sense is altered. The snow beneath my feet has a spongier vibration than pavement. The chirping of birds becomes louder and clearer with the softening of the urban din. As Bachelard writes, "We too are 'swathed' in the blanket of winter".[54] It's sort of like nature's white padded room, within which we are forced to endure tranquility and discomfort simultaneously.

The winter snow transforms the city landscape. When it is stripped of straight lines, I wonder if makes us more at ease? Or does the conversion

[54] Gaston Bachelard, *The Poetics of Space* (Beacon Press, 1994), 39.

from cement grid to snowy pathway cause something more enticing by "creating a kind of pleasant sensation of unfinished-ness"[55] that adds mystery to the journey?

In this environment, my body becomes activated. Each foot is placed carefully to ensure a safe and sturdy step forward. I wander through the snow-shaped streets, navigating their ever-shifting, crunching textures, which allows an innate curiosity to take hold as unexpected sensations invite me to participate. I find the winter beautiful despite my cheeks burning from the coldand the challenge of walking. Indeed, the winter landscape brims with life amidst contradiction.[56]

The anthropologist Edward T. Hall, who coined the term *proxemics*—a cultural theory exploring the human use of space—spoke of the lack of "excitement or visual variation" within modern urban spaces.[57] These visually similar spaces lack opportunities for kinaesthetic experiences and thus create an urban population that is "kinaesthetically deprived".[58] Hall looks to traditional Japanese gardens to illustrate how well-designed spaces can engage the body. While walking through a Japanese garden, visitors are required to alter their step as they place their feet onto the steppingstones, often surrounded by water, without losing balance. Thus, visual concentration and unusual "muscular sensations are built into the experience".[59] Vistas present themselves, not just in front of the viewer but also up high or behind them, forcing neck muscles to stretch, or, as Hall puts it, to be "brought into play".[60] This kinaesthetic way of experiencing space prompts the visitor to become more aware, not just of the aesthetic surroundings but also of their own body. While some architects have utilized this quality by purposefully designing buildings with unusual attributes, such as non-standard stairs or unusual entrances, the responses have often been less than favourable by the people stumbling upon them.[61] However, as cognitive neuroscientist Collin Ellard found

[55] Jenny Odell, *How to do Nothing* (Melville House, 2019) p.104

[56] Bachelard, *The Poetics of Space* (1994), 39.

[57] Edward T Hall, *The Hidden Dimension* (Anchor Books, 1982), 62.

[58] Ibid.

[59] Ibid. 51.

[60] Ibid. 52

[61] The Covel steps at UCLA are also known as the awkward steps for their short, wide dimensions.

with his wearable technology, the absence of visual diversity on city streets led to boredom and fatigue in his participants.[62] With no invitations to connect and to engage with our surroundings, the human body becomes weary and tired. Could this loss of stimulation be connected to a loss of potential?

Spatial Noticing 5. Sensory Activation

Spatial Noticing

Think about which spaces make your body feel most activated or bored?

What qualities provide the most sensory and embodied stimulation?

What do you notice when something in your everyday surroundings changes?

Remembering

I remember sitting at my office computer for the first time after a trip to my parents' house in Victoria to attend a friend's wedding. Mentally, I understood the distance we travelled across the country, by plane, from one place to the other. I had packed my suitcase, drove to the airport, said goodbye, watched movies, ate terrible pizza, drank mediocre wine, and soothed my exhausted two-year-old. The sun was setting when we arrived back in Montreal. The humid air hit my body as we walked through the airport doors and got into a taxi. We went to bed late, our bodies still operating on Vancouver Island time. In Greece, there are two words for the way we experience time. The first is *chronos*, which refers to standardized and scheduled time; it is the time we read on clock and calendar. The second, *kairos*, is less programmed. It is felt; it changes and adapts, lives and breathes. Kairos is rhythm. It calls upon intuition, presence, and awareness to feel it and act within it, rather than itineraries and alarm bells. Jetlag pulls me temporarily into Kairos time. A liminal space in which I am neither here nor there.

The next day, while unpacking my suitcase, I brought a shirt up to my face and took a deep breath. It smelled like my parents' house. I took another breath and closed my eyes. For a second, I was back—or perhaps

[62] Colin Ellard, *Places of the Heart* (Bellevue Literary Press, 2015).

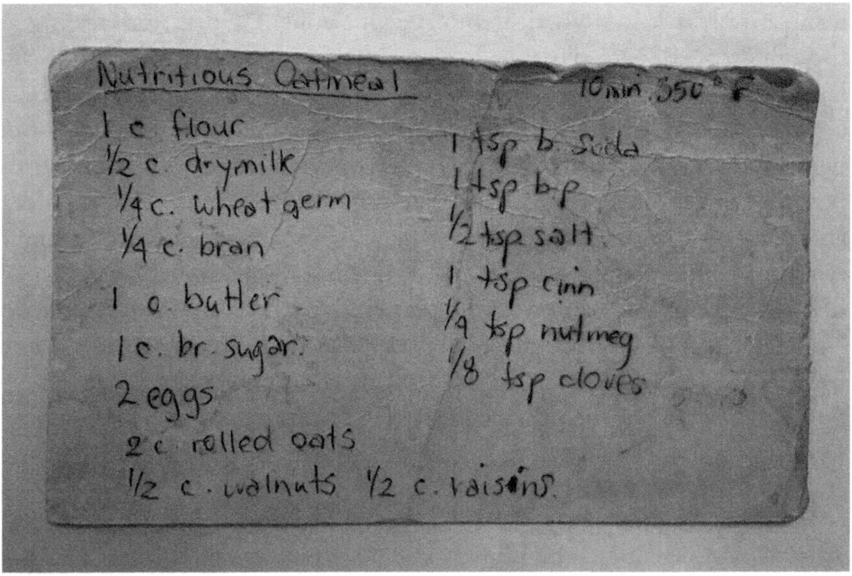
Nutritious Oatmeal
10 min 350° F
1 c flour
1/2 c. drymilk
1/4 c. wheat germ
1/4 c. bran
1 c. butter
1 c. br. sugar
2 eggs
2 c rolled oats
1/2 c. walnuts 1/2 c. raisins
1 tsp b. soda
1 tsp b.p
1/2 tsp salt
1 tsp cinn
1/4 tsp nutmeg
1/8 tsp cloves

Fig. 4.5 Nutritious oatmeal cookies

part of me was still there? My body was still on West Coast time, making us all sleep in late. It was slowly adjusting to the hot, sticky air, which had replaced the cedar- and kelp-scented ocean breezes. I felt out of sync in Montreal.

I took my daughter to daycare and came into the office. I was staring at the screen, looking for something that called out to me. Where do I start? Uncertain and looking for distraction, I took a bite of the snack I brought. It was an oatmeal-and-chocolate-chip cookie, which my mother had baked just before we left. It was the recipe she used to make when I was a kid (see Fig. 4.5). Back then we called them *occasional* chocolate-chip cookies because there were so few chips in them. It tasted like her and my childhood. It felt strange and good to taste home in Montreal—a momentary merging of two different places and times. In the past, I have tried to replicate these cookies, but they are never exactly right. They never deliver my childhood home into my mouth.

Marcel Proust made famous this type of spontaneous, embodied memory when he bit into a tea-dipped madeleine and was unexpectedly transported back to a vivid memory of his aunt. He describes feeling as though "an exquisite pleasure had invaded [his] senses, something isolated, detached, with no suggestion of its origin".[63] In this passage, Proust conveys both the pleasure and disorientation in the experience—not being fully aware of what was happening or where he was being transported. Philosopher Edward Casey describes Proust's notion of memory and place as a moment or essence that "can be compressed into a single sensation, which being reawakened, can bring the place back to us in its full vivacity".[64] Such impressions of places past, he continues, remain "lodged in our body long after we have left [them]", waiting to be released by the correct sensation or trigger.[65] In this sense, memories do not transport us elsewhere; rather, they bring part of ourselves forward. These sensations of memories and bodies' past merge with our present moment to create a melange of time and place.

Similarly, Dylan Trigg, in *The Memory of Place*, describes these memories as "residue" within the body.[66] He defines the act of remembering as "the meaningful retrieval of an experience, encompassing a surrounding world of place, time and corporeality".[67] In this definition, memories are located both in terms of their surroundings and within the body. Regardless of how the memories arrive, their existence within the mind–body influences how we relate to our present environment. Place contributes to how we exist in the world at a very fundamental level, shaping our behaviour, affecting our emotion, and guiding our action. With such powerful qualities, it makes sense that these influences would not simply disappear when we leave a room.

Places are in us. They become part of our physical being, leaving "traces"[68] on our bodies that later resurface through memories often triggered by sensory experience. But past spaces do not only exist as flashes in our mind. Through regular interaction, they can alter and shape our

---

[63] Marcel Proust, *Swann's Way* (Vintage Books, 1922), 48.

[64] Edward S Casey, "Between Geography and Philosophy", *Annals of the Association of American Geographers 91*, no. 4 (2001): 688.

[65] Ibid.

[66] Dylan Trigg, *The Memory of Place* (Ohio University Press, 2012), 11.

[67] Ibid. 51.

[68] Nijs & Daems, "And What if the Tangible were Not", (2012): 190.

movements, our ways of communicating, and how we interact with each other. Because of this, our current modes and experiences are "imbued with the thickness of a past that has not ceased to be".[69] These spatial habits do not immediately disappear when we leave a space or replace an old space with a new one.

While reading about memory and space, it happened to be autumn in Montreal. One of my favourite times of year. The colour infused into the city through the red, yellow, and orange treetops never ceases to feel magical. But there is something even more mysterious that happens when the leaves fall to the ground. They leave an imprint—a perfect, ghostly print as though the leaf's shadow forgot that it and its leaf were supposed to stay together (see Fig. 4.6). The sidewalk is preserving the memory of the leaf in a beautiful display of something that came before—a little time capsule of the fall.

Spatial Noticing 6. Material Memory

Spatial Noticing

Are there certain spaces, smells, tastes, or sounds that trigger memories?
What material residue do you have in your body? When does it surface?
What other elements in our environment preserve moments in time?

Material Past

On a recent trip out west, we stayed in my grandparents' house, which was built (by them) in 1955. The house, nestled among moss-covered rock and expansive oak trees, is where my mother and her three sisters were raised. I also lived there briefly, while I attended university. After class, I would walk up the winding hill to their house. Grandpa would build a fire that filled the room with a smell of smoke as it cracked and hissed, before settling into his armchair to read the paper. I would lay on the couch, listening to Grandma in the kitchen and watching the flames flicker, until my eyes eventually closed.

---

[69] Ibid. 188.

Fig. 4.6 Leaf imprints

The house has always been one of my favourite places. Grandma's exquisite taste in objects, art, and furniture is showcased throughout their home. Her travels and adventures are on display through the wall hangings, photographs, pottery, and sculptures. The house itself embodied their creative spirit through years of handcrafted alterations, as well as every piece of saved string; the drawers of cleaned-and-dried plastic bags, pottery jars of elastics and twist ties, and the endless containers of saved miscellaneous materials. Born in the Depression era, their house was a meticulous assortment of useful and cared-for items, organized and waiting to be repurposed. Their investment and attention to detail were infused in every corner of the house. Many renovation projects were done by my grandfather, a talented woodworker, and my grandmother, who would tackle any project. I remember when she re-modelled the fireplace—converting a drab grey brick hole into a work of art through floral tiles and cement paste.

My grandfather died last spring with my grandmother joining him six months later on her 95th birthday. My family gathered in their home to begin the process of cleaning, clearing, and preparing the house to be sold. My sister and I had the task of sorting through my grandmother's workroom. It was never called an office, but it did contain many years of work—mostly in the form of slides and journals from research in China, Japan, and Nigeria. As a painter, her desk was covered in jars of paint brushes, paints, pens, and various types of paper. I discovered all sorts of little objects that had been converted from their original purpose or created to achieve some other effect—sponges, sticks, bent twigs—known only by Grandma. Over the years, shelves had been added to the walls and desks outfitted with additional levels by my grandfather. The space becoming a finely tuned extension of my grandmother's body. It contained all her tools: cameras and lenses, resource books, paper, pens, clips, and brushes—everything she needed to create, to work.

In his book *The Architecture of Happiness*, Alain de Botton speaks of the house as a witness. He writes: "It has provided not only physical but also psychological sanctuary. It has been a guardian of identity. Over the years, its owners have returned from periods away and, on looking around them, remembered who they were".[70] I found it particularly difficult to say goodbye to that house. Not just because of the memories I had of them in it but also because in many ways it *was* my grandparents. They were woven into every aspect of the house for over seventy years. It held, protected, shaped, and witnessed them. So many traces of their movements were visible in the stains on the carpet, the worn spots on the steps, the hummingbird nest brought in from the garden, the smell of the basement. If we see space as entangled when someone is alive, what happens when that person dies, when the house is part of their remains.

[70] Alain de Botton, *The Architecture of Happiness* (McClelland & Stewart, 2006), 11.

Spatial Noticing 7. Material Ghosts

Spatial Noticing

Have you ever lost someone and felt connected to their physical space or material objects?

Does the material retain someone's life?

What objects remind you of past relationships?

Rearranging

Growing up, once I was able to dress myself, I did so four to six times a day. Constantly trying on new combinations, each outfit felt like I was wearing a different person. The clothes gave me permission to play with and express different aspects of myself that were usually hidden. When I was a little older and physically able to move furniture, my fascination with transformation shifted to the rooms in our house. My childhood bedroom was very small. It fit a single bed, a desk, and not much more. Yet, a few times each year, I rearranged its contents. It was as though my room became a mirror for the emotional upheaval and confusion of adolescence. The obvious position for the bed was lengthwise along the right-hand wall. At the far end of the room was a medium-sized window and, along the other wall opposite the bed, a closet with folding doors. Once, I remember positioning the bed horizontally under the window. In this configuration, I couldn't completely open one of the closet doors. But it didn't matter. It was an experiment. Every time I rearranged, I would tap into a somewhat fantastical hope that something new would emerge—that somehow, if I kept trying, a new, totally different room (me) would be revealed.

My penchant for moving furniture helps me remain attuned to my house and to notice qualities that may have shifted beyond my awareness. Rearranging furniture, plants, and art keeps me more present and engaged with my current environment. Our house has become a subtle but constantly evolving space. Most often, the changes will be very slight. A plant rotates or moves to another location. The rocking chair and armchair switch places. A pillow moves from here to there. But even when the shift is small, the entire room has a slightly different resonance. Unfamiliar shadows appear and new relationships between objects emerge like shifts in the conversation. *Now, my view from the rocking chair is different—from here, I can see the painting.*

Recently I moved a lamp from the bedroom to the dining room for more light now that winter is creating darker evenings. What happened surprised me: the light projected shadows, of the plant sitting beside it, onto the ceiling. Suddenly, giant leaves patterned the wall and the ceiling, once invisible, became part of the room.

Spatial Noticing 8. Rearranging

Spatial Noticing

Move something around in your home or office. Touch it, smell it.
How does it change the space?
What do you notice?
Does cleaning or rearranging make you feel more connected to your space? Why?

Potential

Potential space, a term used by Winnicott in his influential work *Playing and Reality*, is filled with possibility through its indication of presence and absence, a simultaneous joining and separating between subject and object. Winnicott, a psychoanalyst and theorist, introduces the term *potential space* as a quality of the (un)coupling between mother and child and emphasizes the importance of trust and reliability as foundational qualities for the creative play flourishing at its centre. Winnicott does not attempt to resolve this inherently paradoxical term.[71] Instead, it exists as an (im)possibility—the co-creation of material and immaterial during a transitional state of separation and becoming. Rather than isolate these qualities, they are all considered part of a loving relationship, within which—through a creative process of exploration—the child begins to understand themselves as something separate from the mother.

[71] Donald W. Winnicott, *Playing and Reality* (Routledge, 2005), 145.

Accessing this state of *potential space* requires an ontological shift from the "identity logic of Euclidean space to the relational logic of potential space".[72] Repositioning from an objective and rational state to a relational way of being in and understanding the world opens our perspective infinitely. Within this openness, "potential is neither internal nor external, but is the nonfinite difference that emerges through *relation*".[73] One way to access potential is through a spontaneous eruption that guides our behaviour, as opposed to conscious, deliberate action. Winnicott describes this attention as "undirected" contemplation and play that is "deliberate, but without too much deliberateness".[74] It represents those moments when you make decisions without time to think too much about them. They simply emerge from you *and* the situation. The results can be familiar or unexpected outcomes that shift and shape our future directions.

While (un)tangling theories of *affect* and emotion, Brian Massumi connects *intensity* to something "embodied in pure autonomic reactions".[75] Intensity is "static"—almost as if time were suspended "in a state of suspense, potentially of disruption"—while simultaneously "filled with motion" and resonance.[76] It is through this intensity or affect—a simultaneous pause and growth of frenetic energy—from which we get the "unexpected and inexplicable".[77] In this exploration, Massumi separates affect from emotion by positioning it within the body as an abstracted paradox where "opposites coexist, coalesce and connect".[78] It seems that the more we try to comprehend and disentangle such states, the more it is discovered that "outsides are unfolded, and sadness is happy".[79] Instead, leaving room for the unknown, unfathomable, and undefinable becomes part of the process.

[72] Ref. "Metcalfe and Game (2008)" is cited in text but not provided in the reference list. Please provide details in the list or delete the citation from the text.Metcalfe and Game, "Potential Space and Love", *Emotion, Space and Society* 1, no. 1 (2008): 18.

[73] Ibid.

[74] Winnicott, *Playing and Reality* (2005), 147.

[75] Brian Massumi, "The Autonomy of Affect", *Cultural Critique* 31 (1995): 85.

[76] Ibid. 86.

[77] Ibid. 88.

[78] Ibid. 91.

[79] Ibid. 91.

This spontaneous collaboration between the self and situation draws the environment into our lives in a tangible way. These eruptions of potential and possibility are hidden and embedded into every moment. What emerges from the interactions are aspects of ourselves that may not yet fully exist but are revealed or created from the unknown.[80] Kathleen Stewart describes potential as something "stored in ordinary things".[81] Its essence can be "fleeting and amorphous"—something like "residue or resonance" and yet "palpable as a physical tree".[82] We can feel potential; it hides and lingers in the in-between.

Playing with "absence-in-presence"[83] seems to be an essential element for often undervalued aspects such as curiosity, surprise, and mystery. Perhaps the creative potential embedded within *mess* stems from the possibility hidden underneath or behind stacks of books and papers. In *The Poetics of Space*, Bachelard speaks at length about the intimate potential of drawers and chests for this reason. He writes:

> Wardrobes with their shelves, desks with their drawers, and chests with their false bottoms are veritable organs of the secret psychological life. Indeed, without these 'objects' and a few others in equally high favor, our intimate life would lack a model of intimacy. They are hybrid objects, subject objects. Like us, through us and for us, they have a quality of intimacy.[84]

Here secret spaces and objects take on an intimate role. They provide a framework within which our mysteries, treasures and truths can reside. Just like the hidden nature of the mind–body, cupboards and boxes offer distraction and recesses to explore, or fill.

Researchers[85] examining the impact of order and disorder on behaviour and decision-making discovered that participants in an orderly room were more likely to choose more conventional and healthier options,

---

[80] Alfred Margulies, *The Empathic Imagination* (W.W. Norton, 1989), 131.

[81] Kathleen Stewart, Ordinary Affects (Duke University Press, 2007), 21.

[82] Ibid.

[83] Margulies, *The Empathic Imagination* (1989), 132.

[84] Bachelard, *The Poetics of Space* (1994), 78.

[85] Kathleen D. Vohs et al., "Physical order Produces Healthy Choices, Generosity, and Conventionality, whereas Disorder Produces Creativity", *Psychological Science* 24, no. 9 (2013).

while those in a messy room were more likely to exhibit enhanced creativity and favour novelty. This study uniquely links the presence of mess or order to how we make decisions. With tidying being elevated to an art form[86] and a "growing industry centred on instilling environmental orderliness", the study illustrates the creative value of disorder and mess while acknowledging the benefits of a clean, uncluttered space.[87] Perhaps both are possible. Perhaps it is not about the mess or cleanliness, but about the ability to hide.

My daughter loves playing hide-and-seek. When she was little, she would show us where to hide and then return, with boundless surprise and delight, to find us exactly where she left us. Other days, we spend enormous amounts of time taking turns hiding and finding, always stumbling upon new spaces to curl into or lay beneath—holding our bodies still, breathing into the cloth, and sensing the approach of discovery.

It is a marvellous way to play with each other and with the space. My favourite, though, is when my daughter closes her eyes and says, "you can't see me. Where am I?" For her, we instantaneously disappear, and she hides for a second or two in the darkness behind her eyelids. *Found you!*

While we play, the house is both obscured and revealed in novel ways. The game therefore becomes a process of discovery, a practice of absence-in-presence. As we run from room to room, the house unfolds before us, but never all at once. There always remains a part that is unseen and perfect to hide in.

Becoming more sensitive to what is hidden, within our mind and within the physical world, opens a world of possibility and potential. The presence of mystery, mess, or undefined qualities within spaces cannot be reduced to aesthetic preferences; rather, these ingredients are necessary to shape the future. As geographer Doreen Massey wrote, a space cannot be "a container for always-already constituted identities nor a complete closure of holism".[88] This would be a space without relation—of closed, insular, and static action. This description pushes past space as an external framework—which so many are desperately trying to perfect—because

[86] See Marie Kondo, *The Life-Changing Magic of Tidying Up* (Ten Speed Press), 2014.
[87] Vohs et al. "Physical Order" (2013): 1866.
[88] Doreen Massey, *For Space* (Sage Publications, 2005), 12.

regardless of how accurately a space is designed to meet every possible need, as Massey puts it, for "the future to be open, space must be open too".[89] Too often, undefined spaces seem predestined for junk storage—fatalities of collective neglect. On the other hand, to realize the possibility and potential within a space requires a balance of trust, flexibility, engagement, and experimentation. From a relational perspective, there needs to be a certain level of awareness and attunement between the space and those working with it.

Spatial Noticing 9. Potential

Spatial Noticing

What does openness in a space look and feel like?

What mysteries can you invite into your space? What can you find—a drawer filled with forgotten treasures—or hide?

Is there potential in your space? Where is it located?

Curious Shadows

The presence of potential can also be linked to emotions such as optimism, curiosity, and hope, among many others. But why does it feel difficult to justify the need for curiosity in space? In organizational studies, how often do we evaluate a space based on its ability to provoke intrigue? Richard Phillips suggests that we need to actively "make space for curiosity" in everyday work environments.[90] Spaces can be embedded with curiosity through objects of interest, or qualities of the space itself. Throughout his work *In Praise of Shadows*, Junichirō Tanizaki meticulously describes the settings and qualities of Japanese architecture, design, and ritual, often contrasting them with Western aesthetic and cultural norms.[91] His words lead us into a room that is empty yet overflows with detail and mystery:

---

[89] Ibid.

[90] Richard Phillips, "Space for Curiosity", *Progress in Human Geography* 38, no. 4 (2013): 493.

[91] Junichirō Tanizaki, *In Praise of Shadows* (Leete's Island Books, 1977).

> I marvel at our [Japanese] comprehension of the secrets of shadows, our sensitive use of shadow and light. For the beauty of the alcove is not the work of some clever device. An empty space is marked off with plain wood and plain walls, so that the light drawn into it forms dim shadows within emptiness. There is nothing more. And yet, when we gaze into the darkness that gathers behind the crossbeam, around the flower vase, beneath the shelves, though we know perfectly well it is mere shadow, we are overcome with the feeling that in this small corner of the atmosphere there reigns complete and utter silence; that here in the darkness immutable tranquility holds sway.[92]

Here, Tanizaki illustrates the beauty and power held within "the secrets of shadows"[93] by emphasizing their almost-mystical qualities. We cannot help but be affected at a subconscious level, for what we are witnessing is not a gimmick or device, but the dynamic interplay between the built and natural environments.

While lighting is often spoken about in design, how shadows appear on the wall has received less attention. It is fascinating to watch how they constantly shift and change depending on the direction of light and the placement of the sun or moon in the sky. It is one of the exciting things about being in a new space—seeing the shadows for the first time. It is not something you can always predict, which almost makes it a mystery. I recently placed a crystal on a high windowsill to catch the afternoon light streaming in. Instantly, the house was covered in dozens of rainbows gliding, ever so slowly, along the wall, the subtle retreat of the sun now reflected in luminescent colour (see Fig. 4.7).

The presence of curiosity naturally provokes mystery and inquiry, as we attempt to make sense of the unknown. For Maggie MacLure, these liminal moments represent a "threshold between knowing and unknowing, that prevents wonder from being wholly contained or recuperated as knowledge, and thus affords an opening onto the new".[94] Just like seeing shapes in cloudy skies, our imaginations are activated through connections and encounters with the undefined. In this sense, curiosity becomes an essential quality of seeing anew.

---

[92] Ibid. 20.

[93] Ibid. 20.

[94] MacLure, "The Wonder of Data", (2013): 228.

Fig. 4.7 Shadows and reflections

Spatial Noticing 10. Light Show

Spatial Noticing

Does anything in your space ignite curiosity?
What emerges or recedes with the light?
What elements provoke your imagination? Is anything undefined?

Workspace

For the most part, I have written this book while working in an old classroom in an unused school that has been rented to freelancers as office space. There are large black chalkboards that run the length of the walls and tiny sinks in the hallway. There are moving walls covered in textured beige material that divide the room. I occupy a corner space with one large window that is currently open allowing a warm breeze to flow in. Raindrops splat against the leaves on the trees. There is a daycare on the first floor, and, in the morning, I can hear the sounds of the kids playing outside. Even though my daughter does not attend this daycare, hearing the kids laugh, sing, or cry makes her feel present in some way. It is nap time now. I know this because it is quiet. It was also quiet for five months during the Covid-19 pandemic, when all schools and daycares were closed in Montréal. During this time, I came to my office alone. There were no sounds of laughing outside and no other people working. But it was not a peaceful solitude; it felt unnerving, and I had a hard time writing.

The floor of my office is a dingy tan-and-burgundy laminate; no matter how much you clean it, it looks dirty. There are two rows of fluorescent lights, only half of them functional, and the paint on the ceiling is beginning to crack and peel away. I do not like fluorescent light, so I recently invested in a few lamps for my desk, though my office mate turns the overhead fluorescents on whenever he comes in. It is irritating. My wooden desk is covered in photocopied pages from books returned to the library, wobbly stacks of books, scribbles on scrap paper, pens, multiple empty mugs, a dingy glass, and two monitors that seem to emerge from the chaos.

I try to imagine this room as a classroom—its original purpose—lined with rows of little school desks and the storage closet filled with lunchboxes and colourful backpacks. I wonder how the past lives of this space affect me while I work here. Is this a school or an office? Or both?

~

While this chapter has been an experimental and personal exploration in the dynamic and elusive qualities of various relationships with my surroundings, it also provides insight into how we can reflect on and represent office space. Many of the themes I explored are ones that surfaced in my research with the organization, Head & Hands, and their office relocation. By drawing upon ordinary moments, memories, and experiences, my day-to-day surroundings offered a tacit application for the research ahead.

At the beginning, you were invited to participate in this journey, and I want you to contemplate where you are now, both physically and metaphorically in your spatial inquiry. *Has anything changed?*

References

Bachelard, Gaston. *The Poetics of Space.* Beacon Press, 1994.

Bar, Moshe, and Maital Neta. "Visual elements of subjective preference modulate amygdala activation." *Neuropsychologia* 45 no.10 (2007): 2191–2200. https://doi.org/10.1016/j.neuropsychologia.2007.03.008.

Cairns, George, and Tamar Jeffers. "Looking into/out of* Organizations Through the Rear Window" *In Art and Aesthetics at Work.* Edited by Adrian Carr and Philip Hancock, 38–50. Palgrave Macmillan, 2003.

Casey, Edward S. "Between Geography and Philosophy," *Annals of the Association of American Geographers 91,* no. 4 (2001): 683–693. https://doi.org/10.1111/0004-5608.00266.

Davidson, Joyce, and Christine Milligan, "Embodying emotion sensing space: Introducing emotional geographies," *Social & Cultural Geography* 5, no. 4 (2004) 523–532. https://doi.org/10.1080/1464936042000317677.

de Botton, Alain. *The Architecture of Happiness.* McClelland & Stewart, 2006.

Ellard, Colin. *Places of the Heart.* Bellevue Literary Press, 2015.

Fetell Lee, Ingrid. *Joyful.* Little Brown Spark, 2018.

Hall, Edward T. *The Hidden Dimension.* Anchor Books, 1982.

Heerwagen, Judith. "Design, Productivity and Wellbeing: What are the Links?" In *AIA Conference on Highly Effective Facilities.* Cincinnati: OH, 1998.

Heti, Sheila. A Common Seagull. *Yale Review* 107 no.4 (2019): 24–35. https://yalereview.yale.edu/common-seagull.

Howes, David. "Introduction." In *Empire of the Senses: the sensory culture reader.* Edited by David Howes. Bloomsbury, 2005.

Howes, David. *The Sensory Studies Manifesto.* Toronto University Press, 2022.

Kaplan, Rachel. "The Role of Nature in the Context of the Workplace." *Landscape and Urban Planning* 26 no. 1–4 (1993): 193–201. https://doi.org/10.1016/0169-2046(93)90016-7.

Kaplan, Stephen. "The Restorative Benefits of Nature: Toward an Integrative Framework." *Journal of Environmental Psychology* 15 (1995):169–182.

Kaplan, Rachel, and Stephen Kaplan. "The Experience of Nature: A Psychological Perspective." Cambridge University Press, 1989.

Keeling, Trevor, Derek Clements-Croome, Rachael Luck, and Philip Pointer. "How the Sensory Experience of Buildings can Contribute to Wellbeing and Productivity," In *Proceedings of the 7th Windsor Conference: The changing context of comfort in an unpredictable world.* London: Network for Comfort and Energy Use in Buildings, 2012.

Kondo, Marie. *The life-changing magic of tidying up*. Ten Speed Press, 2014.
Lefebvre, Henri. *The Production of Space*. Translated by D. Nicholson-Smith. Blackwell Publishing, 1991.
MacLure, Maggie. "The Wonder of Data," *Cultural Studies - Critical Methodologies* 13, no. 2 (2013): 228–232. https://doi.org/10.1177/1532708613487863.
Magnaghi, Alberto. *The Urban Village*. Zed Books, 2005.
Margulies, Alfred. *The Empathic Imagination*. W.W. Norton, 1989.
Mason, Oliver J. and Francesca Brady. "The Psychotomimetic Effects of Short-Term Sensory Deprivation." *Journal of Nervous and Mental Disease* 197, no. 10 (2009): 783–785.
Massey, Doreen. *For Space*. London: Sage Publications Ltd, 2005.
Massumi, Brian. "The Autonomy of Affect," *Cultural Critique* 31 (1995): 83–109.
Merleau-Ponty, Maurice. *Phenomenology of Perception*. Routledge, 1962.
Nijs, Greg and Amelie Daems. "And What if the Tangible Were Not, and Vice Versa? On Boundary Works in Everyday Mobility Experience of People Moving into Old Age: For Daisy (1909–2011)." Space and Culture 15, no. 3 (2012): 186–197. https://doi.org/10.1177/1206331212445962.
Nute, Kevin Nute and Zhuo Job Chen. "Wind-Generated Movement as a Potential means to Psychological Presence in Indoor Work Environments." *International Journal of Design in Society* (2020):1–9. https://doi.org/10.13140/RG.2.2.16714.11203.
Odell, Jenny. *How to do Nothing*. Melville House, 2019.
Pallasmaa, Juhani. *The Eyes of the Skin: Architecture and the Senses.* John Wiley & Sons, 2012.
Pearson, David G., and Tony Craig. "The Great Outdoors? Exploring the Mental Health Benefits of Natural Environments," *Frontiers in Psychology* 5 (2014): 1178. https://doi.org/10.3389/fpsyg.2014.01178.
Pérez-Gómez, Alberto. *Attunement: Architectural meaning after the crisis of modern science*. MIT Press, 2016.
Phillips, Richard. "Space for Curiosity," *Progress in Human Geography* 38, no.4 (2013):493–512. https://doi.org/10.1177/0309132513506271.
Pink, Sarah. *Doing Visual Ethnography*. Sage Publications, 2013.
Proust, Marcel. *Swann's Way.* Translated by S. C. K. Moncrieff. Vintage Books, 1922.
Satama, Suvi. "Researching through Experiencing Aesthetic Moments: 'Sensory Slowness' as my Methodological Strength," In *Writing differently*, vol. 4. 209–230. Emerald Publishing Limited, 2020. https://doi.org/10.1108/S2046-607220200000004013.

Stewart, Kathleen. *Ordinary Affects*. Duke University Press, 2007.

Tanizaki, Junichirō. *In Praise of Shadows*. Translated by T. J. Harper & E. G. Seidensticker. Leete's Island Books, 1977.

Thompson, Catharine Ward, Jenny Roe, Peter Aspinall, Richard Mitchell, Angela Clow, and David Miller. "More Green Space is Linked to Less Stress in Deprived Communities: Evidence from salivary cortisol patterns." *Landscape and Urban Planning* 105, no. 3 (2012): 221–229. https://doi.org/10.1016/j.landurbplan.2011.12.015.

Trigg, Dyllan. *The Memory of Place*. Ohio University Press, 2012.

Varela, Francisco, Evan Thompson, and Eleanor Rosch. *The Embodied Mind*. MIT Press, 1991.

Vohs, Kathleen D., Joseph P. Redden, and Ryan Rahinel. "Physical Order Produces Healthy Choices, Generosity, and Conventionality, Whereas Disorder Produces Creativity." *Psychological Science* 24, no. 9 (2013): 1860–1867. https://doi.org/10.1177/0956797613480186.

Wilson, Timothy D., David A. Reinhard, Erin C. Westgate, Daniel T. Gilbert, Nicole Ellerbeck, Cheryl Hahn, Casey L. Brown, and Adi Shaked. "Just think: The challenges of the disengaged mind." *Science* 345, no. 6192 (2014): 75–77.

Winnicott, Donald W. *Playing and reality*. Routledge, 2005.

Wölfflin, Heinrich. "Prolegomena to a Psychology of Architecture." In *Empathy, Form, and Space: Problems in German Aesthetics, 1873–1893*. Getty Center for the History of Art and the Humanities, 1994.

5

Emplaced Research

> The picture of method starts to shift. The argument is no longer that methods discover and depict realities. Instead, it is that they participate in the encactment of those realities. It is also that method is not just a more or less complicated set of proceedures or rules, but rather a bundled hinterland. This stretches through skills, instruments and statements (in-here enactments of previous methods) through the out-there realities so described, into ramifying and indefinite sets of relations, places, assumtions that dissapear from view.
>
> —John Law[1]

John Law writes about research not as a way to depict reality, but as a participant in its enactment. Just as words can act to manifest our surroundings, research processes, relationships, and spaces co-create the story. This interactive and co-evolutionary landscape is at the heart of *emplaced* research. Time plays an important role in research of organizational space because it transforms the office from a static container to one that is constantly created, reinforced, and dismantled. It is a

[1] John Law, *After Method: Mess in Social Science Research* (Routledge, 2004), 45.

K. Messer, *How to Work with Space*, Palgrave Studies in Business, Arts and Humanities,
https://doi.org/10.1007/978-3-031-46541-3_5

"performative process" which allows "the researcher to understand the phenomenon in its dynamic becoming".[2] Space, then, is always in a state of becoming through a continual process of co-evolution as the organization acts upon the space (and vice versa) over time. *What do spaces say and how do organizations respond?* In this chapter, I look more closely at how researchers (and organizations) can understand this reciprocal dynamic and work with it. Research, as a procedure, is inclined to tackle complex issues, simplify them, and present them as straightforward data; however, Law suggests this can distort a world that is "vague, diffuse or unspecific, slippery, emotional, ephemeral, elusive or indistinct".[3] As researchers attempting to glimpse and retain these qualities, we must "find ways of knowing the indistinct and the slippery without trying to grasp and hold them tight".[4] This challenge necessitates the inclusion of our aesthetic, sensory, emotional, and material relationships within research practice and sense-making.

Finding the In-between

As we move deeper into emplaced research as a practice, I want to revisit the themes of presence and attention—attunement, as some have called it.[5] If we notice our physical surroundings—giving them more room to breathe and exist with us—will they start to appear more easily and often? Or do they require more than that? If we actively include them, do they become part of our journey, as Scott Slovic[6] illustrated with his once-invisible bike ride to the university?

Incorporating physical space into research requires an ontological shift away from understanding the material world as an external, peripheral object, to seeing it as an entwined, co-productive force. Such a shift yields an entirely new way of seeing. Rather than focusing strictly on an

[2] Federica De Molli, "An Aesthetic Account of Space: A Report on Recent Developments in Organizational Research", *Studi Organizzativi* 1 (2019): 6.

[3] Law, *After Method*, (2004): 2.

[4] Ibid. 3.

[5] see Alberto Pérez-Gómez, *Attunement* (MIT Press, 2016).

[6] Scott Slovic, *Seeking Awareness in American Nature Writing* (University of Utah Press, 1992).

organization as one or more groups of people, the emphasis changes to a relational field, "where *non*-human forces are equally at play in constituting [the organization's] becomings".[7] This shifts the focus from the organization as a purely human system to an emergent state of becoming through its constant interaction with non-human forces.

The push towards research that includes a more-than-human focus and awareness draws the environment into discussions on topics previously disconnected from their surroundings. A more-than-human perspective "invites researchers to open research relationships, thinking, and representations to beings, things, and objects previously ignored as active agents".[8] Explored by Abram in *The Spell of the Sensuous*,[9] including the more-than-human can illuminate the participation of our material and immaterial world. As I have explored, qualities and things (including bodies) that are omnipresent are often forgotten. They pass behind us, above us, and through us—emerging without much thought or notice—while providing support, wisdom, or discomfort from an "indeterminate realm".[10] Abram gives the example of how "the physicist analyzing data is still nourished by the air that she is breathing, by the feel of the chair that supports her and the light flooding in through the window, without her being particularly conscious of these participations".[11] It is an example that reinforces the continuous relationship between the physicist and her environment; neither is separate from the other, but dynamically involved. Abram cautions us not to "forget our active participation" when seeking to describe the life-world.[12] Descriptions of space can be overloaded with minuscule details yet absent of the author, viewer, or participant.

---

[7] Karin Hultman and Hillevi Lenz Taguchi, "Challenging Anthropocentric Analysis of Visual Data: A Relational Materialist Methodological Approach to Educational Research", *International Journal of Qualitative Studies in Education* 23 no. 5 (2010): 525.

[8] Robyn Dowling et al., "Qualitative Methods II: "More-than-Human" Methodologies and/in Praxis, *Progress in Human Geography* 41, no. 6 (2016): 824.

[9] David Abram, *The Spell of the Sensuous* (Vintage Books, The citation "Abram 1996" has been changed to "Abram 1997" to match the author name/date in the reference list. Please check if the change is fine in this occurrence and modify the subsequent occurrences, if necessary.1997).

[10] Ibid. 40.

[11] Ibid.

[12] Ibid.

The emergent qualities of day-to-day living—feelings, emotions, expressions, actions—represent one of the most difficult aspects to express and account for, both personally and within a research context. It is simultaneously a question of the context within which they are produced and the value, or lack thereof, attributed to what can be fleeting moments. Paul Harrison notes Deleuze's observation that a stutter is not just affected language, but the "enactments of a world and an individual".[13] The stutter is not independent of the spoken words, but the means by which they are born and delivered to the world. It is not *affected* language; it *is* the language. The same can be said about a person's environment. Our feelings and actions within a space are not the product of external spatial qualities but are part of, are woven into, our behaviour—they are enacted with the space. That said, these relations are not always as obvious as the shape and construction of language. The point at which the presence of trees outside my window merges with my thoughts and feelings may be beyond my awareness. Unfortunately, such subtlety often leads to the exclusion from research of such emergent, undetectable qualities.

In a thoughtful exploration on making sense of the everyday, Harrison calls upon two ontological terms in an attempt to capture these indefinable and nuanced experiences. The first is Nigel Thrift's "'almost not quite' ontology, an unfinished or processual ontology"[14] which creates value for things that continually exist in an emergent state. The second is Agamben's ontology of the "whatever", which represents that which "is prior to all levels of classification" and exists in the "emergent and never fully determined nature of being (becoming)".[15] In a similar vein, philosopher Doreen Massey refers to the "throwntogetherness" of place, a quality that "demands negotiation" and "necessitate[s] invention".[16] This indeterminate and evolving role contrasts with the "view of place as settled and pre-given".[17] Thus, we confront the integral and productive *throwntogether* nature of our bodies and day-to-day lives, fashioned from

[13] Paul Harrison "Making Sense: Embodiment and the Sensibilities of the Everyday", *Environment and Planning D: Society and Space* 18 no. 4 (2000): 502.

[14] Ibid. 501.

[15] Ibid.

[16] Doreen Massey, *For Space* (Sage Publications, 2005), 141.

[17] Ibid.

whatever qualities, *almost not quite*. If we are in a constant state of becoming, then it is "from the active, productive, and continual weaving of the multiplicity of bits and pieces that we emerge", says Harrison.[18] A fourth notion, *unsiting*, is offered as an "unconcept" by Beyes and Steyaert[19] as they explore the aesthetics of the uncanny in organizational inquiry. Borrowing the term from Miwon Kwon,[20] Beyes and Steyaert examine how unsiting may unlock "affects by reorganizing a site's constellation of material and immaterial forces".[21] The resulting "unsettled" and unfamiliar spatial experience requires that those experiencing it refamiliarize themselves with their environment—essentially a reattunement. It is sort of like getting lost and suddenly starting to pay attention to details and signs you may not have noticed before. Everything in those moments is heightened and alive, until you find your way back again. But this process of reattunement remains as an added layer of sensation and experience. It gives value, by way of a more explicit connection, and attention to bits and pieces—affective sparks that seemingly do not fit together into fully formed thoughts or actions—that elevate the indeterminate while simultaneously eliciting alternative ways of sense-making.

Researching with Space

Over twenty years ago, Thrift and Dewsbury[22] looked to theatre and performance to breathe life into dead geographies. Is it possible—as Alan Latham suggests—to "imbue traditional research methodologies with a sense of the creative"[23] through the addition of space? Just as Annie

[18] Harrison, "Making Sense", (2000): 502.

[19] Timon Beyes and Chris Steyaert, Unsettling Bodies of Knowledge: Walking as a Pedagogy of Affect. *Management Learning* 52, no.2 (2021).

[20] Miwon Kwon, *One Place After Another: Site-Specific Art and Locational Identity* (MIT Press, 2004).

[21] Beyes and Steyaert, "Unsettling Bodies" (2013): 1450.

[22] Nigel Thrift and Dewsbury, "Dead Geographies—And how to Make Them Live. *Environment and Planning D: Society and Space* 18. no. 4 (2000).

[23] Alan Latham, "Research, Performance, and Doing Human Geography: Some Reflections on the Diary-Photograph, Diary-Interview Method", *Environment and Planning A*, no. 35 (2003): 2000.

Dillard's[24] writing became entwined with her experience of place, might greater attention to, and speaking of, our surroundings make room for the material in research? Can a collective murmur or a sensuous conversation draw out heretofore invisible aspects of office space? To express in words how we interact with and perceive our environment can become part of a new way of sensing and interacting with that space. As Scott Slovic demonstrated with his "scheduleless"[25] bike rides, where material murmurs acted to manifest his environment, naming and speaking to and of space calls it into the conversation. While non-verbal forms of research and practice are fundamental to the discovery, articulation, and presentation of spatial experience, the development of aesthetic, sensory, and spatial language is needed alongside these methods to increase the everyday comprehension of material relationships in organizations.

Unfortunately, the affective, unconscious, and fleeting nature of our relationship with space can make it challenging to describe in words—especially in the English language and culture. In an office, where a culture of rational objectivity dominates, accessing less rational parts of our mind–body can be even more difficult. Steven Taylor[26] suggests that this paradigm can produce an *aesthetic muteness* whereby participants are unable to connect, or unused to connecting, with the emotional, aesthetic, or embodied aspects of their work. As a result, questions intended to elicit emotion are often unconsciously reframed into topics or terms to which the participants are more accustomed, "such as 'thinking' rather than 'feeling'".[27] In fact, Taylor implies that organization members, when faced with such questions, may not "recall the aesthetic experience or even deny that they had any aesthetic experience because aesthetic muteness has lowered the salience of their aesthetic experience below their threshold of attention".[28] In this scenario, it is possible to imagine research studies downplaying or dismissing spatial value should participants not adequately convey the nuance of their experience. Just as the physical

[24] Annie Dillard, *Pilgrim at Tinker Creek* (Harper's Magazine Press, 1974)

[25] Slovic, *Seeking Awareness* (1992), 172.

[26] Steven Taylor, "Overcoming Aesthetic Muteness: Researching Organizational Members' Aesthetic Experience. *Human Relations* 55, no.7 (2002).

[27] Ibid. 828.

[28] Ibid.

environment requires noticing to become integrated into our conscious awareness, feelings, emotions, and aesthetic impressions also need to be valued. That is not to say they do not otherwise exist, but if they do not occupy a position of importance, they may be muted. It seems significant then that the research process itself—through emplaced methodologies—raise the level of appreciation for aesthetic, emotional, and spatial experiences.

Emplaced Methods

Emplaced research is a way to create a spatial dimension that is omnipresent—a triple-layering of office space as focus, setting, and participant. This makes for an interesting, multidimensional conversation in which both participant and interviewer are, as Sarah Pink says, "active participants in their environments, using their whole bodies, all their senses, available props and the ground under their feet, to narrate, perform, communicate and represent their experiences".[29] Situating conversations in the space allows participants to share pertinent material objects or locations in the moment. Using practices such as walking can lead to an "empathic and sensory embodied (emplaced) understanding" between researchers and participants as they actively engage with the environment.[30] Physically moving through a space (built or natural) provides opportunities for the space to become actively presented *as it is encountered* by both participant and researcher. This process situates thoughts and conversations that emerge and are informed by the space. This dynamic process brings the participant (and space) into a position closer to that of a collaborator or a co-researcher. Frederica De Molli points out the benefit to research knowledge, which is "richer and more accurate when actors have been informed that they are in fact creating shared

[29] Sarah Pink, *Doing Sensory Ethnography*. (Sage Publications, 2009), 85.

[30] Sarah Pink, "Walking with Video", *Visual Studies* 22, no.3 (2007): 250.

knowledge".[31] Increasing participants' awareness of the topic's materiality is especially important in aesthetic and spatial inquiry, which is often left out of the conversation.

Emplaced research and analysis require purposefully including the surroundings as active participants in the process. Obviously, I cannot interview a chair, and it will not speak words to me, but I can consider how it holds my body, how it is sat in, used, or treated by others, what its design conveys, how it smells and feels against my skin, what memories or thoughts the chair provokes. These questions are not meant to discover an ultimate truth about the chair's effect on me—as their answers may shift and change throughout the day or year—rather, they include the chair in the work being done. Assigning value to these subjective, sensory, or ephemeral qualities gives the material life and influence. Through this attention and inclusion, our surroundings begin to pulse with energy; they creak, shine, slouch, and hum. Attuning to these types of characteristics requires a research approach and methods that are not only sensitive to but can amplify the world around us.

In 1999, Antonio Strati published *Organization and Aesthetics*, which explored an aesthetic framework to organizational research.[32] While aesthetics is commonly thought of as an artistic framework of beauty, the root word, of Greek origin, broadly means "any kind of sensory experience".[33] In this sense, aesthetics encompasses our embodied and sensuous perception and experience of the world. Strati explores "the constant, collective, and social negotiation" of aesthetics in day-to-day work environments.[34] Organizational knowledge and experience are imbued with aesthetic and empathic understanding, transforming it into something foul, banal, or picturesque. These descriptors highlight feelings, bodies, and judgements, as well as the sensuous nature of work. Strati describes how this shift in focus alters the researcher's process and

---

[31] Federica De Molli, "Participatory Interpretation: a way to Overcome Analytical Challenges in Organizational Aesthetic Research", *Culture and Organization* 27, no. 3 (2021): 233.

[32] Antonio Strati, *Organization and aesthetics* (Sage Publications, 1999).

[33] White, "'It's Working Beautifully!' Philosophical Reflections on Aesthetics and Organization Theory", *Organization* 3, no. 2 (1996): 195.

[34] Antonio Strati, "Aesthetic Understanding of Work and Organizational Life: Approaches and Research Developments", *Sociology Compass* 4 no.10 (2010): 886.

capacity to conduct "empirical and theoretical inquiry" as they encounter their own "ability to see, hear, smell, touch and taste".[35] This sensory and felt layer—a source of knowledge, authority, and meaning that is experienced day-to-day within the organization—contains valuable insight into organizational life. This aesthetic dimension bonds the researcher and the organization as inquiry is resituated as an embodied, sensory, and collaborative experience.

Sensory Ethnography

With a focus on the sensoriality of experience, sensory research is situated in the relationship between mind–body and its surroundings. Sensory ethnography, as presented by Sarah Pink in *Doing Sensory Ethnography*,[36] harnesses the senses as a research methodology. Pink guides researchers through the sensory landscape showcasing the many nuanced ways in which the senses transfer information, evoke emotion, dance with memory, and activate the body. By situating the researchers, the participants, and the senses, Pink offers an ethnographic process that is grounded in a theory of place and space. Drawing from Howes'[37] notion of emplacement, Pink reminds us of the importance of the emplaced ethnographer, which positions them *and* participants as part of a social, material, and sensory world, "characterised by, and productive of, particular power configurations that they experience through their whole bodies and that are constantly changing (even if in very minor ways)".[38] While sensory ethnography is not automatically a study *of* the senses, it brings a sensory sensitivity and awareness into the research. In Pink's research on how self-identity is constituted in the home, the concept of a sensory home was useful in "understanding people's everyday practices and decision-making about domestic work".[39] This framework brought her participants' expe-

[35] Antonio Strati, "Putting People in the Picture: Art and Aesthetics in Photography and in Understanding Organizational Life", *Organization Science* 21, no. 10 (2000): 14.

[36] Pink, *Doing Sensory Ethnography*.

[37] David Howes, "Introduction" In *Empire of the senses: The sensory culture reader* (2005).

[38] Pink, *Doing Sensory Ethnography*, 33.

[39] Ibid. 46.

rience and relationship to their home into focus. Whether the topic is the "sensory home", "sensory city", or "sensory office", applying a sensory lens or framework brings otherwise missed details, relationships, and experiences into focus.

Sensory experience and response can be stimulated and prompted through the use of material objects in the research process. Having participants engage with their physical surroundings at a tactile level may evoke memories or other sensory responses. In her work on the home, Pink's use of a video tour compelled participants to guide her and themselves through their home; these embodied "engagements with material objects were central to our explorations of the meanings of home".[40] Eliciting sensory responses during and as part of the research process can take many different forms. Participants can engage with their surroundings directly, or be brought certain objects to touch, smell, or taste. Sounds and smells are particularly powerful in their ability to evoke emotion and memory. As we saw with Janet Cardiff's sound walks, in which prerecorded sounds overlay guided walks through the city, the tangle of sensory cues acts to amplify and draw awareness to them. Walking itself can act as embodied knowing,[41] as an everyday practice,[42] or as an unfolding narrative[43] that connects the human body to a more-than-human world. For Timon Beyes and Chris Steyaert, bodies-on-the-move "are continuously enveloped in a wealth of visual stimuli, in shifting smellscapes and soundscapes and in varied mash-ups of surface materialities and mediated impressions".[44] While Beyes and Steyaert consider walking through its application for teaching and learning, they demonstrate the continuous and spontaneous encounters their students have while walking through the city. The result is a series of sensory impressions that "force them to grapple with the atmospheric and existential consequences

---

[40] Ibid. 93.

[41] Ref. "Beyes & Stewaert, "Unsettling Bodies of Knowledge" (2020)" is cited in text but not provided in the reference list. Please provide details in the list or delete the citation from the text.Beyes & Stewaert, "Unsettling Bodies of Knowledge" (2020).

[42] Michel de Certeau, *The Practice of Everyday Life*. (University of California Press, 2011).

[43] Rebecca Solnit, *Wanderlust: A history of walking* (Penguin Books, 2001).

[44] Beyes and Steyaert, "Unsettling bodies of knowledge" (2020): 5.

of economic theories too often taken for granted" in the classroom.[45] The felt nature of sensory and affective experience sparks a type of learning and reflection that cannot be found in a textbook or through research methods that remove the researcher and participant.

Aesthetic Empathy

Drawing on the work of Antonio Strati, Samantha Warren suggests that the researcher's embodied experience of space influences their "capacity to empathize with others" who work in that space.[46] Emotions and sensory impressions experienced by the researcher may help them to see their research participants as being engaged or enmeshed in aesthetic experiences themselves, though hopefully without shifting the meaning of those experiences. When considering how participants engage and perceive their own sensorial worlds, it is important for the researcher to "identify the sets of culturally constituted sensory modalities"[47] that people connect to their physiological experience. It's possible that the researcher's spatial experiences may be quite different from those of the participants, who are in contact with the space on a daily basis or have different sensory culture.[48] Therefore, rather than filter and interpret the participants' experiences, the researcher's embodied understanding of the space can serve as a guide for the research process itself. Given such a nuanced, ephemeral, and sensed research topic, drawing from our bodies may aid researchers in accessing their participants' emotional and aesthetic experiences.

Warren outlines two common approaches to conducting research on organizational aesthetics that navigate these issues. The first refers to "analyses of cultural and/or organizational examples in the manner of a

[45] Ibid. 11.

[46] Samantha Warren, "Empirical challenges in organizational aesthetics research: Towards a sensual methodology", *Organization Studies* 29, no. 4 (2008): 563.

[47] Pink, *Doing sensory ethnography* (2009), 125.

[48] David Howes and Constance Classen, *Ways of sensing* (Routledge, 2014).

detached commentator".[49] In such depictions of organizational experience, the researcher assumes a "privileged interpretive position"[50] that relies upon personal or established aesthetic sensibilities. The second approach attempts "to foreground the voices of organizational members",[51] which is not always easy. Adopting the second approach shifts the framework "from 'how do *we* (as researchers) take an aesthetic perspective on organizational life?' to 'how do we evoke and represent *others*' aesthetic perspectives on organizational life?'"[52] Because of the fleeting and personal nature of spatial experiences, articulating others' aesthetic experiences is profoundly complex—especially if the researcher's own experience differs from those of the participants. Similarly, drawing experiences from or, as Warren puts it, "evoking"[53] spatial experiences as part of the research process could shift or otherwise have consequences for what type of knowledge emerges.

Certain research methods can aid this process. Pink describes the way in which video and photography can act to emphasize the bodies' movements, showcase material relationships, or amplify sounds. These qualities serve to deepen awareness of the research and become "opportunities to self-consciously reflect on those experiences, and as such arrive at new level of awareness about them".[54] Whether using sound recordings, photography, or video, certain moments or qualities may begin to resonate in a different way. It is important to remember, however, that the range of embodied experience in spatial, aesthetic, sensory, or atmospheric research can make analysis difficult. Often chaotic, sensitive, and challenging to navigate, making sense of the data, especially when the researcher is entangled in the mix, can become "an intuitive, messy and sometimes serendipitous task".[55] What arises from this emplaced reflexivity, in which the researcher shifts continually between experiencing and analysing, may not always be clear.

[49] Warren, "Empirical challenges", 563.
[50] Ibid. 564.
[51] Ibid. 563.
[52] Ibid. 564.
[53] Ibid. 571.
[54] Pink, *Doing Sensory Ethnography*, 124.
[55] Ibid. 119.

Participatory Interpretation

Participation in the research project through embodied experiences or direct collaboration in planning creates an involvement with participants (or students) that can become intwined with the research and analysis. This quality of engagement is particularly beneficial to spatial and other forms of aesthetic research situated in relationships between the social and the material. While participatory research is well established in certain areas of organizational studies—particularly in Action Research (AR) and Participatory Action Research (PAR), which operate on a collaborative model between various stakeholders—it is less common to see *data analysis* leave the hands of the researcher(s). Frederica De Molli suggests this tight grasp tends to "provide a static and descriptive picture" rather than the true "performative nature of aesthetics under study".[56] When more voices and hands become part of the data creation *and* sense-making, the cooperative process cultivates more diverse perspectives and rich portraits. For this reason, Warren advocates for the use of participant photography, not only for presentation, but for the "individual nature of making images" which present a certain immediacy and multiplicity of experience.[57] Under the heading Photo-elicitation, Warren[58] outlines various techniques to invite reflection and discussion using photographs taken by or in collaboration with participants. After photos have been taken and collected, participants are invited to share (in a group or one-on-one) and comment on their "choice of shot, modes of expression, motivations, experiences and anything else that arises for them".[59] This process provides the researcher an additional layer of reflective discussion that may not have surfaced during a regular interview. In regard to aesthetic and spatial information, participant photography allows participants to explore without the direct presence of the researcher, which

[56] De Molli, "Participatory Interpretation", 236.

[57] Samantha Warren, "Photography and Voice in Critical Qualitative Management Research", *Accounting, Auditing Accountability Journal* 18, no.6 (2005): 864.

[58] Samantha Warren, "Photography in Qualitative Organizational Research: Conceptual, Analytical and Ethical Issues in Photo-Elicitation Inspired Methods", In *The SAGE handbook of qualitative business and management research methods: Methods and challenges* (Sage Publications, 2018).

[59] Ibid. 251.

offers a "potentially less intrusive" research method.[60] Warren gives the example of Harriet Shortt's ethnographic work on hair salons, which draws attention to less prominent spaces such as "cupboards, corridors, alleyways and stairs".[61] These more intimate and banal spaces may not have been noticed by a researcher without the participation of those more familiar with the space.

In addition to participant participation during data collection, the potency of this method can increase when the interpretive process is situated in the aesthetic environment under study.[62] This reflective process adds layers and depth to the research as participants and researchers react and engage with the space together. Involving participants and the material environment in the sense-making of the data offers a "self-reflexive analysis of their aesthetic involvement".[63] Meaning-making occurs beyond the singular interpretation of the researcher through a collective process that values the "polyphony of the aesthetic representations of the organizational actors under study".[64] Both Warren and De Molli speak to the vibrancy that reflexive participatory engagement offers research. Extending that level of engagement to the data analysis itself, through what De Molli refers to as *participatory interpretation* increases further the "performative and dynamic emergence" of aesthetic research.[65] Similar to PAR, in which all data collected is presented back to the participants for further discussion and sense-making, participatory interpretation offers not just the researcher but also the research itself a more accurate and ethical process. This process allows participants to build on or contradict any knowledge formed during the research collection.

---

[60] Ibid. 242.

[61] Ibid. 242.

[62] De Molli, "Participatory Interpretation".

[63] Ibid. p.236.

[64] Ibid. p.235.

[65] Ibid. p.234.

Unfolding Worlds Through Words

Presenting spatial research can be difficult for all the reasons discussed in this book. Exhaustive descriptions can lay flat, void of interaction and meaning. On the other hand, narratives can pull us into a particular place through a "multi-sensorial description" or manifest something neither there nor here—"something that does not yet exist [but that] could actually come to life".[66] Engaging with more-than-human research requires a shift not only in *how* we write but in *what* we write. Literary devices have an empathic ability essential to convey the more ephemeral subtleties of place. Through vivid description, aspects of lived experience that would normally be lost or cut out of the process will remain, either by intentional emphasis or by unconscious transmission through the story. These accounts, while conveying experience, also show the reader how to engage with their sensory world. Allowing the subtle invisibility of our relationship with space to show up through words may also cause it to unfold unexpectedly in between the lines.[67] While there are countless examples of descriptive literature, I found myself drawn to writing that pulled space into the foreground—transforming it from something static to something more animated and active.

The following are two examples of academic writing that integrate space in inquiry by weaving the material into the foundation of our understanding of the exploration itself:

Space as Co-author

Co-becoming Bawaka is a unique article in how it explores a relational understanding of place/space. The authors credit and treat the land Bawaka Country, in northern Australia, as the paper's lead author.[68] In

[66] Federico De Matteis et al., "Phenomenographies: Describing the Plurality of atmospheric Worlds", *Ambiances* 5 (2019): 3.

[67] Anita Sinner, *Unfolding the Unexpectedness of Uncertainty* (Sense Publishers, 2013).

[68] Bawaka Country et al., "Co-becoming Bawaka: Towards a Relational Understanding of Place/Space", *Progress in Human Geography* 40, no.4 (The citation "Country et al. 2015" has been changed to "Country et al. 2016" to match the author name/date in the reference list. Please check if the change is fine in this occurrence and modify the subsequent occurrences, if necessary.2016).

this sense, the land extends into the text its form and flow. The research paper itself is seen as "a place/space that is co-emergent and that is active and sentient, a space/place that draws attention to the ways in which dynamic, ongoing, intense webs of connection"[69] can emerge through the research process. The inclusion of Bawaka Country as an author transforms the space from a setting where things happen into a collaborator and, as the authors put it, an "author-ity" on the subject matter.[70] "Co-becoming Bawaka" is rich with description and creative literary writing, which is necessary to convey the ideas and tone the authors wish to create. The land, Bawaka, is not an abstract place but one with texture, substance, and life: "ah, here is a good spot, let's put the *wapitja* (the digging stick) into the sand to see if it is soft enough … In digging *ganguri*, Bawaka becomes Sasha and her long arms. Sasha and her long arms become Bawaka".[71] Through this engagement with the land and text, the authors illustrate how "places/spaces and beings co-become", which are "so wildly diverse, more-than-human, more-than-words, more-than-thought, more-than-feeling, more-than-dream".[72] The way in which Bawaka is treated—with respect and openness—draws out subtle qualities present in the relationships surrounding it that are often overlooked or dismissed as banal. The space/place does not possess agency on its own; rather, it is through dynamic interaction and adaptability with living beings, and day-to-day use and decay, that it too comes alive. While not every space can or should be the lead author of a study, this example highlights the dynamic role that physical space can play through its unique spatial representation.

Relational Materialist Writing

In a thought-provoking photographic study of children playing, Karin Hultman and Hillevi Lenz Taguchi challenge other researchers to adopt a *relational materialist* approach. They take on an ontological shift

[69] Ibid. 4.

[70] Ibid.

[71] Ibid. 4–5

[72] Ibid. 4.

from a human or social-centred perspective to "a space in which *non-*human forces are equally at play and work as constitutive factors in children's learning and becoming".[73] In their paper, Hultman and Lenz Taguchi provide an explicit example of the relational materialist approach being applied to empirical data—something I have rarely seen in theoretical papers on this topic. In their first example—a photo depicting a young girl playing with sand—the authors admit how difficult it was for them to shift their attentions away from the child:

> Although our aim was to specifically look for the force of the material environment, our gazes were nevertheless persistently drawn to the individual child in each photograph. The children in the images seemed to have a magnetic power over our gazes: they stood out from the background and seemed to rise above the material environment. The sand and the climbing-frame and all other non-human matter visible in the photographs seemed inactive, and in our eyes, merely the backdrop for these children's actions and competences. Regardless of how theoretically informed we were of poststructural thinking about children as contextual and situational, our perceptual style and our habits of seeing still seemed to be guided by the same liberal humanistic notions of the child that we so long had sought to escape.[74]

What is significant about this experiential account is the researchers' transparency and openness as they share their difficulties in carrying out this method. The challenge, therefore, exists in how we may go about comprehending the material world as engaging and significant as the human participants in the research. This type of shift is not easy or possible without conscious awareness, attentiveness, and practice. How we write our words to describe the situation becomes a direct tie to the ontological shift underpinning the relational materialist perspective.

Having successfully applied their method to the photograph, Hultman and Lenz Taguchi's description shifts away from a girl playing in the sand—in which the "girl as the subject of the photograph is separated and detached from the sandbox"—to one in which "both the girl and the

[73] Hultman and Taguchi. "Challenging Anthropocentric Analysis", (2010): 527.
[74] Ibid. 525.

sand can be thought of as *performative mutually intra-active agents*".[75] To put it another way, the sand and the child are each acting upon one another simultaneously. Each account describes a shift in which the sand's materiality comes into an active, affective relationship with, and causes macro or micro shifts within, the child. A relational materialist understanding of the photograph captures the world *in-between* the girl and the sand:

> The uneven foundation of the sandbox forces the body of the girl to adjust to find the perfect balance to be able to perform her task. She directs her whole body around the sand. The force of gravity, the uneven foundation, the bucket and the quality of the grains of sand are all active forces that intra-act with her body and mind and that she has to work with and against. She is most obviously active, but in a relational materialist perspective she cannot be thought upon in terms of a superior autonomous and intentional humanist subject. Rather, in line with Deleuze's (1990) thinking, the sand and the girl, as bodies and matter of forces of different intensities and speed, fold around each other and overlap, in the event of sand falling, hand opening, body adjusting and balancing, eyes measuring height and distance and observing the falling movement of the glittering sand into the red bucket.[76]

In this description, even the play of light and the movement of the eye form part of the relationship between child and sand. Their movements and qualities are woven together, producing each other in the ever-shifting moment. We see how the girl and the sand are momentarily entwined and co-produced within the experience.

These two examples illustrate what a relational materialist approach can achieve through a seemly simple shift in focus. They both include spaces in different ways, one as co-author and one as dual focus; however, the result was equally effective at elevating the material presence in the writing. Space was an active participant in both the research *and* the writing, highlighting the significant role played by our surroundings during

[75] Ibid. 527.

[76] Ibid. 530.

even the simplest tasks. These interactions showcase the entangled socio-material relationships at play and the constant evolution between them.

Researching space does not require a specific tool or a method; rather, it requires an emplaced relational approach that may draw from variety of methods. The key with any method you choose (be it photography, video, interview, questionnaire, map-making, etc.) is to consider how (and if) it invites space into the process. Will it include the material as an active participant and contributor? Is it sensitive to the atmospheric, sensuous, or ephemeral qualities of space? Does it capture the inter-subjective, emotional, and affective nature of experience?

References

Abram, David. *The Spell of the Sensuous*. Vintage Books, 1997.

Beyes, Timon, and Chris Steyaert. "Strangely Familiar: The Uncanny and Unsiting Organizational Analysis. *Organization Studies* 34, no.10 (2013): 1445–1465. doi:https://doi.org/10.1177/0170840613495323.

Beyes, Timon, and Chris Steyaert. Unsettling Bodies of Knowledge: Walking as a Pedagogy of Affect. *Management Learning* 52, no.2 (2021): 1–19. doi:https://doi.org/10.1177/1350507620979713.

Country, Bawaka, Sarah Wright, Sandie Suchet-Pearson, Kate Lloyd, Laklak Burarrwanga, Ritjilili Ganambarr, Merrkiyawuy Ganambarr-Stubbs, Banbapuy Ganambarr, Djawundil Maymuru, and Jill Sweeney. "Co-becoming Bawaka: Towards a relational understanding of place/space." *Progress in Human Geography* 40, no. 4 (2016): 455-475. doi:https://doi.org/10.1177/0309132515589437.

de Certeau, Michel. *The Practice of Everyday Life*. (University of California Press, 2011), 118.

De Matteis, Federico, Mikkel Bille, Tonino Griffero, and Andrea Jelić. "Phenomenographies: Describing the Plurality of Atmospheric Worlds," *Ambiances. Environnement sensible, architecture et espace urbain* 5 (2019): 1–23. doi:https://doi.org/10.4000/ambiances.2526.

De Molli, Frederica. "An Aesthetic Account of Space: A Report on Recent Developments in Organizational Research." *Studi Organizzativi* 1, (2019): 36–63. doi:https://doi.org/10.3280/SO2019-001002.

De Molli, Federica. "Participatory Interpretation: a way to Overcome Analytical Challenges in Organizational Aesthetic Research," *Culture and Organization* 27, no. 3 (2021): 1–15. doi:https://doi.org/10.1080/14759551.2020.1806839de.
Dillard, Annie. *Pilgrim at Tinker Creek*. Harper's Magazine Press, 1974.
Dowling, Robyn, Kate Lloyd, and Sandie Suchet-Pearson. Qualitative methods II: "More-than-human" methodologies and/in praxis. *Progress in Human Geography* 41, no. 6 (2016): 823–831. doi:https://doi.org/10.1177/0309132516664439.
Harrison, Paul. "Making Sense: Embodiment and the Sensibilities of the Everyday." *Environment and Planning D: Society and Space* 18, no. 4 (2000): 497–517. doi:https://doi.org/10.1068/d195t.
Howes, David. "Introduction." In *Empire of the Senses: The Sensory Culture Reader*. Routledge, 2005.
Howes, David, and Constance Classen, *Ways of Sensing*, Routledge, 2014.
Hultman, Karin, and Hillevi Lenz Taguchi. "Challenging Anthropocentric Analysis of Visual Data: A Relational Materialist Methodological Approach to Educational Research." *International Journal of Qualitative Studies in Education* 23, no. 5 (2010): 524–542. doi:https://doi.org/10.1080/09518398.2010.500628.
Kwon, Miwon. *One Place After Another: Site-Specific Art and Locational Identity*. MIT Press, 2004.
Latham, Alan. "Research, Performance, and Doing Human Geography: Some Reflections on the Diary-Photograph, Diary-Interview Method." *Environment and Planning A*, no. 35 (2003): 1993–2017. doi:https://doi.org/10.1068/a3587.
Law, John. *After Method: Mess in social science research*. Routledge, 2004.
Massey, Doreen. *ForSpace*. SAGE Publications, 2005.
Pérez-Gómez, Alberto. *Attunement, : Architectural meaning after the crisis of modern science*. MIT Press, 2016.
Pink, Sarah. "Walking with Video." *Visual Studies* 22, no.3 (2007): 240–252. doi:https://doi.org/10.1080/14725860701657142.
Pink, Sarah. *Doing Sensory Ethnography*. Sage Publications, 2009.
Sinner, Anita. *Unfolding the Unexpectedness of Uncertainty*. Sense Publishers, 2013.
Slovic, Scott. *Seeking Awareness in American Nature Writing*. University of Utah Press, 1992.
Solnit, Rebecca. *Wanderlust: A History of Walking*. Penguin Books, 2001.
Strati, Antonio. *Organization and Aesthetics*. Sage Publications, 1999.

Strati, Antonio. "Putting People in the Picture: Art and Aesthetics in Photography and in Understanding Organizational Life." *Organization Science* 21, no. 10 (2000): 53–69.

Strati, Antonio. "Aesthetic Understanding of Work and Organizational Life: Approaches and Research Developments." *Sociology Compass* 4 no.10 (2010): 880–893. doi:https://doi.org/10.1111/j.1751-9020.2010.00323.x.

Taylor, Steven S. "Overcoming Aesthetic Muteness: Researching organizational members' aesthetic experience." *Human Relations* 55, no.7 (2002): 821–840. doi:https://doi.org/10.1177/0018726702055007542.

Thrift, Nigel and John-David Dewsbury. "Dead Geographies—And how to Make Them Live. *Environment and Planning D: Society and Space* 18. no. 4 (2000): 411–432. doi:https://doi.org/10.1068/d1804ed.

Warren, Samantha. "Photography and Voice in Critical Qualitative Management Research." *Accounting, Auditing Accountability Journal* 18, no.6 (2005): 861–882. doi:https://doi.org/10.1108/09513570510627748.

Warren, Samantha. "Empirical challenges in organizational aesthetics research: Towards a sensual methodology." *Organization Studies* 29, no. 4 (2008): 559–580. doi:https://doi.org/10.1177/0170840607083104.

Warren, Samantha. "Photography in Qualitative Organizational Research: Conceptual, Analytical and Ethical Issues in Photo-Elicitation Inspired Methods." In *The SAGE handbook of qualitative business and management research methods: Methods and challenges.* 239–261. Sage Publications, 2018. doi:https://doi.org/10.4135/9781526430236.

White, David A. "'It's Working Beautifully!' Philosophical Reflections on Aesthetics and Organization Theory," *Organization* 3, no. 2 (1996): 195–208.

6

Case Study: More than a Relocation

> Ordinary affects, then, are an animate circuit that conducts force and maps connections, routes, and disjunctures. They are a kind of contact zone where the overdetermination of circulations, events, conditions, technologies, and flows of power literally take place. To attend to ordinary affects is to trace how the potency of forces lie in their immances to things that are both flighty and hardwired, shifty and unsteady but palpable too.
>
> —Kathleen Stewart[1]

The following case study documents my experience exploring socio-material relationships within an organization during a period of spatial transition and change. The fieldwork and analysis were conducted during my PhD studies and are presented here as a learning model. The project is not a blueprint to follow, rather a spatial experiment—complete with its inescapable mistakes and nuanced errors. As Kathleen Stewart writes of her book *Ordinary Affects*, this exploration commits "not to the demystification and uncovered truths that support a well-known picture of the world, but rather to speculation, curiosity, and the concrete".[2]

---

[1] Kathleen Stewart, *Ordinary Affects* (Duke University Press, 2007), 3.

[2] Ibid. 1.

K. Messer, *How to Work with Space*, Palgrave Studies in Business, Arts and Humanities,
https://doi.org/10.1007/978-3-031-46541-3_6

At the start of this process, I struggled to balance my desire to remain open and emergent with a need to set limits and achievable goals. I wanted to prove that space *affected* an organization at a tangible level–that it mattered in a significant way. However, it soon became evident that realizing that goal was trickier than I had imagined. I let go of my original aims, instead documenting how the office was articulated and how it manifested for the staff. My exploration became less about finding definitive answers on the impact of office design to more of an emergent inquiry rooted in day-to-day experience. I worked on my ability to notice what had always been there, partly through a greater attunement with the environment and by experimenting in my own surroundings. The questions I took into my fieldwork are as follows:

- *What happens when we see space as a co-creator in an organization's evolution?*
- *How do changes in an organization's material environment affect the staff and organization?*
- *What phenomena surface during the experience of changing spaces?*

The answers to these questions are not the same for everyone; they are conscious and unconscious, visible and invisible, held within the space and within one's body. They are emotional, circumstantial, essential, and unimportant, present within the day-to-day but visible year-to-year.

Research Process & Methods

Locating Space

With space habitually relegated to the background in day-to-day life, it was my intention to work with an organization that was renovating or relocating. This moment of change seemed important as a means of drawing the physical office out of its day-to-day normalcy and thereby tapping into the heightened spatial awareness of the staff. A physical relocation is a pivotal moment for an organization that involves a disruptive process of displacement and replacement. This change in environment can lead to fresh perspectives and opportunities for the organization to reflect, reorient, and make conscious modifications.

Finding an organization that was undertaking an office move in a timeline parallel to that of my research was difficult. However, I was familiar with Head & Hands, a not-for-profit youth service organization, having served on their board of directors three years earlier. In addition to knowledge of their staff and culture, my past engagement with Head & Hands deepened my relationship with the physical office space, strengthening my ability to empathize with and contextualize the experiences of the staff without being a staff member myself.

After meeting with the organization to present the study, I began a series of conversational interviews that focused on the staff's experience and relationships with the space. Towards the end of these initial conversations, Head & Hands won a bid for a ten-year, rent-free lease of a space in an old neighbourhood library and thus took the decision to move. Shortly after this, I gave birth to my daughter and took a two-year maternity leave. After a lengthy renovation process, Head & Hands moved into its new premises. Roughly six months after the move, I resumed the research with the organization in their new office. All in all the data collection spanned just over three years.

Gathering Socio-Material Experiences

While my initial project included an inclusive participatory research process, over time these plans faded. Attempts to create a research committee interested in collaborating on the topic amounted to little more than unanswered emails, though many staff came forward for conversational interviews. Interviews may not seem the most obvious method for sensory, experiential spatial research given the numerous studies illustrating the benefits of alternative methods;[3,4,5,6] but part of my initial exploration

---

[3] Nigel Thrift and John-David Dewsbury, "Dead Geographies—And how to Make them Live", *Environment and Planning D: Society and Space* 18 no. 4 (2000).

[4] Samantha Warren, "Photography and Voice in Critical Qualitative Management Research", *Accounting, Auditing Accountability Journal* 18, no. 6 (2005).

[5] Sarah Pink, "Engaging the Senses in Ethnographic Practice: Implications and Advances", *The Senses and Society* 8, no.3 (2013).

[6] Robyn Dowling et al., "Qualitative Methods III: Experimenting, Picturing, Sensing. *Progress in Human Geography* 42, no. 5 (2017).

included a curiosity in the staff's awareness of and language about their space. The staff's enthusiasm to speak about the space displaced my attempts at participant photography and other group practices as not enough staff were interested or available to participate. This was in part a failure in my research design that I will explore later.

To enrich the interviews,[7] I situated the conversations using a relational materialist approach. As Antoni Strati says, the oscillation between social and material "assigns greater complexity to the aesthetic dimension in organizations than transpires from tangible and visible elements".[8] With two rounds of interviews in two different locations over a period of three years, the conversations provided a comparative snapshot—fleeting moments—of the organization's multifaceted spatial experience. The somewhat ephemeral narrative that resulted "is the tangle of their interpretations",[9] in which the staff shed light on moments with and within their surroundings. This research method may not be a radical departure from tradition, which some may believe is required to produce "spaces which flirt and flout, gyre and gimble, twist and shout";[10] however, it does offer an account of an office space that "is no longer passive"[11] but responsive and open to "a manifold of possibilities in time".[12] The space's influence, as a force acting upon the organization, emerges through the staff's thoughts, feelings, and dynamic relationship with the space.

Interview Process and Participants

The first round of interviews took place in the spring and summer of 2016, at the old Head & Hands office. I interviewed ten out of fourteen staff members over a period of four months. The interviews lasted roughly

[7] Robyn Dowling et al., "Qualitative Methods 1: Enriching the Interview", *Progress in Human Geography* 40, no. 5 (2016).

[8] Antonio Strati, "Organizations Viewed through the Lens of Aesthetics", *Organization* 3, no. 2 (1996): 216.

[9] Ibid.

[10] Thrift and Dewsbury, "Dead Geographies", 412.

[11] Ibid. 415.

[12] Ibid. 415.

from one hour to one and a half hours. To participate, staff members responded privately to an email which I had sent to all staff to introduce the project. During this time, the organization was considering a move, but the decision and details were not yet finalized. The second round of interviews took place over the winter of 2018 and spring of 2019, about six to ten months after the organization had moved into the new building. To recruit participants, I emailed approximately ten staff members individually. I interviewed five of them; three more responded to the call, but due to various schedule conflicts were ultimately unable to participate. Between the two rounds, only one person was interviewed twice, but all staff participants worked in both offices.

Within the organization as a whole, I focused my research on permanent staff members—those who were in the office *daily*. The embodied relationship between staff and office is most acute when it is lived on a day-to-day basis. While the organization's board of directors and its clients have their own unique relationships to the office space, I wanted to get at the minutiae of daily interaction, rather than monthly (board) or occasional (client) experiences. Therefore, I did not pursue interviews with board members or youth clients. However, I admit that limiting the perspective to staff members provides an incomplete view of the organization as a complete entity. This would be problematic from a systems thinking approach, which requires experiences from the entire system.[13] While it could be valuable to the organization to compare and contrast the spatial experiences of its staff, board members, and clients, ultimately such an approach did not benefit my study, in large part due to the inherently *collaborative* relationship between staff and space—a quality less present for the board and clients. Insight into the staff's numerous relationships, which evolved within and with the two spaces, might have been obscured or lost had the research also encompassed comparisons of their experiences with those of board and clients. While there can be little doubt that the board members and clients would offer rich perspectives, for this particular study the depth of the staff's connection to the space offered greater and more particularly interesting insights into the shifting

[13] Marrelyn Emery, *Participative Design for Participative Democracy*. Centre for Continuing Education, Australian National University (1989).

and morphing relationships as the office changed over time. Keeping the staff members' dynamic interactions with the office space at the forefront afforded me the opportunity to focus my attention on this nuanced and already-voluminous data. For this reason, I limited the study's size and scope in this manner.

Emplaced Conversations

To bring space into my interviews, I conducted all but one in either the old or the new offices. Engaging a collaborative approach of spatial exploration with the staff and the space increased the self-reflexive engagement of the participants. Having the participants fully aware of the research topic and aim gave staff time to reflect on and consider their surroundings with closer attention.

Bringing the environment into the interview process by using physical means of engagement transformed our material surroundings into an active participant, which in turn created a more dynamic relationship between me, the staff, and the space.[14] In answering questions, staff could glean inspiration from what they saw, felt, or smelled and in many instances actually "show me".[15] With each interview, staff chose the location, leading me through the office to their preferred place. Most often, staff members selected their own offices, but not always. One interview was held at the front desk, while another took place in a co-worker's office. As we settled into each location, arranging our chairs, glasses of water, and the recorder, we were actively creating the interview setting. Meanwhile, other events continued to occur as layers around us: phones rang and were answered, toddlers cried, clients came to collect food bags, and staff chatted nearby.

As I participated in the interviews, I became "embedded in the situation"[16] through my emplaced presence with the staff and in the

---

[14] Sarah Pink, *Doing Sensory Ethnography*. (Sage Publications, 2009).

[15] Samantha Warren, "Having an Eye for It: Aesthetics, ethnography and the senses, Journal of Organizational Ethnography 1, no.1 (2012): 109.

[16] Federico De Matteis et al., "Phenomenographies: Describing the Plurality of Atmospheric Worlds", *Ambiances* 5, (2019): 9.

office. Although this dynamic was not always explicitly acknowledged, my mind–body engaged in relationships with the sounds, smells, textures, light, and people in the office. These details are woven into the transcripts, their meaning bound within them. As Strati suggests in his aesthetic approach, "the understanding of organizational life is conditional on the researcher's capacity to immerse him/herself empathically in organizational action and interaction".[17] Situating myself in the organization's office space provided a socio-material basis from which I could directly connect to the staff's relationships and interactions. These experiences helped me shape both the interview questions and how I understood the staff members' responses.

In addition to the emplaced interview setting, I structured the conversation to deepen awareness of the space. I asked participants to visualize and feel the office and to describe it, in their own words, to someone who couldn't see it, smell it, hear it, or feel it. This reflexive approach allowed the staff time to physically sit in the office, while imagining it through descriptive verbalization. This immediately brought the richness of the office into our discussion; giving name to these various qualities helped to form the foundation of descriptive language, which simultaneously drew the walls and textures that surrounded us into the discussion. This aesthetic exercise mitigated "aesthetic muteness"[18] by building a foundation of spatial noticing, awareness, and a shared vocabulary between me and the participant. My questions did not conceal the focus of the interview; rather, staff were asked to consider connections between the physical space and their emotions, behaviour, and work as co-explorers.[19] As our conversations continued, I asked staff members to explore specific moments of tension or happiness as well as their personal history and relationship with the office. Together we explored the affective qualities of smells and sounds in the office, as well as moments the space provided or prohibited certain opportunities.

---

[17] Antonio Strati, "Aesthetic Understanding of Work and Organizational Life: Approaches and Research Developments", *Sociology Compass* 4, no.10 (2010): 886.

[18] Steven Taylor, "Overcoming Aesthetic Muteness: Researching Organizational Members' Aesthetic Experience", *Human Relations* 55, no. 7 (2002).

[19] Federica De Molli, "Participatory Interpretation: a way to Overcome Analytical Challenges in Organizational Aesthetic Research", *Culture and Organization* 27, no. 3 (2021).

Participant Perception

In addition to situating the interviews and consciously evoking emotive and sensory descriptive introductions, I purposefully timed this research during a period of spatial change. Everyday spaces tend to fade, almost disappearing, into the background of social life. By conducting research at these moments when the office space was uniquely present to the staff and to the organization—first, when the old office building was under scrutiny, and second, when the new building was still fresh—the comparison of the two provided subtle, nuanced insight into the organization's evolving and entangled relationship with its office. Prior to the first round of interviews, Head & Hands had been through a lengthy and vigorous process of self-evaluation and dreaming as they created the bid for, what eventually became, their new office. This created a heightened awareness of their current office as conversations and imaginations were used to evaluate and construct potential spaces, which ultimately enriched our conversations. Before the second round of interviews, the organization had been in, and in many ways were still in, an intense spatial transition, which contributed, even more so, to the staff's spatial awareness. Conducting research at a moment of change and transition afforded me a unique glimpse into the role of space. When the "familiar is defamiliarized and unsettled", previously unseen or "hidden" insights tend to emerge.[20] Such "uncanny" moments present researchers and organizations with opportunities, as they enact an "intertwining of affective, spatial and aesthetic approaches".[21] In addition, the open and whimsical culture of Head & Hands meant emotive conversations about their space were not uncommon. However, as Taylor explores, when conducting sensory and spatial research, it is important to recognize the level of comfort and familiarity with aesthetic ways of being.[22]

The following list contains sample questions I drew from during my interviews:

---

[20] Timon Beyes and Chris Steyaert, "Strangely Familiar: The Uncanny and Unsiting Organizational Analysis. *Organization Studies* 34, no.10 (2013): 1447.

[21] Ibid.

[22] Taylor, "Overcoming Aesthetic Muteness", (2002).

- How would you describe the H&H office space to someone who couldn't see it, smell it, hear it, or feel it?
- When first you come into work, how do you feel as you walk into the office? What do you notice as you enter?
- What would you say is the spirit of H&H?
- When you think about that spirit, what aspects of the physical office space contribute to these qualities? Are there any aspects that aren't part of H&H's spirit?
- What qualities of the office stand out when you're stressed or tired?
- Is there a place you go when you're feeling tired or need downtime? What's comforting about it?
- Have you made any changes to your personal space? If so, what? Why?
- What changes have been made to the office in general?
- How would you describe your personal relationship to the office?
- How does this space help and or hinder your work? The organization's work?
- Describe your favourite part of the office? What do you love about it?
- When you think of all the smells and noises, or of touching the surfaces and textures in the office, what comes to mind?
- What does this space mean for H&H? For its future direction?
- What do you think H&H's space is communicating to people?
- …
- Renovating a building, moving, settling in—it's a big transition for an organization. What was the process like for you and the team?

  - What's been hard/easy?
  - What surprised you?
  - What's been most meaningful?

- Has the new space disrupted any patterns—the way you see or do things?
- Do you think the space is still changing?
- Since moving, have you had any reflections on the role that the space plays in the organization?
- Are there any new processes, services, opportunities, or ways of working that have been initiated since moving?
- Do you miss any aspects of the old space?

Office Images

In addition to my conversations with staff, I have included photographs taken by a Head & Hands volunteer, Margot Flores Torre, who was asked to document the space as well as pictures I took during my visits to the organization's old and new offices. In my original vision of this research project, I had hoped the *staff* would take photographs of the space and as a result took less of my own photographs. Unfortunately, this idea did not gain momentum; only two staff members in the old office responded to my request. Part of this failure stems from the overload of demands already placed on staff—but there was another factor, for which I take responsibility. Rather than place photography at the heart of the inquiry, as a way "to *generate* data rather than [as] images" to be analyzed, I saw the images as another text to be read—albeit a visual one.[23] Understanding photographs simply as records of physical objects or settings can be limiting without accompanying insight into "how these objects are experienced or made meaningful" by those in contact with them.[24] When I received the images created by the two staff who did respond, I immediately realized that I was unable to decode their significance on my own. Even if staff had been keener on the assignment, my assumption that as a researcher it was my responsibility to conduct a photo analysis undermined the significance and knowledge bound within the photograph.

The power of photographs rests not only in their ability to *show* us things but also as a tool used as part of the exploration. Warren[25] delineates a method she calls *participant-led photo interviewing* in which photographs can be used as part of the interview process to aid participants in expressing emotional or aesthetic experiences that may be challenging to express in words. Had I made photographs a part of my interview process, I believe they would have taken on a more significant place in the project. In asking staff to take photographs *after* our interviews, they

[23] Samantha Warren, "Photography in Qualitative Organizational Research: Conceptual, Analytical and Ethical Issues in Photo-Elicitation Inspired Methods", In *The SAGE handbook of qualitative business and management research methods: Methods and challenges* (Sage Publications, 2018), 239.

[24] Pink, "Engaging the Senses" (2013): 80.

[25] Warren, "Photography in Qualitative Organizational Research", (2018).

became *homework*—a mere add-on to our conversation. Of course, this was not my intention; however, after receiving just two responses to my email request and upon viewing the photographs sent without accompanying discussion, I realized my mistake.

In the end, I have combined my own and Margot's photos as way to show the space to the reader. Had the photographs been taken by staff, they would be extensions of *their* "voice"[26] and experience. However, the images (included in this case study) provide a thought-provoking glimpse into the two very different offices of Head & Hands. They provide visual representation of *my* (and Margot's) point of view. Sarah Pink reminds us that "the meanings of photographs are contingent and subjective; they depend on who is looking and when they are looking".[27] Images are fluid. They shift and morph. As you read the case study, consider how the images appear to you? Do they change after you read about the experience behind them?

For me, the photographs enhance and ground the narrative; however, when I look at the pictures, they do not convey the same emotional aspects I felt when I was in the office or that I heard described by the staff. As Holtham states, photographs of "offices rarely provide sufficient significant insights into the organizational reality" on their own.[28] One element missing from most of the photographs is people, something I only realized when looking at the photographs months later. The spaces in the pictures feel empty and lonely. They are uninhabited and thus represent only half of the story. In *The Dictionary of Obscure Sorrows*, John Koenig has coined a word—*kenopsia*—to describe this eeriness, the forlorn "atmosphere of a place that's usually bustling with people but is now abandoned and quiet".[29] Although empty offices have become the norm during the Covid-19 pandemic, these photos lack the lively and emotive social presence that I was used to feeling when visiting the office. I realize

---

[26] Warren, "Photography and Voice", (2005): 870.

[27] Pink, "Engaging the senses" (2013): 75.

[28] Clive Holtham, "Designing Spaces for Knowledge Work: Can the use of Fiction Help Construct New Realities?" In *Managing Knowledge, Conversations and Critiques Conference* (University of Leicester: UK, 2001), 1.

[29] John Koenig, *Dictionary of Obscure Sorrows* (Simon & Shuster, 2021).

how difficult it can be to capture an "affectively charged spatial situation"[30]—to transmit every sensation or atmospheric impression. For these reasons, the stories and experiences surrounding the images remain the focus of *this* narrative.

Attuning to the Research

The spatial focus of this project propelled me to immerse myself in two ways. Parallel to the emplaced relationship I was forming with Head & Hands was the less structured, exploratory journey of my own spatial experience. Although some may label this an autoethnographic process—one which "allows for an understanding of personal experience intersecting with a social and cultural context"[31]—I considered it to be more of a spatial attunement (though there are obvious similarities). Rather than focus strictly on Head & Hands' relationship with their office environment and my experience within that space, I included my day-to-day material surroundings in my sense-making. It speaks to the reflexive and intersubjective elements of autoethnography in regard to how researchers position themselves "in relation to self-other, self-culture, [or] self-social context".[32] In this project, I positioned myself in relation to the physical environment.

As I researched and read the philosophies of space and place, I actively brought these concepts into my daily life. This was not a formal or planned component of the research, and, as such, I have no consistent journal entries tracking my experience. Instead, I have a more rhythmical and sporadic account written on scraps of paper buried within the pages of notebooks, as well as embodied imprints of reflexive experience. Actively drawing space into my lived experience increased my sensitivity and attention to everyday spatial relationships. *How* these relationships with space affected me was not always clear, but attending to certain

[30] De Matteis et al., "Phenomenographies", (2019): 4.

[31] Kathryn Haynes, "Autoethnography", In *The SAGE handbook of qualitative business and management research methods: Methods and challenges* (Routledge, 2017), 17.

[32] Ibid. 18.

aesthetic qualities drew them into the foreground of my experience. Over time I became more aware of how my environment was present or in certain situations less visible. Walking down the street while actively calling out my material surroundings felt as though I was exercising a spatial muscle. A material, sensory and atmospheric, exercise against the mundanity of the every day.

Strati spoke about how his two separate passions (conceptual photography and the sociology of organizations) seemed to not merge but inform one another; over time, he began to "look at organizational life with the eyes of an artist", which ultimately led to an "aesthetic understanding of organizational life".[33] Tapping into the wealth of knowledge housed within and travelling through both the researcher's and the participant's bodies encourages a nuanced and emotional understanding of lived experience. In this project, the two processes were simultaneously separate and entwined. My reflective practice allowed the themes and interview transcripts space to percolate and surface over time—a dance between my developing spatial awareness and the experience of Head & Hands.

Time

Time was an important factor in this project, in terms of both alignment and process. The timing of the research overlapped with the organization's own investigation of office space, the two enquiries together providing a heightened awareness of spatial dynamics. Being involved in a collaborative design practice with their architect, together with the physical move itself, afforded the Head & Hands staff with a greater knowledge of office design against which their lived experience in the new space could be compared. The timing of my maternity leave, which serendipitously happened in parallel to the organization's move, allowed for interviews in both spaces.

The period of time spent away from the project, as well as the time I spent immersing myself in the literature and the first round of interview transcripts, led me to an intuitive and embodied connection to the data.

[33] Strati, "Aesthetic Understanding", 54.

It took me a long time to see the meaning in these relational, aesthetic experiences, to feel comfortable exploring and presenting this story—the kind of story that is often dismissed as too subjective or cut altogether. My visits to the offices, combined with my personal exploration and experimentation with the theory, created for me a nuanced and empathic understanding of the staff members' experiences. Sumara and Luce-Kapler articulate how "research emerges from day-to-day lived practices" such that "the lines between 'research' and 'researcher' become blurred".[34] The more I became immersed in the research, the more fluid and immersive my research practice became. Similarly, Linstead & Höpfl speak to the "integrity and coincidence of self-identity" and expression, which the researcher creates through the merging of "text and experience".[35] They suggest that this is a form of "reconciliation between theory and practice" in which the researcher's embodied process exists on the page.[36] I am woven into the story as a character (the interviewer or the narrator); at once, the story is a reflection of the staff's experiences as well as my relational experience.

Limitations and Failings

While supplementary data collection, which included spatial visioning exercises and participant photography, was originally planned for this project, empirical constraints limited the feasibility of these avenues. Time constraints and demands on the staff's workload interfered with my ability to collect a wide range of experiences. In addition, the organization hired an architect to renovate the new building. As she began conducting her own research, it created duplication of processes. My attempts to collaborate with the architect were promising yet I was never officially brought into the planning process. In the end, I attended one group visioning and planning meeting for the new space. Although I was

[34] Dennis J. Sumara and Rebecca Luce-Kapler, "Action Research as a Writerly Text: Locating Co-Labouring in Collaboration", *Educational Action Research* 1, no.3 (2006): 391.

[35] Stephen Linstead & Heather Joy Höpfl, eds. *The Aesthetics of Organization*. (Sage Publications, 2000), 3.

[36] Ibid.

initially disappointed by this turn of events, it was not catastrophic to the study. After reviewing all the data from the research, the interviews—specifically the second round—provided the richest accounts of the staff's spatial experience. Ultimately, the group discussions became my grounding and provided context for the staff's emplaced experiences in the space.

The organization's small size made the exploration of inter-employee dynamics, race, and power structures almost impossible without additional protection—though I touch on some experiences that were shared openly by staff. Additionally, because the second round of interviews represented less than half of the organization, I was unable to get a complete picture of larger socio-spatial dynamics. While these limitations are important to consider for future research, this research was never intended to provide a complete picture or grand truths, but rather to expand our relational understanding of office space.

Lastly, and perhaps most unfortunately, the arrival of the Covid-19 pandemic stalled further meetings with Head & Hands personnel and derailed the collective analysis and meaning making process that was originally planned. While several attempts were made to present and discuss the data, pandemic office closures, safety limitations, and staff shortages proved too great a hurdle. Because of this development, the case study lacks staff impressions that could have benefited the study and created new organizational knowledge.

As such, I am left wondering if any new insights or changes emerged for staff members following the interviews? And what additional changes to the space and organization have continued as Head & Hands further settled into their new office space.

Relational Materialist Analysis

To keep the data pertinent to day-to-day experience and to guide their presentation, I have organized my results in overlapping themes rather than a highly structured format. I want the reader to experience the tangled web of nuanced encounters and tacit knowledge as it exists in the day-to-day, criss-crossed and inextricable. Similar to the ephemeral, embodied, and complex encounter with physical space, these paragraphs constitute an active exploration of the socio-material relationship. Shawn Wilson, in writing about Indigenous research methods, suggests that "the data and analysis are like a circular fishing net. You could try to examine each of the knots in the net to see what holds it together, but it's the strings between the knots that have to work in conjunction in order for the net to function".[37] It is this *between relationship* that holds meaning for the data and analysis—something connected and whole that creates form, rather than disconnected parts. Four broad themes emerged from the data, which I explore in two parts, though in reality they are intertwined:

- *Displacement*: the disruption, transition, and bonding process between the staff and the old space;
- *Imprints*: the memories and ghosts that shape our surroundings;
- *Supportive space*: the emotional and empowering value of health and well-being in the new space; and
- *Potential space*: the possibility embedded in spatial change and evolution.

In this presentation, the participants' experiences come through their own words. Through the use of participant testimony, coupled with observations from pertinent literature, the text is intentionally open to the reader's interpretation and collaboration.[38] As with most qualitative presentations, there are many ways to connect with the staff members' experiences, and it was impossible to explore all the various threads in their accounts. As such, I encourage the reader to find additional knowledge and insight from the research presentation.

Although conversational interviews are an established research method, my attempt to foreground co-productive moments *between* the space and the staff lent the data a new energy. These relational moments show up in staff members' emotional, sensory, behavioural, and atmospheric experiences in the space as well as through their physical encounters with and changes to the space itself. By "employing incredibly sensitive and

[37] Shawn Wilson, *Research is Ceremony: Indigenous Research Methods* (Fernwood, 2008), 120.
[38] Sumara & Luce-Kapler, "Action Research" (2006).

nuanced analysis to data collected from interviews",[39] the material world can become a more active part of the focus. Just as Hultman and Lenz Taguchi demonstrated with their example of the girl in the sandbox,[40] how the researcher positions the material surroundings can transform an object, such as sand, from something detached and inert into something connected and active. The spaces—in this case the office spaces—are a setting and, at the same time, "become characters in these stories' plots".[41] This creates a double role in which "organizational spaces are both medium and message".[42]

Emphasis is placed on everyday spatial negotiations, while my observations draw from the literature in an attempt to broaden connections and expand the context. This way of working with the interview transcripts represents a "shift from interpreting texts to seeing them as agents in action" in and of themselves.[43] In the staff's accounts of their experience, socio-material ties can be understood in "terms such as enactment, performance, and practice", which shift the dialogue around space to an active and interactive relationship.[44] By remaining grounded in the words and space of the staff, I have tried to illuminate rather than overshadow their experience. This engagement with space opens a "reservoir of possible perceptions, filled with unique connections and characteristics that simply need to be presented in a new light".[45] The result is a messy overlapping of combined participation that trace the organization's experience of moving. In this spirit, this research is meant to be an opening—an exploration of lived spatial experience—rather than a confirmation or a conclusion.

[39] Robyn Dowling et al. "Qualitative Methods II: "More-than-Human" Methodologies and/in Praxis", *Progress in Human Geography* 41, no. 6 (2016), 824.

[40] Hultman and Lenz Taguchi, "Challenging Anthropocentric Analysis", (2010).

[41] Dvora Yanow, "Space Stories", *Journal of Management Inquiry* 7, no. 3 (1998): 215.

[42] Ibid.

[43] Mike Crang, "Qualitative Methods: Touchy, Feely, Look-See? *Progress in Human Geography* 27, no.4 (2016), 498.

[44] Alan Latham, "Research, Performance, and Doing Human Geography: Some Reflections on the Diary-Photograph, Diary-Interview Method", *Environment and Planning A*, no. 35 (2003): 2012.

[45] Klaske Havik and Kristen Van Haeren, "A Story of Three", *Spool* 3, no. 2, (2016): 6.

On the Move: Getting to Know Head & Hands through its Office Spaces

This story consists of two parallel narratives, each following the organization, Head & Hands', office relocation. One is the turbulent yet remarkable journey of the staff as they dislocated—physically removing themselves and their departments from a rundown yet beloved house—and relocated into a newly renovated, intelligently designed space. The other story follows the transition of Head & Hands through a period of disruption and potential and as the organization adapted and reformed itself with and within the new space.

I begin by introducing the main characters. These descriptions are an amalgam of my own observations, public information about the organization, and sentiments and imagery paraphrased from interviews with the staff.

The Participants

The Organization: Head & Hands

Self-described as down to earth and informal, Head & Hands is a grassroots, not-for-profit organization focused on providing a variety of vital resources (medical, legal, and social) to local youth. In addition to these main areas of support, two additional branches of the organization offer care through a young parents' programme and a youth drop-in centre. In operation since 1970, the organization employs between ten and fourteen full-time staff members,[46] supported by volunteers and part-time workers. Their approach is holistic, harm-reductive, non-judgemental, and inclusive. According to its website, Head & Hands' mission is to "empower youth, and to facilitate social change based on the needs of youth" within the community.

Head & Hands is located in the residential neighbourhood Notre-Dame-de-Grâce, commonly referred to as NDG. Situated southwest of

[46] For reasons of privacy, all names of staff members have been changed for this chapter.

downtown Montreal, NDG is a diverse area with multiple socio-economic strata. Although Head & Hands primarily serves youth, certain outreach initiatives, such as their street work programme, broadens the organization's mandate by offering support to those working or living on the street. Striving to be an inclusive environment, Head & Hands works diligently to ensure that the most vulnerable and marginalized youth can receive the help they need.

The Old Office

The old office occupied the first two floors of a rundown traditional Montreal triplex with a lower-level storefront on a busy street in the neighbourhood of NDG. The third floor, accessible via a shared stairway, was rented (by the landlord) to a family. The entrance, directly off the street, gave into the waiting room: a light-filled space, somewhat chaotic and overflowing with plants, posters, pamphlets, books, and chairs whose backs faced the large window facing the street (see Fig. 6.1). Beyond the waiting room were a half-dozen makeshift cubicles with partial walls, constructed from donated lumber and old window frames and hand-painted a deep orange and burgundy. Curtains of different fabrics hung from some of the open windows. Opposite the cubicles were three closed offices, also perforated by old window frames opening up to rest of the office. An open corridor ran down the middle, between cubicles and office, leading away from the natural light towards a small, dingy bathroom and a large, windowless room, known as the cave, filled with mismatched old couches, chairs, and a desk or two. Beyond the couches was an exam table and a doctor's stool, while medical tools hung from a blue wall. A ceiling track with a light-blue curtain accorded a degree of privacy (see Fig. 6.1).

The second floor, originally designed as a residential apartment, had bedrooms that were repurposed as offices and an exam room. A double living room housed a legal office and health services; broken windowpanes in the glass door separating these offices afforded more of a conceptual separation than an acoustic one. The kitchen was functional, though dirty—a tragedy of the commons—and was used primarily by staff to warm lunches.

Fig. 6.1 Street front and the "cave" (photos by Margot Flores Torre)

Many of the staff considered the office space a second home. Its atmosphere was frequently described as homey and warm, and at least one staff member admitted to occasionally sleeping there after working too late. Haphazardly cobbled together, the office was an agglomeration of patchwork fixes, paint donations, and staff turnover—unique and endearing—littered to overflowing with boxes, meeting notes, filing cabinets, and years' worth of handmade posters and decorations. Brightly painted walls and buckets of condoms distracted from the crumbling floors and disintegrating sofas in the waiting room. The linoleum floor tiles, peeling or missing, were etched with a patina of dirt and decay.

As part of its whimsical aesthetic, the office was intended to be unpretentious and welcoming to youth, especially those marginalized in our society—a space where they could find the services and support they needed without judgement or bureaucracy. This was not a sterile, faceless medical clinic, but somewhere youth could go and be comfortable while speaking with somebody who cared about them and prioritized their needs.

The New Office

Echo, Echo, Echo. The new office *feels* and *sounds* new. It is shiny, clean, and bright, with a smell of fresh paint. Its layout, converted from an old

Fig. 6.2 H&H exterior and main room (right photo by Margot Flores Torre)

church that was later a library, allows words whispered at one end of the building to be heard at the other. The new office sits in a small, green park on a tree-lined residential street about a block from the busier main street it used to be on. It is owned by the city and was donated to the organization for a ten-year period. The church spire and sloped roof still preside over the building (see Fig. 6.2).

The entire office sits on a single floor spread over two wings. The entrance, accessible by wheelchair (a quality lacking in the old building), leads into a large waiting room, which sits in the centre of the building. Plastic chairs and an old wooden church pew line the neutral walls, which are decorated in framed posters from the old office. The reception desk is painted with black chalkboard paint—it is covered with drawings depicting a diverse group of faces. Sunlight beams through a large window, where plants hang in baskets and various brochures line the sill.

To the right of the reception area, past the wall and through a wooden gate, are staff offices and a small kitchen, which look out onto a large, central space for meetings and volunteer work. This area is not visible from the front door as you first enter the building. Beams of light enter the space through circular light tubes in the ceiling—an ingenious design strategy to increase natural light. For the most part, the walls—painted in neutral blues and greys—remain unadorned. Two banks of large, white, almost floor-to-ceiling storage cabinets line the far wall, separated by a bright window with a built-in desk below it. Miscellaneous tables, mix-and-match chairs, and textured couches sit about the open space—a contrast to the flatness of the new walls, flooring, and institutional fixtures (see Fig. 6.2). A pile of boxes, unpacked and leftover from the move, awaits a permanent location. The vastness of the space makes it feel empty.

To the left of the reception is the childcare centre for the Young Parents Program (YPP). The back wall is painted, floor to ceiling, in black chalkboard paint and is covered in children's drawings. Colourful desks, shelves, and toys fill the room with a playful energy, while the sounds of kids playing interweave with the voices of staff chatting at the front desk. Just past the YPP room are the health services office and exam room. It would be easy to miss the large kitchen and workshop—used by the YPP—tucked in directly behind the reception area. This is a large space with multiple worktables, shelves, and stoves. From here, the smells from the instructional cooking classes waft through the building. Sometimes they bake cookies.

Part I: Embodied Encounters

Moving as an emotional experience—the sorting, the packing, the decision-making, the unpacking—is rarely spoken about in research on office transitions. Management literature on office moves has tended to describe employees more like objects being "relocated" to new spaces.[47,48] These transitions are often framed in terms of organizational goals, productivity, or cost-cutting; however, the lived experience of moving can be stressful, disruptive, emotional, and physically challenging. Here, I explore the emotional journey the staff experienced as they navigated a shifting foundation. This transition blurred

[47] George Cairns, "Aesthetics, Morality and Power: Design as Espoused Freedom and Implicit control", *Human Relations* 55, no.7 (2002).

[48] Cornelia Gerdenitsch et al., "Need–Supply fit in an Activity-Based Flexible Office: A Longitudinal Study During Relocation", *Environment and Behavior 50,* no. 3 (2017).

the boundaries between the past, present, and future as the staff encountered organizational memories and histories. The old office contained many traces of the organization's past iterations, in the form of physical documents and artefacts, with the building itself a major contributor to the organization's identify and culture. The domestic architecture of the old office had become entwined with how Head & Hands functioned and identified. In the first part of this investigation, we begin before the move as a way to ground ourselves in the old space with the staff.

Emplaced Memories and Spatial Imprints

The Domestic Office

The old office building, like many in the neighbourhood, was built as a traditional ground-level storefront with two upper storeys for residential apartments. Head & Hands occupied the storefront and the second-floor apartment. Every staff member I spoke with commented on the office's homeyness—a trait that was clearly a defining quality of the organization. As we sat together in her space, Jenna described how her apartment-style office contributed to the clients' comfort (see Fig. 6.3):

> So, upstairs has a really nice, chill, calm vibe that I like. I love my actual office, itself. I find it very comfortable. I guess I've decorated it in a way that reflects me or things that I like. I've got my Bruce Springsteen poster on the wall. [laughs] I get so many comments about my office from clients and patients really liking it. It's always nice to get that external validation—hearing people say "I like your space, I feel comfortable here. It feels like an old apartment." It *is* an old apartment! And then, yeah, you can just watch how they kinda relax in it and they're more likely to share the important information about their lives that you need to know about to take care of their health, you know? (Jenna)

Fig. 6.3 Office curtains (photo by Margot Flores Torre)

I asked Jenna how her office makes her clients feel comfortable. She continues:

> I think it's the homey feel. I think it's the old-apartment feel. I think it's the creaky old wooden floors and there's just some character. Especially upstairs. My office is contained, it's got closed doors and walls … . And I think that helps clients feel kind of *held* a little bit. It's comfortable, it's not austere, it's colourful—the walls are yellow and turquoise and burgundy and stuff. And you know, it was my predecessor who painted the office, but I just kept them. It works. Yeah, and to see the artwork up, and the pamphlets, and the things I put around—I mean, sometimes it's kinda messy. Right now, it's messy. I need to tidy it. Generally, it's a space that I feel really comfortable and at home in, and maybe that also influences the cli-

Fig. 6.4 Upstairs office detail (photo by Margot Flores Torre)

> ents coming through. It reflects me, and maybe if they see that I'm really at ease in the space, maybe it helps them to be that way as well. (Jenna)

In her description, Jenna mentions things like creaky wooden floors, colourful walls, and character (see Fig. 6.4). There is a history, evidenced through the painted walls, posters, objects of those who came before.[49] It's messy, but it feels like home—to her. In this sense, clients enter into a more personal space. Here the building's construction as a residential apartment shapes the mood and interactions within the upstairs offices. There is more of an expectation that a home may reflect its occupants than an office. In Jenna's description, these two spaces merge. Her office, like a home, is lived in. It is very different than the more sterile medical centres her clients may be visiting. The colours (burgundy, turquoise, and yellow)

[49] Harriet Shortt, "Scarred Objects and Time Marks as Memory Anchors: The significance of scuffs and stains in organizational life", *Human Relations* 74, no. 10 (2021).

themselves contribute to this less formal atmosphere, whereas we would expect a medical clinic to be layered in neutral greys, beiges, or blues.

Louis, who also worked upstairs, attributes the warmth of the Head & Hands as an organization to its physical homeyness:

> First thing I would say is it's a warm environment because it's very homey—like, you know, to someone who had never been here, I would describe this place as your old-architecture Montreal, but inside looking like a non-profit organization. But it's warm inside because it looks like an apartment. The way it's set up—the configuration is set up in a way that it is very warm from like the colours that are selected [for] the space. And I'd say it looked pretty much like an apartment—like a home.... It makes you feel very comfortable in the space, you know. For sure, there are a lot of things that need to be changed here. Since it's an old building, and you see some windows missing and cracks and whatever, but I could say it almost looks like my old house when I used to live in the Plateau, for example. (Louis)

Through these descriptions, we get a sense of how spatial identity is manifested. The building's construction calls to mind other homes clients and staff may have visited or lived in themselves. Its residential past exists through its physical layout and construction, but it is also enacted on a daily basis. Elements like wooden desks, old doorknobs, nick-nacks, French doors, and inadequate lighting are very tangible contributors to the present. I asked Louise what quality of his office he felt most attached to; he banged on his desk and said: "I like the smell of wood. Some days it's more prominent. Sometimes it's more fragrant. Weirdly, you know, sometimes it's less. I like that." The smell of wood from his beautiful old desk connected him to the space (see Fig. 6.5).

These sensations represent important qualities of relational interactions with the space. Listening to a co-worker or client walk down the hallway—*creak, creak*—becomes an auditory reference of home and the building's long history. For Louis, memories of his house in the Plateau-Mont-Royal neighbourhood become intermingled with his embodied experience of the office. In this sense, the office is lived both in place and in memory. Trigg speaks of how our "memories pursue us as we pursue place, both forming an ambiguous zone somewhere in between".[50] The

[50] Dylan Trigg, *The Memory of Place* (Ohio University Press, 2012), 9

Fig. 6.5 Upstairs office desk (photo by Margot Flores Torre)

office was a constant reminder of what made Head & Hands unique and different from other youth services. Its aesthetic was, in many ways, a material manifestation of their values.

A Material Divide

While the upstairs office was filled with homey warmth, the main floor of the office had a separate energy. The physical separation between upstairs and downstairs was often blamed for creating a division in the staff between those who worked upstairs and those who didn't. The reception area was downstairs (see Fig. 6.6) along with the administrative staff offices (fund-raising, office management, outreach, etc.), while the upstairs offices housed the various service programmes (legal, health, social). These physical divides, as Katelyn articulates here, were felt by many of the staff:

> There is that divide where I feel like upstairs people are a lot closer to each other. It's not cliques, but sometimes something will happen in a staff meeting and you can tell there is a divide. I think that being on two sepa-

Fig. 6.6 Downstairs reception (photo by Margot Flores Torre)

> rate floors creates different formations. I wish that we were all on the same floor. (Katelyn)

While these divisions could be explored through a strictly social lens, another element that manifested was more atmospheric. Each floor had very different energies. The main floor was lively and boisterous—an open space where clients and staff congregated, the atmosphere was filled with music, conversation, laughter, and, on busy days, a frenetic spirit. Upstairs was quieter and gentler. While all staff took shifts at the front desk, the programme staff mainly worked in larger individual offices upstairs. Geneva, who worked upstairs in the medical office, spoke of feeling a stress in her body that physically dissipated as she walked up the stairs to her office:

> I try to check in downstairs and then, going upstairs for me, I always get calmer going up the stairs because that's my area. I think it's a different vibe for me downstairs than upstairs.
>
> When I have to work downstairs, I'm definitely not in the same mindset or in the same zone than I am when I'm upstairs, because my office is upstairs. But also, we're four permanent workers upstairs. There's this kind

> of vibe that we have altogether because, even if my door is closed or when my door is open, I can hear everything that's happening in some ways. So, I really feel more at ease and calmer when I'm upstairs. (Geneva)

Geneva's account confirms the bond of the upstairs staff, while her embodied experience of walking upstairs speaks strongly to her varying comfort in the two spaces. Having programme workers upstairs, in private offices, while administrative staff crammed into an open space reinforced a social, hierarchical, and physical divide in the office. Without judging the positive or negative repercussions of that, these separations manifested two very different atmospheres within Head & Hands; they created a unique aesthetic and diverse resonance that became entangled with the staff and work taking place.

Haunted by ~~Im~~Material Ghosts

Rearranging

As an organization evolves and new staff become part of the space, it is interesting to notice how a relationship with the space develops. During the first round of interviews, I spoke with Amanda, who had been with the organization for about six months. She was just settling into a different room following a collective staff decision to rearrange who would occupy which office:

> I definitely feel a lot better about this space, actually, because I inherited the office I came into, and there was a lot of furniture and I couldn't move a lot of things around. Like I started to try, especially, to make a space so that we're not sitting across a desk from one another. So, that was some of the first steps, and then, when time came to switch offices, I was able to take that time to really consider how I wanted things arranged and what would I want to keep or had no choice but to keep. But this led me to a space that I'm happier with. (Amanda)

The office originally given to Amanda had been her predecessor's. New to the organization, she found it difficult to make substantial changes to that space. This was in part because the physical desk, cabinets, and other furniture were too heavy for her to move on her own. The oversized filing cabinets, filled with years of organizational documents, could not be thrown out, leaving very little space for creative rearrangement. Jacqueline Vischer examines how a truly supportive environment is evaluated not only in terms of "receiving support from, but also being able to act on the environment".[51] Acting on the environment underlines the importance of a reciprocal connection with space, with changes to one's own space being an integral part of that relationship. When Amanda moved into a new office, she was able to create a functional space that felt good and supported her work.

While I was waiting to speak with Amanda, she came out of her office, which was down the hall to the left, and poked her head through the open part of the window to speak with a colleague. The exchange, which only lasted a minute or so, was framed by the makeshift structure of the office (see Fig. 6.7). While Amanda could have opened the office door, she chose a more informal route of communication. At the time, it felt playful and familiar—an act that had been performed dozens of times. It is easy to imagine the staff member on the other side of the well speaking to this head peeking through the window, half-in and half-out of the space. At the end of the hallway is the large window-less meeting room, also known as the "cave", which doubles as an additional medical exam room.

Another staff member who experienced the same office reorganization was Katelyn. For different reasons, she, too, found it hard to make changes to her initial workspace—a small desk squeezed in behind a cubicle with office thoroughfares on three sides. Her desk was next to a noisy fan, a public bathroom, and a large meeting space. She describes it here:

> For the first three years that I was working here, I was in that space and I actually didn't make any changes in that space. I really hated it. Then the fan broke and I was right next to the fan, and the by-product of it breaking, or the consequence, was that it was on all the time, and so my ability to be in that space deteriorated. This was not a good working condition—there's no light, it's right next to the bathrooms clients use—so I used to hear people having all sorts of experiences. And it was right next to the "cave," where people have bigger meetings, which means people often leave gar-

[51] Jacqueline C. Vischer, "Towards a User-Centred Theory of the Built Environment", *Building Research & Information 36*, no. 3 (2008): 237

Fig. 6.7 Downstairs hallway (photo by Margot Flores Torre)

> bage or dirty dishes, and it just wasn't a good space. So, for a while, I wasn't working there. I would try to work out in a café or at home. (Katelyn)

Katelyn's account provides a visceral description of her unhealthy workspace. Without walls, the noises of fan and bathroom became part of her space. It was dark. Other uses and users of the space impinged upon her area. There was no privacy. Katelyn was haunted by the lingering smells—apple cores and forgotten dirty dishes—and the cacophony of sounds that permeated her space. Ultimately, these residues were stored in her body, contributing to her sense of self as she existed in relationship to the office and her work. What is important about this list of sounds, smells and feels is the "meaning and function" of these qualities for Katelyn and the other staff members.[52] In this situation, Katelyn found it difficult to feel motivated or inspired. She did not make any changes to the space, but instead found somewhere else to work.

In *Places Through the Body*, Heidi Nast and Steve Pile trace the "intricate webs" of relationships woven between space and bodies, which embed themselves into bodies and onto places.[53] Just as buildings are constructed, so too are bodies shaped through their interactions with other humans and non-humans. The built environment becomes a visceral language, communicated through symbols and forms, which we "ingest" sensorially through our bodies.[54] The word *ingest* is powerful; it leaves a sour residue on my tongue and conjures sensations of indigestion as I speak it. Ultimately, its use implies an intimate connection between ourselves and our space through a consumptive relationship. Food is a substance we consume both for pleasure and for sustenance. *How do we consume spaces? What do they taste like?*

It is hard not to imagine the old Head & Hands space from this sensuous, boundary-crossing perspective. Katelyn, in her description of her desk in the old office, spoke of being situated beside the washroom and forced to listen to "all sorts of experiences." In another other conversation, Amara described the smell of the old office as "putrid, like rotting wood". Smell is a quality that literally enters the body; sound does this, too. Tamira spoke of the constant din of fluorescent lights and not being able to hear over the bathroom fan. Other aesthetic qualities may not physically enter the body, but they can still have an effect on it. Amara described the old office as painted in "oppressive burgundy, weird green, and pee-yellow". Being surrounded, day after day, by a colour you find oppressive must surely infiltrate and affect one's mind and body.[55]

These qualities and descriptions explicate the reciprocal relationship taking place and transform it into something animated and alive. During these spatial experiences, we may be "stretched, opened, compressed,

[52] Hariett Shortt, "Sounds of the Salon: The Auditory Routines of Hairdressers at Work", *International Journal of Work Organisation and Emotion* 5, no. 4 (2013): 352.

[53] Heidi Nast and Steve Pile, *Places Through the Body* (Psychology Press, 1998), 4–5.

[54] Ibid. 4.

[55] Timon Beyes and Christian De Cock, "Adorno's Grey, Taussig's Blue: Colour, Organization and Critical Affect", *Organization* 24, no. 1 (2017).

relaxed, shocked, or moved emotionally".[56] To speak of one's relationship to physical space as alive may seem overly descriptive, but it also feels appropriately invasive and lush. As Trigg puts it, "the body activates place. But the same is true in reverse: Place activates the body".[57]

Dislocating

Our confrontation with the material world is accentuated during a move, personal or professional, as every item requires some level of attention. The logistics of organizing and packing while maintaining an organization's services adds an extra layer of complexity. One detail that often accompanies a move is the relentless stream of micro-decision-making[58] that occurs as documents and objects are assessed and categorized. *Which box do these papers go in? Will I need them before we move? Should I pack, scan, shred, or recycle these documents?* As the office is disassembled, chaos and mess increase, and while a certain amount of mess has been linked to creativity and innovation,[59] the dismantling of an environment can be chaotic and challenging. Especially when it is felt and sometimes mirrored in our bodies. The combination of uncertainty and disorder creates an environment brimming with heightened emotion and fatigue—accentuated in turn by individuals' different approaches in navigating unfamiliar terrain. For Head & Hands, maintaining relationships with clients and other staff members added an additional challenge.

When I spoke with staff members about the moving process, it was consistently described as long and hard, but also meaningful. The coordination and time required to sift, sort, and scan decades' worth of documents and memorabilia made individuals involved in the process dependent upon one another for help. Closing services to clients in need was an additional and emotional burden for the staff. For one staff member, the loss of services to clients weighed heavily on her and the

[56] Patricia Pringle, "Spatial Pleasures", *Space and Culture 8,* no 2 (2005): 142.

[57] Dylan Trigg, *The Memory of Place* (Ohio University Press, 2012), 11.

[58] See Barry Schwartz, *The Paradox of Choice* (Harper Perennial, 2004).

[59] Kathleen D. Vohs et al., "Physical Order Produces Healthy Choices, Generosity, and Conventionality, Whereas Disorder Produces Creativity", *Psychological Science* 24, no. 9 (2013).

organization during what was already an exhausting time. Her experience illustrates the organizational and interpersonal challenges of negotiating varying levels of motivation, commitment, and preparedness:

> It was really hard and clients didn't stop having crises. You know, so even though we weren't physically open, we still had client interaction and the holidays is a tough period for people who are marginalized. So yeah. Yeah. That was—that was tough.
>
> And just getting everyone on board. Like some people were not packing or shredding or doing things and then they were like hustling last minute. When other people were very methodical and planned out, so—and also, like my physical space on Sherbrooke then was filled with boxes for weeks—stuff everywhere. Yeah, like it wasn't the most welcoming space while we're preparing to leave, you know, so yeah. (Amara)

With all staff members contributing in different ways, times, and capacities, the office was constantly filled with diverse and sometimes competing energies. While some people packed systematically over time, others rushed at the last minute. Amara describes the disarray in her office as unwelcoming. Piles of boxes and papers left to be sorted became part of her temporary physical landscape as she continued to work in the weeks before the move.

The chaos of a space in the weeks before a move can be confusing. All the familiar cues—posters on the wall, tools accessible in drawers or on desks—are no longer there. The spatial disorder creates a disruption in our mind–body's automatic process, which we rely on to function absent of excess contemplation. A familiar place is "habitually sensed and manoeuvred through and around, becoming 'sedimented' in a habituated body".[60] Drew Leder suggests that we are not (nor should we be) always aware of our bodies in everyday experiences.[61] The body, says Leder, has a "tendency toward self-concealment" and thus is seen as freeing us from its confines.[62] While meditative processes to deepen awareness of our surroundings can bring elements to the surface in a controlled and pleasant way, more sudden interferences in the environment force the background to the foreground, ousting our tacit knowledge. Speaking in terms of the

---

[60] Cathrine Degnen, "Socialising Place Attachment: Place, Social Memory and Embodied Affordances", *Ageing & Society* 36, no.8 (2015): 1647.

[61] Drew Leder *The Absent Body* (University of Chicago Press,1990).

[62] Ibid. 69.

body, Leder suggests it materializes when its typical function is disrupted, such as by sickness or injury. Disorder or pain heightens and diverts attention to our once-absent physical form. Similarly, the disarray of space can thrust the environment into our day-to-day reality, creating a heightened and disorienting experience. At Head & Hands, some staff chose to avoid the situation by not packing, while others attempted to regain control and stability.

Oscar spoke of his frustration with the chaos and a lack of leadership during the move. From his perspective, the physical and emotional work required of the staff in moving the organization exceeded what was reasonable:

> I don't feel like anybody liked the process of moving. Like let's be clear about that. People injured themselves! … You know, it's the kind of thing where we were like, "we need all hands on deck," but everyone was very passive and just being like, "I guess I gotta be here, but I don't know what I got to do." And I feel like I would have paid people. I didn't need to be there. It was a lack of leadership. And like fine, you know, this is something that happens a lot at Head & Hands. Like counting on everybody—scraping energy from individuals and being like, "if we all put energy into this, it is gonna work." But I'm like, "no!" We need leadership and structure, you know, to make things happen. (Oscar)

Oscar's experience radiates with frustration and confusion. The disruption and chaos of the space became mirrored in the disorganized structure of the group. A lack of leadership became evident as all staff members were expected to do their part. In not-for-profit organizations, staff are often expected to do work outside their job description as part of their shared commitment. Cora's account also references the chaos and difficulty of the move, but she frames it as a collective problem—one that required empathy and compassion from fellow staff members:

> Just having to sit there and not judge people, and be like, "okay, I don't do this program. So, I don't know what it's like to have all these files and I really cannot judge this person for having their life and this many files and being afraid." So, it's really an intimate process of being in each other's business because we have to. Yeah, so a lot of things came up with that—helping people and then also just being like, "who's going to handle these

> logistics? Who's going to like, handle the truck? Who's gonna handle the movers? And who's going to make sure that all these things are in place?" And just kind of trusting each other to do that. (Cora)

Cora frames this process as a collective problem rather than one of leadership. For her department, which stored most of its documents online, packing was not especially difficult, but she observed and spoke about the link between certain departments' day-to-day functions and their ability to sort and pack. The range of emotions staff encountered speaks to the intensity of the process. The act of helping one another with shredding or packing documents is an intimate one, with the documents and their "symbolic significance" acting as an extension of our private selves.[63]

Cora's experience of the move, serving in a helping role, seemed to allow her the ability to recognize and respond to the ebb and flow of others' experiences and needs. Asked what advice she would give to another organization, Cora's response describes the feelings and intimacy associated with the moving of personal objects—details that require tenderness and empathy:

> I'd make sure that every single person is being supported and held, because it's really easy to fall through the cracks and be like, "oh, I just need to move my things or something." But you forget that a lot of other people might be feeling very overwhelmed, and that it's a whole team that has to move, and that it becomes a very personal process because all your things are being added to other people's things. It's hard to explain, but it's a very personal thing to have all of your things being moved to another place and essentially leaving memories behind, so it's just something that is inevitably hard and just has a lot of feelings and emotions attached to it. (Cora)

Cora's comments on the challenge of having your "things" taken and piled with "other people's things" emphasizes our complex connection to the material world. It is difficult for her to find the words to express these nuanced emotions—how she feels about seeing her personal papers and objects in moving boxes. This challenge to describe socio-material relationships[64] is one of the reasons why researching spatial relationships can

---

[63] Shortt, "Scarred Objects" (2021): 1693.

[64] Steven Taylor, "Overcoming Aesthetic Muteness: Researching Organizational Members' Aesthetic Experience", *Human Relations* 55, no.7 (2002).

be difficult: people are not often used to speaking emotionally and descriptively about physical or aesthetic relationships. Cora also mentions how she is "leaving memories behind". She describes these memories as though they too are physical objects that will remain behind in the old building.

Another staff member, Tamira, also reveals the heavy burden moving can place upon staff, as well as certain contradictory feelings and moods inherent in intense situations:

> The packing process was my nightmare. I vividly remember. It was like 10 p.m. Like the week before we moved. And I was throwing out old documents from like bins and bins and bins and bins of fundraising shit and I just started crying. So hard. When I'm overtired, I cry, and I was so tired. I started sobbing uncontrollably.
>
> But I really like organizing and I like throwing things out. So that part of it was nice, because I was like throw this out. Throw this out. Throw this out. Scan this. Downsizing is super fun for me. (Tamira)

Despite Tamira's love of organizing and downsizing, the stress of physically moving and making these micro-decisions under pressure became too much for her.

The physical task of sorting old papers can also become an embodied trigger of memories. Whether as momentary flashes or lingering emotions, the recollection of past events surfacing vis-à-vis a stack of documents or an object can be pleasurable, painful, tedious, joyful, or all of the above. Dylan Trigg reminds us that memories are not "confined to our heads" but in fact also exist in "*things* in the world" that serve to "activate our brains".[65] As a staff member packs material objects, these "things act upon the body" through a process of remembering.[66] Understanding this entwined and affective aspect of the office space as acting upon the staff as they act upon it—dismantling, sorting, and packing it in cardboard boxes—immediately intensifies and personalizes it.

As Tamira and I continued our conversation, she spoke of the more meaningful elements in the process—specifically while sorting through the organization's old historical documents:

[65] Trigg, *The Memory of Place*, 47.

[66] Ibid. 48.

> Going through all the old documents was really special.... And it's really an honour. I feel honoured to be part of this process and to witness the organization go through this huge transition into this like really nice, sustainable space....
>
> We went through all these old documents and we found some documents about a fire in the old, old, old, building in—whenever—the nineties or eighties. We found a bunch of old documents about why Head & Hands had to move—we had a fire! And we found photos from the aftermath of the fire, that kind of stuff. And it just felt like really, really important and meaningful to me because it like brought up those legacy feelings and like the continuing of the work and, you know, people come in and out of this organization really quickly....
>
> We're just flashes in the pan of this organization, but then being able to revisit that in the middle of this transition was like, oh no, I'm actually part of like a lineage rather than just like in another phase. It felt like building on that continuity and being like, so many people have invested so much love and care and energy into this space, and it's so like incredible that we get to be part of that too. (Tamira)

In her description, Tamira describes uncovering historical documents—organizational memory—that reveal the cause of the organization's last move more than three decades ago: a fire. The merging of past, present, memory, and place created a meaningful moment and context for Tamira, who became, in a sense, timeless. As Tamira's experience connected her with those who came before her, her employment no longer felt isolated but part of something larger. The physical interaction with boxes of old papers surfaced an organizational memory that allowed Tamira to "situate [herself] in time and place".[67] Just as our personal memories "co-constituted who we are at present",[68] these organizational documents and history represented a collective memory of which Tamira is now a part.

The experience shifted some of the staff's sense of the move itself, from logistical and burdensome to significant and historic. Trigg speaks of the unique fusion of time, place, and event during moments of profound change when, "precisely through their strangeness, places become

[67] Shortt, "Scarred Objects", (2021): 1694.

[68] Ibid.

memorable by disturbing patterns of regularity and habit".[69] As the staff uprooted their patterns and disassembled the space, the old office took on a certain significance through its unfamiliar state. By disrupting the staff members' usual ways of being in the space, the moving process provided an opportunity for reflection and reconnection to the space and the organization. Cora, for example, saw her participation in the move as an important moment in her commitment to the organization: "for me, having gone from this building to the next was very much me being like, 'oh, wow, I'm moving forward with this organization'".

How memories accompany and influence one's journey into both new and familiar spaces is a topic that seems essential when thinking about an office move. While the staff was packing, Cora mentioned how she felt like she was leaving her memories behind—as though they were part of the building itself—while Tamira handled physical pictures from the old office fire, which elicited feelings of connection and belonging. When we move through a space, an embodied process of encounter and adaptation is simultaneously mediated through past experience and interwoven with our collective identity. Therefore, the ways in which we orient ourselves and the imprint spaces leave in our memory are, as Trigg said it, "existing through the porous retention of our bodies".[70] Looking at the physical environment as something or somewhere that is retained within us evokes a very tangible and real notion of space as part of us, waiting to be felt and remembered.

Material Ghosts

During my first round of interviews, one exchange stood out as particularly relevant to spaces of memory. I was speaking with Emma about her relationship with her office space—a tiny, windowless room tucked beside the radiator at the rear end of the main floor—when she told me about the death of her colleague, Owen. This was the only interview I had outside of the office; Emma wanted to meet in a café. As one of the Street

---

[69] Ibid. 9.

[70] Ibid. 11

Work[71] staff, her office, she said, was the streets. As we talk, her description of the room becomes fluid with past events that took place. I'll let Emma tell the story:

> I left all his things the way they were for almost a year—*so*. I felt in a lot of ways comforted, I think. I think some people were weirded out by it and they were like, "you should get rid of stuff," and I was like, "no, it's kind of comforting," just having these things around. So, yeah, it's kind of a loaded question for that reason. I have slowly been taking his things down and trying to make space for somebody new, and his posters that he put up and stuff are still there. And he put up a dreamcatcher.
>
> Yeah, so it's also a room that's had a lot of shit go down. I was a street worker in 2013—sorry, 2011—when we lost our funding. It sucked. Rebecca and I had a month to sort of pack up and let our clients know. It was terrible in terms of having that happen to you. Like, "wow, what am I going to do next month?" But mostly because we weren't able to reach clients in time. At any rate, while that was happening, we were having a Save Street Work meeting in the director's office, and it was thundering and lightning and raining out. All of a sudden, we hear all this water rushing in and it flooded the street work office. Like there was this much water on the floor. I've never seen anything like that. And previously, there was water damage in the street work office when I started. So, water was kinda dripping … and all the files and street work computer was water damaged, and nothing was really done about it and so we're just like, well, we're not going to set up in this office. We're just going to make a new space. So, there is sort of history of this office being waterlogged. It did get redone when I came back, but it was storage, so I moved everything out and got myself set up. (Emma)

In this profound description, the objects in Emma's office *become* Owen after he is no longer there. She is comforted by their presence yet forced to justify their existence to her colleagues. Removing the items, slowly, is a way of grieving and processing his absence and her loss. The disruption

[71] Street Work is an outreach programme that supports youths and drug users working or living on the street. Two staff members ran the programme until a funding cut in 2011 temporarily halted its activities. It resumed a few years later.

to the space, as *he* is removed, simultaneously and powerfully transforms the space for Emma, who is also imprinted by the objects.

Overlapping this account is Emma's memory of her job coming to an end, which is forever marked with the physical destruction of her office during the rainstorm. The precarious nature of her job—which at the time depended on government funding—and the lack of an uplifting, clean, dry work environment are entwined, the facts compounding each other. In the following account, Emma continues to describe the effects that her office had upon her personally and on her work conditions, which were sometimes unsafe situations as she met with clients. Tucked away next to the radiator, her little space was in a location mostly invisible to the rest of the office:

> It's very loud because the heater is right outside, and the fan. So, I always have to close the door if I'm in a meeting with a client, which I might not always want to do, honestly. Like sometimes I won't know someone very well and I'm not sure where they're at in their mental health.... It's a bit sketchy, where, like my de-escalation training—I hope I really let that sink in, if I really needed to leave the room with someone between me and the door.
>
> I think it's a space where people can sort of forget about you. Like I've been in the office with a client after we'd closed, but usually whoever is doing the front desk will knock and be like, "we're going to leave," and I would be like, right, "okay we have to wrap up." But we were about 10 minutes after we had closed, and I opened the door and all the lights are off and we'd been locked in, and it's just not ideal to have that. (Emma)

In this memory, Emma is simply forgotten by others in the building; her office hides her and her client away from everyone else's attention. Instead of offering protection, the walls become a hazard. The precarious conditions which Emma continually experienced while working in her office reinforce the active role the room played in these scenarios. Her way of interacting with the client, having to close the door, all become part of her mindset, behaviour, emotions, and ability to work. In a way, this traumatic experience of her office scarred her and the office itself. Harriet Shortt extends the corporeal "concept of a scar" to scarred objects themselves as a reminder of and connection to past experience.[72] For Emma, it is impossible to separate the material (past and present) from her way of being and working. The way she relates to herself, her co-workers, and the work itself are all shaped by the environment.

Emma's office also seems to be a physical manifestation of her programme's place in the organization. The programme's funding situation within the organization is replicated in its space—unstable, unsecure, and unreliable.

Later in the interview, Emma returns to Owen's presence in the space:

> When [Owen] came on, he had this vision and just like drew out a little map of the office and how we … I wanted him to feel comfortable in the space, because I'd been there for six months and I wanted him to feel like that was his office too. And so, we moved stuff around and he put up shelves and, honestly, he made the space functional and livable, and I always just feel so grateful about that because there's a lot of materials in that office. Like, it's where I put all the different needles and steri-cups. There's just boxes and boxes of gear back there and condoms galore, and all that stuff. (Emma)

In many ways, for Emma, the office is a manifestation of Owen. His investment in the space through decoration and reorganization is part of her relationship with him, in the past and in the present. This happens through her memories of creating the space with him, but also through her relationship with the material objects themselves. Stevenson suggests that the "development of emplaced knowledge" can become "inseparable from the development of emplaced, often material, memories".[73] How Emma interacts with the space—a space that Owen helped shape—is a continuing of their relationship albeit carried out via the material space. Emma's ghostly connection with her office "requires that the present is understood as composed by the past, and that these, indeed, anticipate future".[74] The blurring of time, space, and materiality co-create an experi-

[72] Shortt, "Scarred Objects", (2021): 1694.

[73] Andrew Stevenson, "We Came Here to Remember: Using Participatory Sensory Ethnography to Explore Memory as Emplaced, Embodied Practice", *Qualitative Research in Psychology* 11, no. 4 (2014): 338.

[74] Arja Ropo et al., "Embodiment of Leadership Through Material Place", *Leadership* 9, no.3 (2013): 384.

ence that simultaneously allows the past, and future to merge with the present.[75] These connections through spatial memories also obscure the boundaries between material and immaterial. As Nijs and Daems observe, these moments "are enacted and actualized through elements that are neither totally material nor immaterial".[76] The entangled nature of such encounters makes them impossible to separate and quantify by category or time. Emma's experience illustrates how places and people not only leave traces of themselves as memories and imprints but also become part of a potential and "uncertain" future.[77] Because memories are not static—they shift and morph over time—how a space is experienced in the present cannot be "disentangled from these features".[78] As Emma's memories evolve, so does her relationship to Owen and the office in the present.

Reorienting (Challenges), Embodied Encounters

Reverberating Echoes

When Head & Hands moved into its new offices, there were many lingering histories to negotiate in the new space. Initially designed and used as a church, the building retained some of its original religious forms, such as the spire and peaked roof. Following the church's deconsecration, but many years before Head & Hands' occupancy, the building served as the neighbourhood library. These past lives were present for the organization and its staff, who sought to establish their programmes and make the building feel like it was theirs. In the photograph (see Fig. 6.8), the colourless snow adds an eerier quality to the building—as though we have been transported backwards in time. In one conversation, Amara spoke of the community's well-established familiarity with the building:

[75] Ibid.

[76] Greg Nijs and Amelie Daems, "And What if the Tangible Were Not, and Vice Versa? On Boundary Works in Everyday Mobility Experience of People Moving into Old Age: For Daisy (1909–2011)", Space and Culture 15, no. 3 (2012), 189.

[77] Ibid.

[78] Fabio James Petani, "Space and Process: The Organizational Importance of What we Leave Behind", In unpublished doctoral dissertation (Università della Svizzera Italiana, 2016), 16.

Fig. 6.8 New Office exterior (photo by Margot Flores Torre)

> A lot of people know it and have fond memories about the library where our offices are. Like my department, it's where the children's library used to be. A lot of our clients are from 12 to 25, so when they come here for services, they're sort of like, "oh, I used to, you know, get books in this section." So, it's kind of cool in that way. I think people enjoy it. (Amara)

Similarly, Oscar appreciates the familiarity that people have with the building. When giving workshops at schools in the area, he uses people's memory of the library to introduce Head & Hands:

> But when I'm doing the FEELS project and I'm telling people like, "who remembers the old Benny Library?" And like half of the classroom raises their hand and I'm like, that's where *we* are now. Everybody has a clear idea of where Head & Hands is, you know, and that helps a lot in terms of like visibility. Like having the kids knowing where we are, right? (Oscar)

On the other hand, Mary mentions some confusion regarding the office's appearance:

> When we first opened and I started seeing clients again, I had clients who didn't think this could be it because it was a church. And, you know, who

> are so confused.... Sometimes I get an email, "oh, I couldn't find the place," so, you know, like "I just saw this church." Yeah, that was it. Now, I tell people it used to be a church, it used to be a library. Now it is us. So, that has gotten easier. Clients come in and they're like, "wow," you know? But I've had clients also come in and say "oooooh, your other room was so cozy." (Mary)

The new building, which sits atop a little hill in a park, still has the old façade, the grandeur of a church. Walking up to it feels very different than approaching the old office's storefront windows on a busy street. For older clients coming to the new office for the first time, walking across the grassy, tree-filled park towards what looks like a church is a drastic change from Head & Hands' former aesthetic. Mary mentioned some of her clients' initial responses to her new office, their laments at the loss of coziness, a quality that defined every aspect of the old space. Similar to the impact of the church facade, this immediate recalling of the old office draws past into present, momentarily merging the two spaces. The new office is haunted by these overlaid memories and comparisons; it "is inseparable from how [it] 'used to be'".[79] It is a church, a library, and now an office *all at once*. Interestingly, this lineage is also experienced through sound. The architecture of the church was designed to channel and move sound through its structure to accentuate the voice during services. Cora describes this effect:

> Yeah, it is spacious. It's really roomy. It's like you can definitely hear a lot of the sounds, because there's not a lot of like ... it's just the way that the building was built, from what I understand, is that it used to be a church and then it was a library. So, that means that the way that the space is set up, it's like so that somebody can hear you from far away. And so, sometimes, it can be a little bit hard for people to kind of not eavesdrop. (Cora)

Mary described how sound moves through the office as transforming the space into "an echo chamber", adding that she could hear the front-desk person from her office on the other side of the building. When I interviewed Tamira at the front desk, I noticed immediately that she was

[79] Nijs & Daems, "And What if the Tangible Were Not", (2012): 189.

speaking at a level barely above a whisper to avoid being heard by everyone. Oscar also changed his work patterns due to the “distracting” sound: “I often have to work with my door closed, which I feel is like not with the spirit of Head & Hands”. The noise level led to micro-adjustments, a sort of repatterning, in how the staff members worked and related to one another, with some new behaviours moving away from the organization’s culture of openness. Cora speaks to other, more nuanced ways in which the sound affected the office atmosphere:

> The noises are very—it can be good and bad, because, like if you’re feeling kind of down, like you never feel too alone. Mmm, and then just like the, just the echoes in it feel very like … it can be like a really nice feeling, because it’s just like, it’s just everybody can really hear each other clearly. Hmm—but it’s obvious that sometimes it can be a little overwhelming, because you don’t you feel like you can do anything discreetly. So sometimes, depending on the mood, it can feel really nice or very hard to kind of manage, so it depends on the mood. (Cora)

The permeating contact of sound resulted in a comforting connection between the staff, located in different parts of the building. On days when few people were in the office, the space felt large and empty; hearing someone at the other end of the building made staff feel less alone. On busier days, however, this very connection overloaded staff by creating an overwhelming and chaotic environment.

For Mary, the noise directly affects her job. As a counsellor providing support to youth in need, the atmosphere in her office can influence how her client feels. She takes pride in providing a safe and supportive space within which she can concentrate and focus on her client. However, unlike her old room, which was upstairs and separate from the gathering area, the new space has private offices surrounding the collective spaces. This creates conflicting energies and needs within the same space:

> Sometimes when I’m in here with clients and, you know, it can be very intense, like my client experience can be very intense. Telling me stories that are you know hard to tell and then, you know, we hear gales of laughter out there, and you know, the kitchen is there, right? And, of course, my colleagues are allowed to be happy. But I’ve had to, a couple of times, open my door and just say like “please?” (Mary)

The frustration that Mary feels comes from a lack of privacy. The newly constructed walls are what Blesser and Salter refers to as "acoustically transparent".[80] This means that despite being able to close her office door, "the auditory channel, which supports voice communication" remains open.[81] The original acoustic design of the church creates an unsupportive aural experience for a contemporary office. Excessive noise and "reverberating clatter produces stress, anxiety, isolation, and psychological tension" while compromising employees' ability to accomplish their tasks.[82] Exposure to loud noise can increase heart rate, blood pressure, and can interfere with sleep.[83] Sound, unlike sight, enters into our bodies. It can provide immense connection—bringing our environment to life—but its intimacy can also quickly become an intrusion.

While the building's construction as a church affected the staff internally, it also provided an external presence that was new for the organization. Its meaning and legacy, both as a church and a library, are entwined in a role that was now being passed on to Head & Hands. Tamira explains what the building offers the organization:

> Longevity—for sure, longevity. We get to be here for a long time and then even longer, if we want. I think it offers a commanding presence. I think that this is just so big, you know, and it's just kind of like *plopped* in the middle of a park. And so, it feels like the park is our backyard. And I think that that makes us seem more commanding in this neighbourhood. Which, in addition to that and the fact that this is a historic building, adds reputation. Not reputation—validation. In the city or in the borough? Validation in the borough and the support of the community and politicians. (Tamira)

The building offers the organization a more "commanding" voice through which it may speak to the community. In this example, the building is directly connected to how the organization perceives itself. It is like getting a new body. Petani suggests that organizational memories are key to

[80] Bary Blesser and Linda Ruth Salter, *Spaces Speak: Are you Listening?* (MIT Press, 2007), 21.

[81] Ibid.

[82] Ibid. 3.

[83] Esther M. Sternberg, *Healing Spaces: The Science of Place and Well-being* (Harvard University Press, 2009).

informing current realities. It is in moments of change where "intentional and powerful histories and organizational remembering of space inform the way in which available possibilities are represented".[84] In this sense, how the organization perceives and reacts to the new building and its future potential are connected to its past experiences and physical form.

Looking at Head & Hands' move through a lens of ghosts, memories, and imprints emphasizes a time–space relationship. Understanding how spatial memories create present realities, or how past spaces infiltrate current experiences, underlines a rich dimension to spatial transitions. While all of these themes would benefit from further exploration, the aim of this discussion is to surface a multiplicity of experiences in the hope of inspiring further research and consideration of spatial affect in organizations. In that vein, I continue the exploration with the displacement and reorientation of staff as they adjust to the new office.

Displacement and Reorientation

Moving into a new space was not simply an adjustment for the organization, but a fundamental rearrangement. As Bachelard suggests, "an entire past comes to dwell in a new house".[85] Staff members had performed their jobs in the old space for months or years, and their emplaced skill sets—now embodied memories—were coming into contact with a new space within which they would have to perform their jobs. In line with the discussion of immaterial ghosts, above, the staff's experience and perception of the new office was "constructed between places, rather than merely (confined) in them".[86] This in-between manifestation ultimately formed a collaborative presence between the old space and the new.

As I spoke with staff members about the new building, I noticed that the conversation would often turn to the old office. Frustrated, at first, I attempted to keep the conversation on the new building, steering the focus back to the present. Nijs and Daems encountered a similar dynamic as they tried, "rather unsuccessfully", to keep their conversations "in the

[84] Petani, "Space and Process", 17.

[85] Gaston Bachelard, *The Poetics of Space* (Beacon Press,1994), 5.

[86] Stevenson, "We Came Here to Remember", 341.

immediacy of the unfolding moment".[87] Soon, however, I realized the old space *was* the present moment. Through our conversations, staff members were experiencing a blending or a layering of memory and experience. How they encountered and oriented themselves in the new space was being informed by their embodied memories of the old space.

When I asked Tamira how the new office helps or hinders her work, her reply immediately recalled the old space: "It helps my work. Because my old office, in the old space, was incredibly depressing and a horrible colour, and had no windows". Tamira's improved experience in the new space was almost entirely based on the negative memory of the old space. In another question exploring how the new office affected the staff interactions and work processes, the old space surfaces again as a comparison or framing of Tamira's answer:

> There's a good balance between taking space from each other and still being social that is enabled by this building. It's not like … so, in our old space on the first floor, there were no doors except for two offices, and those offices had a wall of windows. There was no space. People would be walking by all the time and talk to whoever or whatever…. So, I think that overall staff health—not health, but the way we are with each other—is better. Also, having staff meetings not in the cave is the most incredible experience. Everything feels easier when we're not crammed together in a dark room that smells weird. (Tamira)

To demonstrate how the new building enables a balance between taking space and being together, Tamira draws on patterns from the old office. Even months after the move, staff members continued to interact with each other as if cloaked in the essence of the earlier office. These emplaced memories are interwoven with the staff's perceptions of both their behaviour in the new office and the physical office itself. Appraisals of new elements are continually held up against the old and familiar. The new office feels good—not just because it is bright and fresh, but because it is not dark and smelly.

---

[87] Nijs & Daems, "And What if the Tangible Were Not", 189.

Such comparisons appeared throughout the interviews. In responding to a question about what makes the new office inviting, Cora's response moved fluidly between the new space and the old:

> Just the fact that we actually have a place for everything, so it's not going to look like a makeshift place anymore. Where it was like, "oh, we're just going to put this here" because we have to, because we don't have the space. It's a space that has dedicated areas now, so it just feels like our clients know that it's for them. (Cora)

Later, Cora mentioned how the memory of the old space shaped her impression of what was important in the new office. Qualities like light, plants, and spaciousness seemed to take on a greater significance and value after having gone without for so long:

> We have so many more plants. We moved [everything] around so that whenever we have staff meetings, we actually have room and there's light. I think everybody is definitely very aware of all the things that we didn't have in the old building in this building. We make sure that there's always light and plants, and that we can walk in and not feel too crowded. (Cora)

This fusion of space and time draws a particular attention to the office space that allows staff members to see that space, and their relationship to it, anew. Elements that are new and different from the old space stand out, making the lived experience of the office more conscious and dynamic.

Encountering Displacement

Settling into the new space surfaced moments of uncertainty and challenge. Oscar found it difficult to create the structures he needed in the new space. After losing elements of his old office set-up in the move, he seemed uncertain about how to figure out a new solution:

> I'm really having a hard time rebuilding my shelf where my volunteers can pick up the stuff they need. Because in the old space, there was something

> built for this. And now I'm just like, "where am I putting it?" I have to reorganize it. And I've just gone along the whole last year not having it and preparing the stuff myself for volunteers, because I was like, it's just going to be easier like that. But then like, no, it's a lot more work for me and I'm just like, I have to do this. But then I just I don't know how, yeah, so this disrupts my work. (Oscar)

Losing the physical structures—in this case an accessible shelf—completely disrupted Oscar's work. Rather than have his volunteers grab the documents and pamphlets they needed on their own, Oscar had to create packages for them. The physical structure was no longer there to support this part of his work and he felt incapable of creating a solution. Suddenly, Oscar had to address part of his work that heretofore had functioned on autopilot. His tacit, subconscious way of working had been shaken up.

New spaces can force changes to habitual ways of working that are rarely thought about. Mary mentioned how the size of the new medical office had affected one of the doctors: "I think Dr. B. is struggling. He's got [a] very small office there and he has to step out when women changed, because there's no room for a curtain. Yeah, there's some problems there". Adjusting to new technologies was also challenging for staff. A new phone system was installed, and, all of a sudden, something that used to be very basic and automatic required thought and learning. For Mary, this was particularly challenging:

> Even our phone—it's different. We've got this fancy phone system and it's a problem. Nobody really knows how to use it. I've asked people, "please help me use this." Yeah, and nobody seems to really be able to help me… . So, it's tricky for me. I generally just put people on hold to go and tell whoever it is that the phone is for them—you know, transferring calls, etc. It's not easy. And also, the concern that some of us have about clients calling and getting that system and not hearing a human voice…. It just says the extension you want to reach, and we're not happy about that. (Mary)

Mary speaks about feeling confusion and a lack of agency. This physical tool, once so familiar and comforting, is suddenly transformed into something much less trustworthy and distant. Mary circumvents the phone's complicated system by getting up and walking across the room to deliver messages. She also mentions the impact that this technology could have on youth clients, who may have a harder time reaching a human. Instantly, the phone becomes worrisome for its impact on the warm and caring qualities the organization strives to provide.

The feeling of being displaced during the move was evident in my interview with Mary. She was the first person I interviewed after the move and the only person I was able to interview twice—once in the old space and again in the new. The following is Mary's response to my question: When you first come to work, how do you feel in the space and what do you notice?

> It's a really good question. It's different. There's a different feeling here, for sure. Often I feel quite alone and it's probably also the result of staffing—which is different. We've had a lot of problems with the front-desk staff position and so often when I come in, I'm the only one here—sometimes for an hour. I don't answer the phone. Sometimes I do. It's a bit … there is sort of a sense of, um, a bigger responsibility. A bigger building. Well, it's actually not, space-wise. I think it's a different space. But we had two floors there, you know, and um, I don't have the beautiful sun pouring in my window that I had there and that view onto Sherbrooke Street that I really loved. It was a very small space, but it was a very cozy, comfortable space.
>
> This is less so. I mean it's a little bigger, but it's a lot colder. I tried to cozy it up. The sound is terrible—it carries. I can hear Maya on the phone at the front desk here. If my door is open, I hear everything. That's been a huge adjustment. The other space was so quiet. This place is pure echo. When you come in the morning, it's very echo-y and it doesn't feel very warm. So yeah, we're trying to figure out how to warm it up because, I'm not the only one, I think, who feels that way. But it's clean and it's fresh, right? And there's a lot better storage space. (Mary)

Here is Mary's response to the same question in the old space:

> I'm usually the first person here except for Tuesdays, so it's kind of like getting the place ready for the day. Turn off the alarm. I feel really good. I feel like this place, this community is really lucky to have this place, and I feel very blessed to be here. Very privileged to be here, and yeah, I feel good. It's a good feeling…. I love that there's trees that I look out on here. The sun

> moves across the sky this way, so there is sun here all day, every day. Even in the winter, it's bright. And it's like I'm blessed. And I have this sense of aliveness without it being imposing. I see the birds, the squirrels, the pigeons, come. I have a sense of things happening out there, without them really being imposed upon me. So yeah, I really love this space. It's really great. I have lots of personal things that I bring in. And my whiteboard that I also like…. It's great. (Mary)

The difference between the two responses is stark. Mary's comfort and familiarity with the old office comes through in the confidence with which she describes the space. As she spoke, her routine and presence emerged in the details. We can visualize her walking into the space and turning off the alarm, setting up for the day in an environment that is familiar. The sun moves across the sky as she attends to her clients and works at her desk. She is not alone here, even though she is the first to arrive.

In contrast, Mary's testimony regarding the new space is less cohesive. When she arrives at work, she is alone in an unfamiliar environment. It feels bigger—a greater responsibility. It is "echo-y" and cold. The question she is seeking to answer gets lost in her meandering thoughts about the space. However, sometimes these non-words can provide "valuable information" on how she feels.[88] When participants cannot find the right words to describe their spatial relationships or experiences, "nonverbal expressions or even stammering related to spatial experiences provide a valuable proxy to atmospheric perception".[89]

There is no question that Mary misses some elements of her old office. A period of loss and grieving can occur when a staff member loses such aspects of their space. Mary loved her old office. Her new one is not quite as cozy, and it does not have a big window overlooking a treelined street. However, the value in comparing her two accounts is not in determining which space was better, but in understanding the disorientation and adjustment that occurs for staff after a move. Such periods of adjustment

[88] Ulrike Mackrodt, "How Atmospheres Inform Urban Planning Practice: Insights From the Tempelhof Airfield in Berlin", *Ambiances* 5 (2019): 7.

[89] Ibid.

are rarely given empathy or attention, but rather dismissed as necessary hurdles to overcome. *Moving is difficult. Buck up.*

In a comprehensive look at the experiences of newcomers to organizations, Meryl Reis Louis[90] outlines three features of the entry experience that could also be applied to an organization in a spatial transformation. In a sense, after all, the entire organization becomes a newcomer as its personnel are forced to adjust, to learn how to perform in the new space. Louis' three entry features for "understanding the process of newcomers' coping, or sense making" are change, contrast, and surprise.[91] *Change* is the "objective difference" between the past and current settings. These changes are publicly noticed, meaning they are visible to everyone. Such changes may be small or large, depending on the situation. The second feature, *contrast*, represents the personal shifts or adaptations that "emerge when individuals experience new settings".[92] The personal basis of this feature emphasizes the individuals' lived experiences and memories, which inform their perspectives and actions. The final feature, *surprise*, deals with a person's preconceived or anticipated notions. These anticipations can be "conscious, tacit, or emergent" and both "overmet or undermet anticipations can produce surprise".[93] Often emotional and affective, these encounters may produce joy or disappointment.

In Mary's experience, the presence of all three features can be identified. As she describes navigating the changes in the office, she reports a high degree of contrast to how she used to work—especially in relation to her experience with office noise interfering in her work with clients. Her tacit knowledge, once dependable, no longer supports her as she is forced to learn new ways of working and communicating. Meanwhile, she lives with her disappointment at the lack of warmth and coziness in the new office, two qualities that she previously identified as extremely important.

[90] Meryl Reis Louis, "Surprise and Sense Making: What Newcomers Experience in Entering Unfamiliar Organizational Settings", *Administrative Science Quarterly* 25, no. 2 (1980).

[91] Ibid. 235.

[92] Ibid. 236.

[93] Ibid. 237.

Louis uses the phrase "reality shock" to describe the experience of a new "physical and social world" in which one's "senses are simultaneously inundated with many unfamiliar cues".[94] When an organization moves into a new space, there is "no gradual exposure and no real way to confront the situation a little at a time".[95] Everyone is tossed into an unfamiliar situation and must navigate their personal trajectories (excitement, disappointment, or apathy) as well as their organizational tasks and functions. Sometimes the physical space can accentuate, or obscure, this process. Cora spoke of the emotional transference that occurred in the new space:

> If I am feeling something, I have to go outside or close my door. I have to shut myself off because it's such an open building. And if I'm not trying to have those emotions or I don't want to stress everybody else out, I have to be careful—because it is a very, like even just the way that you hear noises … like your energy can come off if you're stomping or even walking loudly. Like you can feel it in the building. (Cora)

Feeling others' emotions in the space occurs on a regular basis, but even more so during times of change and transition. As the organization adapts to the new space, it is in a state of forming. The anticipations of the staff are continuously "tested against the reality of their new work experiences".[96] This creates an ongoing sequence of individual and collective processes occurring in relationship with its new surroundings. While this time can be challenging, it is also ripe with potential and possibility.

Conclusion

This emotional and aesthetic collection of moments and experiences is intended to illicit further questions and inquiry into the entangled relationships between organizations and their space. I have offered only

---

[94] Ibid. 231. "reality shock"—a term borrowed from Everett Hughes.

[95] Ibid. 231.

[96] Ibid. 232.

glimpses into the experience of the staff during this time and yet have provided a rich and sensuous portrait of Head & Hand's office during a period of change. The intention of sharing these accounts, mostly from the staff directly, is to illustrate the depth of emotion woven within the staff's inter-subjective spatial relationships. This relocation was more than moving parts from one location to another.

Spaces reinforce our way of being. During times of change, moving or creating a new space, there is a unique opportunity to re-examine ourselves and our organizations. Through an explicit or unconscious process that manifests itself through our bodies and the placement of objects, delving deeper into these iterative relationships provides a new aesthetic and more-than-human perspective on work. Arguments about what belongs where might be less about taste and more about who we are.

Part II: Shape Shifting

The second part of this study focuses on the opportunity or potential embedded in spatial shifts and transformations. As such, I will explore some of the micro-shifts that took place as Head & Hands settled into its new office. These shifts represent the co-productive, entwined nature of people's relationships to space and provide a basis for understanding larger organizational shifts that may emerge in the years to come. As with the previous section, this exploration is a collection of snapshots intended to raise questions and inspire future research potential; they do not offer conclusions or attempt to solve problems.

Loose themes hold these collective transformations together. However, just as one's experience is not felt or perceived according to isolated categories, this written exploration shifts between, and among, these themes. I start the discussion with the organization's iterative and creative process of material change, highlighting some specific changes to the physical office. The conversation then shifts to the benefits of a healthy, supportive space on staff members' well-being and their ability to perform their jobs. Finally, I explore how Head & Hands' feelings of pride and ownership lead to organizational dreaming and future possibility.

Iterative Change

Emplaced Engagement

After all the packing and upheaval of moving comes the unpacking—settling in and getting to know the space. While larger companies often hire people to unpack, arrange furniture, and hang artworks, not-for-profit organizations like Head & Hands do it themselves. This process requires a substantial investment of time and energy. With the space still fresh and unfamiliar, unpacking becomes an emergent process of testing, adaptation, and rearranging (see Fig. 6.9). This somewhat chaotic period thus provides a unique setting for change, reflection, and opportunity. Unlike our everyday environment, in times of spatial change the material office emerges as a set of hyper-present, malleable structures that elicit a range of emotional responses. New space is not a "known place that exists prior to our engagements with it"; rather, it is through a process of engagement and decision-making that eventually "we become the spaces to which we

Fig. 6.9 Rearranging (photo by Margot Flores Torre)

have invested our practices".[97] As organizational practices and embodied knowledge carried over from the old space, they shifted and adjusted to fit the new space.

While the office took shape, the group adapted and evaluated, making more and new changes, and then repeated the process. Like Lewin's action research model, these micro-feedback loops of reflection, learning, and change happen consciously and unconsciously.[98] When the space shifted with new objects, arrangements, and encounters, emergent views about the space and new ways of feeling in it surfaced. Michel de Certeau describes the transformation that occurs with "the awakening of inert objects … which, emerging from their stability, transform the place where they [once] lay motionless".[99] These micro-transformations—a couch moved to another spot, a painting hung, the addition of shelves—can shift the feeling or atmosphere of space as well as its functionality. Altering the space changes how staff and the organization engage with-it and therefore how they are supported and held by that space.[100] Such rapid changes can produce an atmosphere of disruption and chaos—but these are not always negative qualities. Periods of change are often filled with moments of surprise or shock, which momentarily offer "glimpses into other possible worlds of reality".[101] Often unintentionally or out of desperation, spaces and objects are used in ways never intended or realized. These moments hold the capacity to spur the "realization that the world can be experienced in ways beyond the taken-for-granted meanings that construct our experience of it".[102] With habitual ways of being disrupted, a new embodied co-presence can emerge.

When Head & Hands began the unpacking process, it soon became evident that creating the new office would entail more than just unpacking boxes. One staff member recalled a particular "now what?" moment

[97] Alberto Corsin Jiménez, "On Space as a Capacity," *Journal of the Royal Anthropological Institute* 9, no. 1 (2003), 141.

[98] Chris Argyris & Donald A Schön, *Organizational learning: A theory of action* (Jossey-Bass, 1978)

[99] Michel De Certeau, *The Practice of Everyday Life*. (University of California Press, 2011), 118.

[100] Paddy O'Toole & Prisca Were, "Observing Places: Using Space and Material Culture in Qualitative Research," *Qualitative Research* 8, *no.*5 (2008).

[101] Kjersti Bjørkeng et al., "Becoming (a) Practice. *Management Learning* 40, no. 2 (2009), 156.

[102] Ibid.

that occurred *after* the unpacking was done. All the essentials had been unboxed, yet questions such as *Now what do we envision? How do we expand it? How do we make it perfect for us?* remained unanswered. In our interview, Tamira spoke at length about this time in the space:

> I think there was a period where we were rushing to get it perfect. Eventually, we got lost in other things. And so that sitting happened naturally, because we were distracted and so, when you don't think about something too much, it comes to you. So that's kind of what happened. I think we started thinking about events and summer and everything else, and then things would come to us when we weren't looking at them anymore. (Tamira)

Although this period of place-making and experimentation with the space was not intentional, the organization ended up experiencing a very open and creative moment. Tamira illustrates the process by which staff explored how they *felt* in the space and formed tacit and explicit wisdom about the organization. Frank Barrett describes such moments as poetic wisdom, which "involves intuiting glimpses of immediacy and fluidity, experiences of awe, reverence and wonder".[103] Accessing these moments requires a certain letting-go—an "absence of certainty and a fresh perception" of what was once ordinary and common.[104] Tamira continued to describe the process as a state of experimentation and dreaming:

> It looks like sitting in the space for a while and then feeling your way around a little bit—you're in the dark and kind of touching things and seeing things, and being like this doesn't make sense. This isn't working. This doesn't make sense, and then trial and error to get it right. And then a little bit of dreaming and asking what would make this feel beautiful? What would make this feel homey? What would make this feel *like us*. I have a tendency to like want to nest really fast and that was not something we're able to do. But in the end, I think it was nice to have like a long process to do that work with each other. (Tamira)

[103] Frank J Barrett, "Cultivating an Aesthetics of Unfolding," In *The aesthetics of organization* (Sage, 2000), 230.
[104] Ibid.

As Tamira mentions, the staff had been more-or-less stumbling about in the dark—touching, feeling, and dreaming their way through the space. As the space appeared to them in states of discord or harmony, questions around beauty, homeyness, and identity presented themselves. Sitting in this ambiguous and fluid state can be destabilizing, and for this reason, the wisdom and revelation that are born out of such fresh encounters may benefit from some support and stability. Barrett suggests that organizations cultivate an ebb and flow of practice and learning, grounded in a flexible structure that "keeps agents richly connected as they respond to one another in non-linear ways".[105] Being in this exploratory state was not a comfortable or positive experience for everyone. Oscar felt the ongoing spatial adjustments were too much:

> I feel like there's been a lot of change in the big common area—I mean, in the way we organize for meetings. What do we put there? What do we do there? It's an ongoing conversation? It's *always* a conversation and *never* a conversation. Never an official conversation. That tires me. This is not the kind of thing I really care about. (Oscar)

To Oscar, the informal and continual change felt tiring; perhaps there was not enough structure for him to feel grounded and supported. It is also possible that the atmosphere of constant change simply did not feel good to everyone.

Emergent Talent

As the staff went through the intimate process of moving and unpacking, they got to see different sides of each other. In part, this happened during the height of the move, when staff were the most stressed, anxious, exhausted, and emotional, but other traits also surfaced after the move, when the organization was settling into the new space—before daily work routines had taken shape. Mary spoke with praise about how her co-workers helped set up the space:

[105] Ibid.

> We've had to build this place from the ground up. So, for example, people's talents have been used—like Mia. She is so fabulous around staging. Things coming in, and her finding its place and putting things away, and you know, moving this plant over here instead of there. I mean, she is so talented. And Terrell and Otis, you know, really helped out a lot with the electronics and getting computers going, getting the photocopy machine going. I mean really, really helpful. And to us, we haven't really seen that before, because the old place, well, there wasn't necessarily room, right? (Mary)

Because the old office was so entrenched in routine, so full of material accumulated over many years, little room remained for staff to exercise their creativity, passion, and talent. Immediately after the move, the space was full of unknown, which invited participation in a fresh way. Staff engaged with the new space in ways that were necessary for the organization, but also personally and creatively motivated. A few staff members I spoke with mentioned Mia's talent for spatial organizing, while Tamira commented on the staff's willingness to invest in the new space as it evolves: "we're willing to put that investment in and be flexible with how it will change, and Mia, especially, keeps changing lots of stuff". Moving into the building together seemed to spark a tangible investment on the part of the staff. It created a dynamic relationship in which the space served the work and the organization through the interventions and alterations made by the staff.

Spatial Adjustments

Similar to the iterative process of setting up the space, I will focus on some of the specific ways in which staff interacted with the material space itself. I am sure there were dozens of small changes staff made to the space; for those I interviewed, however, it was difficult to remember them. Most of these examples emerged at other points in the conversations rather than being elicited from a specific question on spatial change.

The first example is the reception desk, which had been larger and more rectangular originally. However, it felt too tight for Mia, who

Fig. 6.10 Modified front desk

wanted additional space behind the desk. To create more room—so that multiple staff could move through the space—Mia had it cut out. Its substantial width was replaced with a crescent-shaped desk, which curves around the person who sits at it (see Fig. 6.10). Tamira mentioned that in the end, "they cut it deeper than [Mia] wanted". They thought it felt "a bit exposing". The openness of the now-thinner desk no longer imposes a barrier between those to either side of it.

In the image, you can see the curved desk with a staff member behind it. The cut-out creates a larger, rounder space behind the desk, and one can imagine how the space behind a wider, straighter desk might feel more confining. Now, whoever is working there has greater freedom of movement, including room for an additional person. The front desk is the first place guests arrive after walking through the front doors. In this photograph, we see a brilliant sunbeam strike the chalkboard drawings on the side of the desk. On the wall a sign reads "what is the opposite of a prison?" Farther down the hallway, a staff member crouches by the stairs visiting for a moment with their son who is cared for by the Young Parents Program.

Cutting down the desk altered the space's functionality and energy. The decision to change it was an embodied one; in its original form, the desk did not feel right. Edward T. Hall once described a woman who assessed whether her office was large enough based on her body's experience of the space.[106] Unconsciously, she would push her chair back from her desk and stretch out her arms and legs. If the chair hit the wall, it was too small; if not, it was adequate. There is much to be learned by how our bodies feel in relation to material objects and spaces. Listening to these feelings and experimenting with a space can lead to unique outcomes (when it's allowed).

Another story that illustrates this material interaction was the evolution of Cora and Tamira's office after their first design attempt, a modern and minimalist style, ended up feeling plain and boring. Tamira tells the story:

> At first, we wanted a white office. First thing, [Cora] and I put up old posters—all the "Sunday in the Park posters"—on the wall. We wanted it to look nice and minimalist, but like decorated, and then at some point we felt our office was boring. *How do we make it feel more like us?* We're very silly people. So, we got a graffiti artist to come in and spray-paint a tag on our wall. It says "since 1970," and it's humongous, and that really cinched my office for me. Where I was like, we have this really minimalist "professional" quote-unquote office, with nicely curated posters and nice little wooden furniture, calendars on the wall and stuff like that.
>
> But then I was like, it needs to feel younger! Yeah, you just feel younger, it needs to be more fun. It needs to feel representative of our clients. Cause fundraising—you can get lost in it, and you have to find some sort of way to connect and remember that connection when you're not seeing clients or building relationships with them. So, I think adding [the graffiti] felt

[106] Edward T Hall, *The Hidden Dimension* (Anchor Books, 1982), 53.

> like part of that for us. Cora and I are both Black, and having a big graffiti thing on our wall adds a sense of ownership of our office. It's very unique to us—very *ours*. That helps make it feel good for us. (Tamira)

Similar to the front desk, Tamira and Cora's office did not feel quite right. It did not represent them or the organization's clients. Even though they wanted a minimalist design with white walls and curated posters, something was missing. Hiring a graffiti artist to come in and tag the wall with a date meaningful to the organization shifted the atmosphere in the space by connecting Tamira to her youth clients and to her Black culture. By literally putting a stamp on the wall, Tamira and Cora became part of the space, creating a sense of ownership and connection. These performative interventions illustrate the symbiotic process by which Tamira and Cora imprinted themselves onto the space. Sarah Curtis writes that although graffiti can be seen as vandalism or symbolize "social disorder", its symbolic impression shifts with the "content and location".[107] At Head & Hands, the "since 1970" tag conveys "playful emotion and illustrates how graffiti may communicate and symbolise messages in ways that support psychological wellbeing" (see Fig. 6.11).[108] Whenever Tamira feels lost or disconnected, her office walls now serve as a connection to herself and to those she is serving.

Understanding how the space shaped experience gave the organization deeper insight into ways they could adjust and interact with the office and their community. Noticing the sounds, textures, or aromas of the office added another layer of knowledge about the organization. One of the biggest challenges with the new office was its acoustic design. As I have already mentioned, being originally designed as a church, the sound carried and echoed throughout the building. With personal and confidential subjects being discussed, the front-desk staff mentioned that they play music to camouflage voices. Cora described how the new building's sonic environment led to more music:

[107] Sarah Curtis, *Space, Place and Mental health*. (Lund Humphries Publishers, 2012), 181.

[108] Ibid.

Fig. 6.11 Desks "kissing" below their "Since 1970" graffiti tag

> We definitely try to play more music now—just to make sure the clients don't necessarily hear what we're doing and so they feel like it's more confidential. If we have somebody coming in, we do try to separate the working space—like *our* working space—with like the client space because we're trying to make sure that there's some kind of separation. And so, we've been kind of coping by just like playing music and making sure that the client space where they sit down is as like cozy and welcoming as possible. (Cora)

In Cora's account, music takes on multiple roles. First, it protects confidentiality by surrounding people's voices with melody. Second, it becomes a barrier or wall providing a clear separation between public and private spaces.[109] Last, it attempts to create a cozy, welcoming atmosphere around

[109] see Blesser and Salter, *Spaces Speak* (2007)

the front desk. In this sense, sound is used to foster a particular energy in the space, and contribute to clients moods and or behaviour in that space.[110] In *Spaces Speak, are you listening?*, Bary Blesser and Linda-Ruth Salter explore the often unrecognized ability of "humans to sense space by listening".[111] Sound has the power to shift atmospheres, independent of their physical amenities; it can encourage or discourage certain behaviour, give or remove aesthetic meaning and value, and provide orientation or navigational support. The musical intervention at Head & Hands illustrates how sensory experimentation can lead to both changes in the atmosphere and function of the office.[112] These musical adjustments altered how staff members interacted with the space and consequently the affect it had on them and their clients.

I experienced the office's acoustic atmosphere first-hand during my interview with Tamira, which took place at the front desk as she was doing her community shift. We had just begun our conversation when I noticed that she was almost whispering:

> Karen: I've heard voices can really travel, is that why you're speaking quietly?
>
> Tamira: Yeah, but to be honest, if her door was open, Mary can probably hear me right now, because it carries. It's the church. It's designed that way. (Tamira)

Tamira was whispering because she did not want to disturb Mary. The sound in the building heightened Tamira's awareness of others' experiences in the office to such an extent that it motivated her to modulate her own voice.

Sound played an important role in understanding the experience of staff in this building,[113] whether it is the music playing, the staff whispering, or the lights humming. Noticing how staff enacted themselves within the building and through their bodies to shape desks and spray-paint walls gives meaning and texture to those experiences.

[110] Shortt, "Sounds of the Salon," (2013).

[111] Blesser and Salter, *Spaces Speak*, (2007): 1.

[112] Ibid. 11.

[113] (See Shortt, 2013, for a more comprehensive look the importance of at sounds at work.

Illuminating Atmospheres

A contributing factor during the Head & Hands transition had to do with the mood and atmosphere that surrounded and emanated from the interaction between staff, office, and organization. This "hazy and vague in-between phenomenon" contributed to how staff experienced the building.[114] Atmospheres are constantly shifting and evolving. They combine "objective parameters, such as materiality, shadow, light, dimension [and] temperature", with subjective ones, "such as mood, memory, and sensitivity",[115] into a complex interplay of "something more".[116] As the perceivers of such atmospheres, the staff were part of their creation—in collaboration with the surroundings—and were simultaneously affected by it.

When Head & Hands moved from an old, dark, rundown building into their well-lit, spacious new premises, the impact on the atmosphere was substantial. This new environment shifted how the staff *felt* in the space; the spaciousness and lightness of the new office seemed to manifest itself physically within their bodies. In addition to the new space's architectural features, its energetic, emotional, symbolic, and sensory qualities all seemed to come together into a brighter and lighter atmosphere. Working in a space that is sunny and clean, spacious, and functional affected the relationship of the staff to their work and their building. Asked about how the new building helped or hindered her work, Tamira drew a connection between the new space, her mental health, and the organization's health:

> Tamira: [The new space] helped my work.
>
> Karen: So, you feel better?
>
> Tamira: Yeah, 100 percent. Our office is white, which I like. I need the most open, the most-bright space, to feel focused. Yeah, I think that because there's so much space, empty space, and the ceilings are so high, I feel open and relaxed in the space. I think the natural light is really vital to

---

[114] De Matteis et al., "Phenomenographies," (2019), 3.

[115] Klaske Havik, "TerriStories: Literary Tools for Capturing Atmosphere in Architectural Pedagogy. *Ambiances. Environnement sensible, architecture et espace urbain* 5 (2019) p. 3

[116] De Matteis et al., Phenomenographies," (2019): 3.

> my health, my mental health, and my workflow. So, having one of the offices, maybe the only one, with one of the solitudes [ceiling light wells] in it—which is part of why I took it—we have a lot of natural light in there and that helps a lot… .
>
> Hopefully, if we feel more well-lit emotionally and physically, then maybe we can give that back to our clients. All of our services are direct human-to-human, so if our frontline staff don't feel good in this space, then our clients won't feel good in the space. (Tamira)

Tamira describes the bright natural light as vital to her mental health and workflow and the reason she picked her office. Despite conclusions from the Hawthorne experiments, in which light was not found to improve performance,[117] important connections between light and well-being are being made. Understanding the value of "luminous conditions that match what the occupants want and expect" is leading to associations with what psychologists call *positive affect*.[118] This "pleasant emotional state" is being connected to benefits in "mood, comfort, and environmental satisfaction".[119] Light shifts how we see, Mikkel Bille and Tim Sorensen explain, because it actively contributes to our everyday connections and social interactions with a space.[120] In this sense, light becomes a socio-material factor by influencing the meaning and experience of a space. Through design or general mood, light can determine how a room looks or feels. It is like sound in the way it enters, permeates, and transforms a space. Bille and Sorensen argue that light is not only a filter through which we view the world but also an active contributor to our experience. For Tamira, the light makes her feel "well-lit emotionally and physically", which shifts how she connects to the space, her co-workers, and her work. In one of the offices pictured (see Fig. 6.12), a large window dominates the room adding natural light and a view to the outside. The large wooden beams framing the window echo some of the homeyness felt in the old space.

---

[117] Jennifer A. Veitch, "Lighting for High-Quality Workplaces," *Creating the Productive Workplace* (Taylor & Francis, 2006).

[118] Ibid. 212

[119] Ibid. 212–213.

[120] Mikkel Bille and Tim Flohr Sorensen, "An Anthropology of Luminosity," *Journal of Material Culture* 12, no. 3 (2007).

Fig. 6.12 Office with window

Not everyone felt the light to be purely positive. For Mary, the light was beautiful, but it also brought an element of coldness to the office:

> Well, there's a lot of beautiful things in terms of the light. You know, the light is so much fresher and more inspiring than the old space, but there is sort of a coldness about it that we're sort of trying to figure out—what we need to do to warm it up a bit. (Mary)

Once again, experiencing the space's brightness as cold speaks to the atmospheric qualities of light. Bille and Sorensen have researched the coziness of low lighting (including candlelight) in homes.[121] In these inti-

[121] Ibid.

Fig. 6.13 Main foyer of office

mate lightscapes, "the movement of the shadows and the inability of the candlelight to fully light up the room are considered more hyggeligt (cozy) than what the light of a bare electrical bulb would offer".[122] Pallasmaa explains how "homogeneous bright light paralyses the imagination in the same way that homogenisation of space weakens the experience of being".[123] The picture of the main office (see Fig. 6.13) was taken about six months after the move. The kitchen and closed offices line the left side, while the open area on the right is a mixed-use space for

[122] Ibid. 275.

[123] Juhani Pallasmaa, *The Eyes of the Skin* (John Wiley & Sons, 2012), 50.

meetings, group work, volunteers, or other miscellaneous tasks. The glowing circles on the ceiling are light wells, or "solitudes", which consistently beam natural light into the building.

While darkness and poor lighting are often unhealthy traits for a work environment, these qualities can also contribute to a space's warmth, coziness, and mystery. For Head & Hands, although their old office was falling apart and was sometimes depressingly dark, it often exhibited an atmosphere of homeyness. Its haphazard, whimsical construction and layout were endearing, offering endless nooks and crannies for light and dark to explore. Having various and varied light sources with different levels of illumination creates flows of light, rather than an omnipresent sheet of brightness. While the organization has gained a clean, well-lit, solid space, it is evident that some of the cozy, intimate and, as Katelyn has put it, "higgledy-piggledy" characteristics have been lost.

When staff members described the old space *in* the old space, there was a sense of fondness for its ramshackle nature (most prominently, from those who worked upstairs). Jenna suggests that the old building possessed a sort of "humanness" that was represented by its many cracks and faults:

> It's always felt like a very organic space. So, for example, nothing matches; there's no coherent paint scheme or decoration theme. Everything you see in the space has just grown organically over the 16-or-however-many years we've been in this space. It's very cobbled together—like a collage—which, I think, contributes to its charm and to the whole comfortable, homey feel of it. So, you know, the couches downstairs were donated to us at some point along the way, probably. And now they're falling apart and they've got cracks in them that have duct tape over them, and that's gross and we should replace them—but you know, it is what it is. I think if you focus on a little detail like that, you're like, "eeeeew!" But if you take the space as a whole, I think it actually contributes to the positive vibe in a sense ... within reason—the humanness. (Jenna)

This way of speaking about the old office—tinged with fondness and acceptance—was shared among many of the staff members in the first round of interviews. Staff saw the wear and tear of the office—its "scars"—as a reminder of their "resilience when facing adversity".[124] The collaged nature of the office meant that it was filled with historical reminders of what had been experienced.[125] Replacing these makeshift, organic qualities with new, clean, solid features changed the atmosphere of the office. How it felt to come into work changed. For all the staff we spoke to, it was ultimately a positive change—but even a beneficial transformation requires an adjustment time. Mary's experience of the space evinces an ebb and flow between sadness and contentment as she grapples with the changes. She misses the friendly spirit, but enjoys the new cleanliness:

> I'm not like "Oh, yay, I love it here!" It's got some drawbacks. I find it very, very cold and very sterile. Well, it's been great in the heatwave, because we've got air [conditioning]. We've got a system. "How do I turn that fan off?" But yeah, it doesn't feel as warm and friendly to me. It just doesn't. But maybe that that will come. Yeah, you know, that will come.
>
> The big echo. It sort of makes you feel sometimes like you're in a factory or something, you know? So, there's that. It does feel cleaner. The air feels cleaner. The surfaces stay cleaner. The place is so much cleaner. And you know, I think we all deserve that and so do our clients. So, it's sort of lacking that old charm—which is a very valuable cosmetic point, you know, there's a lot of charm in those little places. We don't have that here at all—quite the opposite. (Mary)

Of the staff members I spoke with, Mary struggled the most in her transition to the new space. Her sensitivity to the sound, light quality, and institutional aesthetic wove itself into her discomfort and insecurity in the office. In sharing her experience, Mary contends that some of the "warm and friendly" qualities she missed might come back over time. Just as the old space was a collage co-created over time, the new space will shift and be shaped as the group uses it. Having a foundation that supports change and development in a positive and healthy way enables the staff to grow more consciously.

The new office and its staff kitchen shifted the energy of lunch, food, and breaks at the office. For Cora, how this impacted the staff was surprising:

---

[124] Shortt, "Scarred Objects," (2021): 1703.

[125] Ibid.

> I was surprised by how much a building can effect like the mood of workers. Like, I knew that, but just seeing it in action was still surprising. How just having a little bit more light and having like a common area to eat that's more accessible can make a huge difference in the way that we relate to one another. (Cora)

Cora remarks how the new kitchen (see Fig. 6.14) changed how the staff relate to each other. Something echoed by other staff. The new kitchen became a sanctuary or respite from work, where staff can interact without work demands. Oscar mentioned how nice it was to "sit down and have your lunch. It's nice not having to eat in your office and it's understood

Fig. 6.14 New staff kitchen

as a break room". While it was common in the old office to sit at your desk and eat, now staff had somewhere comfortable to go. These seemingly small details had had a huge impact on how staff members felt and behaved in the space. While the kitchen is a physical room, it created an atmosphere of respite and comradery—a place to eat, chat, and take a break.

Part of the shift in how the staff interact and work relates to the space's comfort and cleanliness—qualities absent in the old space. Amara explains:

> It's not perfect, you know, but it's a massive improvement over the other place. The other place had crumbling walls, and a toilet that didn't work and would back up all the time. And, you know, the rooftop would flood. It was just a mess. It was a big, big mess. So being here, where it's nice and clean and well-lit, feels so much better. (Amara)

Being in a space that is clean and bright *feels* good. One staff member described the windows as "comforting". Research on the impact of windows and light on wellness[126] confirms that a lack of light is connected to increased cortisol, lower levels of melatonin, and depressive symptoms.[127] Amara's frank comparison between the new and old spaces emphasizes the contrasts. Words such as "crumbling", "mess", and "flood", or the description of toilets backing up, express visceral sensations. On a metaphorical or symbolic level, it's impossible not to consider that two so very different spatial contexts might impact the work occurring within them. When I spoke with Louis in the old space, I asked him to name the first thing he noticed when he arrived at work. Most staff mentioned the person greeting them at the front desk, but for Louis it was the cracked and broken front steps leading up to the old office. For him, every day that he stepped on it was reminder of their landlord's neglect and broken promises. While hardship was often rallied around as something to overcome, the crumbling building was a constant reminder of going without.

---

[126] Roger S. Ulrich, "Effects of Interior Design on Wellness." *Journal of Healthcare Interior Design* 3, no. 1 (1991).

[127] Francine Harb et al., "Lack of Exposure to Natural Light in the Workspace is Associated with Physiological, Sleep and Depressive Symptoms. *Chronobiology International* 32, no. 3 (2015).

Office Kids

Merging spaces with Young Parents' Program (YPP), which before the move had been housed off-site, was a palpable change for the office (see Fig. 6.15). Almost every staff member mentioned the unity of being together in one building. But adding YPP into the main office also provided a more intimate relationship with the young parents and their kids in unexpected ways. For Mary, it enabled greater interaction with some of her clients:

> The nice part is that the Young Parents' Program is here now. And so, I get to see those clients a lot more and there's so much more available and the

Fig. 6.15 Young Parents' Program (YPP)

> children and everything. It feels so much more in touch with that program, which is a very integral part of the H&H philosophy, right—just in terms of that holistic approach. I have been very helpful in accompaniments. I've gone to court with a couple of clients. I have provided supervision for a family that had to have supervision in order for the father to see the children. So, you know, that wouldn't have happened, I don't think, if we were in the other building. So, there is that. It's nice thing. (Mary)

Having the YPP physically present in the same building has allowed Mary to better serve those clients and offer services she might not have provided in the old building. This account offers a tangible example of how the new office is already influencing Mary's day-to-day work. Over time, YPP's inclusion in the office could lead to other more substantial shifts in Mary's job description and mandate. While these changes may feel incidental, they are a clear correlation between the organization, YPP, and the new office.

Staff mentioned how YPP's presence just *feels* better, being more aligned with Head & Hands' "holistic" philosophy to serve youth. With YPP in the new building, the atmosphere of the office now includes a quality of babies, kids, and youth. I remember entering the new office before an interview and seeing a staff member with her two-year-old child (same age as mine at the time) sitting on the stairs with one of the YPP workers. As I negotiated my own experience being back at work, it was meaningful to witness an organization that had managed to make it possible for parents and kids to coexist in the workplace. I couldn't help but wonder how it would feel to have my child so intimately connected to my work.

Having kids and babies in an office rapidly connects all staff and clients to the sounds, objects, and energies that accompany them. While speaking with Amara, she described how she can hear and smell their presence:

> I'm [working in a space] off the entrance, so I hear everything that happens—like earful conversations to the reception. I hear other programs running and I hear the children, you know, being children, and so I'm going to say it's highly stimulated every day in my office.

> If the Young Parents Program are cooking lunch, I always know what they're having for lunch because I can smell it, which is actually nice and comforting. They often make cookies—yum. They hire cooks from the pool of their clients, too. So, I know that they're learning a skill. It's actually kind of neat to smell what they're cooking and knowing it's a skill they're acquiring too, you know? It's kind of … it's kind of neat. It gives me the warm-and-fuzzies. (Amara)

Amara's descriptions of the comforting smells wafting into her office from the YPP kitchen and the sounds of children "being children" illustrate some of the more sensory shifts in the atmosphere of the new building. These smells and sounds within the office are contextualized within Head & Hands' larger culture and mandate to serve youth. While the sound of kids and the smells of lunch might be off-putting in other office cultures, for Head & Hands they are tangible markers of success.[128] As Riach and Warren explain, smell is more than a singular sensation; it is "one element of an experiential system that summons us to the world so that both the world and ourselves are constituted through that experience".[129] Knowing that the smells of lunch mean young parents are learning how to cook healthy meals determines how Amara feels about them: it gives her the "warm-and-fuzzies" (see Fig. 6.16).

Material Support

It was hot and sunny on the day of my first interview in the new building. I arrived a bit early and sat at a little picnic table outside. Though I could hear the distant sounds of traffic, the sound of leaves rustling in the breeze dampened them. I watched an old man fold up his bed of cardboard in the park and walk along the sidewalk in front of me. He asked for the time before heading through the Head & Hands' front door. At the same time, a staff member exited the office through the back door into the park; she sat on a bench under a tree while checking her phone.

---

[128] David Howes and Constance Classen, *Ways of Sensing* (Routledge 2014).

[129] Kathleen Riach and Samantha Warren, "Smell Organization: Bodies and Corporeal Porosity in Office Work," *Human Relations* 68, no. 5, (2014): 790.

Fig. 6.16 YPP Menu (photo by Margot Flores Torre)

Although I was quite nervous, being about to begin my second round of interviews after a lengthy maternity leave, being at the office physically was immediately calming. I felt the warm air against my skin as the light glimmered through the trees. Then I walked into the office for my interview with Mary. Cool air hit my whole body. The old man I encountered earlier was loudly asking the staff member at the front desk for a bag of food while pouring himself a coffee. I hear a baby crying in another room. Some posters on the wall read: *Health Care for All* and *We Didn't Cross the Border, the Border Crossed Us.* The old man leaves the office, and another staff member approaches, asking why he was yelling. The person at the front desk responds: "He was hungry". My presence in the office during this exchange feels normal. The space is here for me too. I am part of what unfolded.

Head & Hands is a service organization offering aid to youth and at-risk groups. Exploring how the office supports the staff in fulfilling that mandate is vital to understanding how the new building is entwined with the organization. While the old office had its charm, it ultimately worked against the staff, draining their energy, and stretching their resources. During our conversations, Amara spoke a lot about the new building's impact on staff and clients. In describing how the new building might affect clients seeking services, she uses the metaphor of a person's "spoon inventory" as a measure for how well they are doing:

> Being able to walk into a space that is not crumbling is helpful. Like you can clear your mind. As a user of the organization, if you're walking in and you're already at minus five spoons and you're having a hard day, but you walk into a space that smells or looks smelly, is crumbling, the couches have tears in them, it doesn't help. But if you walk in here and it's nice and lit-up, and there's fresh coffee and, you know, you sit on the chair that is not falling apart, your spoon inventory has increased, you know? So, I think that it has a huge impact. (Amara)

Here the space becomes *part* of the services that are offered—an extension of the organization's mandate in providing support to youth. The new building helps clients by offering somewhere clean to sit, fresh coffee, and brightness, whereas the old space was unable to offer such supports. This set the old space out of alignment with the organization's values and mission. Where previously the organization offered services *despite* the building, now the building enhances the service. Even if it is just for a moment, the structure and atmosphere of the building are entwined, offering those who enter a solid and welcoming place to "exhale and be".

The new building has wheelchair ramps entering the building and throughout, bringing together the building design and the organization's values. A comment that came up repeatedly in the first round of interviews was the lack of accessible access to the old building. Its offices located atop a steep staircase, staff members felt that their building was in direct conflict with their organization's safe, accessible, nonjudgemental policies. Cora explains how the structure and design of the new space helps make clients feel welcome:

> I feel like the space is designed in a way that is very thoughtful of the clients. The fact that we have become an accessible building—it's because we're trying to be better than all the other kinds of institutions that are not equipped or are failing people. So, I feel like we're really trying to try to fill

> those gaps… . So, I feel like the building reflects that and that there are little parts of it that are really like trying to keep in mind like who [we] are trying to serve. The fact that we have a waiting area where we have toys for people who have children. We have a changing table. The fact that we have a ramp outside and inside. (Cora)

These material elements become a way for the organization to send a message of inclusion to those who come through the door, whether they arrive on wheels or with children in tow. Various posters and pamphlets and jars filled with condoms, all brought over from the old space, line the walls and shelves (see Fig. 6.17). They have become a material manifestation of the organization's values. This alignment between the social and material contributes to the well-being that staff (and visitors) feel when in the new space.

In the old space, the relationship between the office aesthetic and the organization was in its warm homeyness. The new space offered the organization something that went deeper than a home; it became an active

Fig. 6.17 Condom wall and positive space, breastfeeding signs

part of their services. The physical alignment, atmospheric and material support offered to the organization, supported the staff in their roles, not to work more efficiently, but better. Cora described how the new space is working *with* them:

> We actually are able to serve our clients and their needs more instead of having to work harder. It feels like we have a space that's working with us. So, it means a little less work for certain things.
>
> It also means that we are growing. Because we actually have moved into a space that helps our needs more. It doesn't make me feel like we're regressing. It really makes me feel like we are just going to keep growing and we're going to keep being able to offer more services in a way that is more tailored, and like in ways that like work more for clients and less of us trying to like stretch and ways that don't work. (Cora)

Cora speaks to the energy and hard work it took just to function in the old space, where the staff had to "struggle to perform their tasks because the built environment" had failed.[130] Not only did the old office fail to provide basic support, the "adverse environmental conditions" sucked morale and creativity from the staff and the organization.[131] Without this burden, the organization is free to work *with* the space, imagining and transforming it in ways that help them reach their goals. In this sense, the space itself becomes leader in the organization by providing an "aesthetic, relational experience"[132] that both inspires and supports the organization.

Pride, Ownership, and Legitimacy

In addition to acknowledging the new space's better capacity to support the organization (the mind–body experiences of its staff and clients as well as practical work functions), the staff expressed a sense of pride and ownership. Shifting from a rental tenancy with an absentee landlord to

[130] Jacqueline C. Vischer, "Towards a User-Centred Theory of the Built Environment," *Building Research & Information* 36, no.3 (2008): 237.

[131] Ibid.

[132] Ropo et al., "Embodiment of Leadership," (2013), 378.

being one's own landlord had tangible and symbolic significance. Rooted in this deeply emotional shift were other qualities, such as hope, optimism, and opportunity. These powerful traits were not present in the first round of interviews. It is as though the old space drained all the energy from the organization, leaving no room to dream. Mary's account clearly illustrates the transformation that occurred when the organization stepped into its new role:

> The other place was so depressing—honestly, it was falling apart. The ceiling was caving in there. It was just disgusting. You know, we had rats and mice, and it was just uninspiring. And the windows were old and freezing, and it was dirty—the kind of dirt that you could never actually clean very effectively. But now we're the landlords! If something happens, we fix it! Yeah, or we get it fixed. We don't wait for the landlord and that is very freeing. This is ours. So, there is a sense of belonging and ownership. And that also feels like growth, it feels like a new step up for Head & Hands. (Mary)

Moving from a space in which the organization had no authority or freedom to make changes to one where the organization is accountable is empowering. As Mary indicates, there is a feeling of belonging, of ownership and of new opportunities. There is more investment in the space as a resource of the organization. As a side note, I would point out that Mary loved her old office, as illustrated by her comments in the previous section. At the beginning of her interview, she expressed her difficulty feeling at home in the new space, feeling its coldness. Now she speaks about the new building's effect on the organization as a whole, of which she is a member. It is a reminder of the conflicting emotions that are emerging, not just *between* staff members but also within the same individual.

Similar to Mary, Tamira speaks of the possibilities for future growth, for next steps, which the new building offers to Head & Hands. You can feel her sense of pride—almost a surprise for Tamira—at the organization and its new space:

> When you see the office spaces and the big open space, you're like, "*oh wow*. I work here!" And it kind of demonstrates that like we've got our shit

together. The old space didn't really communicate that. It was more scrappy. It's not saying that's a bad thing—I like scrappy. That part of the spirit is like fun to me and why I wanted to work here. So, we've moved away from scrappy to a little more professional/institutional, but I think that it just seems like we kind of like left high school or something. And for returning clients, I think that's the feeling they get. And for new clients, I think it adds like a bunch of … it's like *trust-able* to have that mix of the cool posters and the plants and weird mess with this like really beautiful, really high-end-looking space… . I think it offers a lot of opportunity. I think that the space is so versatile and so malleable that it has endless possibilities within it. (Tamira)

As she spoke, the sound of a baby crying and cooing quietly wafts through the space—a constant reminder of who is creating the space. In Tamira's account, there seems to be a convergence of possibility and potential with pride and strength—all of which radiates from the new office space. Pride is a profound emotional experience that can result in a more meaningful experience of work.[133] It can be the result of a momentary achievement or a more enduring interpersonal (or inter-spatial) relationship. Connecting pride to office space expands an emotion, often tied to feelings of self-achievement to a "cumulative experience" of pride that evolves with the organization.[134] As Head & Hands continues to modify and alter the space based on it and its clients' needs, these feelings of organizational pride may regenerate.

For staff members who were more closely involved in the design process—as staff consultants for the architect—the feeling of investment in the building is even greater. Amara explains her sense of pride:

I have a lot of pride in the building because I literally helped design every nook and cranny of this building. Yeah. It was a massive labour of love and it's not perfect—which irritates me to no end. So, I walk in with a sense of pride and a sense of accomplishment, but also a bit upset because there are things that need to be addressed and various people are involved in address-

[133] Yichen Lu & Virpi Roto, "Design for Pride in the Workplace," *Psychology of Well-Being* 6, no. 6 (2016).

[134] Ibid. 6.

> ing this. But I've worked in a lot of community organizations where it's just like dodgy—where our working conditions were very dodgy—and so when I come in here and it's nice and bright, and open and airy and clean and mold-free and accessible, I have a lot of pride. (Amara)

Not-for-profit organizations often end up in less-than-ideal spaces because they do not have the resources—money, time, and knowledge—required to maintain and potentially renovate a building. There is also sometimes a subtle antagonism towards spaces considered too slick or too corporate. The value of a rundown space is in understanding it as a badge of honour given to those who neglect themselves in the service of those in need. In a first-round interview, Michelle referenced the old building's shabbiness as emblematic of the organization's spirit:

> It's very much a community organization that probably doesn't have a lot of money to re-plaster the walls all the time… . People are really committed to what's going on here… . I think a huge part of that is that there is clearly no money being spent on things that aren't absolutely necessary, and that links to the spirit of wanting to provide the absolute best service for youth and so everything is very functional. (Michelle)

The same resourcefulness and functionality are qualities which Mary reiterated in her first interview. We were speaking about what the space communicates to those who enter. Mary saw the organization's ability to exist in the old office as part of its identity:

> I think it's communicating that we're really trying to make the best of a not great situation. I think we're really communicating that—just with the curtains we put up downstairs and the barriers so people can sit on that side when they're here for the doctor's visits—it says we're really trying to respect confidentiality and warmth, and being kind of informal and yet comfortable. Like we're really trying hard to make it work. You know, that's what I think the big message is. (Mary)

Mary felt pride at making something work, despite difficult conditions. This sentiment was shared by some of the staff, but not all. Geneva lamented how the organization's "quality of service [was] not represented with the quality of space". The not-for-profit "culture of adversity" can become a problem if it leads to poor and unsafe working conditions. Oscar described the unhealthy energy within this culture, calling it "devotion discourse". The term refers to the reward or satisfaction that comes from "doing the work" in marginalized communities, which may be assumed to obviate otherwise normal requirements such as adequate pay, functional office space, or other personal and organizational supports:

> I don't feel like a lot of community orgs have had the chance to have a space that is good-looking, has a lot of light, and is functional. And it's so important! But it's like … people are going to do it anyways and not fight for shit, because they're like, "I'm just lucky that I could do this work. It is so important." Well, I'm just like, "fuck this." I hate this devotion discourse. Like to me, this is my work. Of course, I love my work and am passionate about it and will do everything so that my program is on top of what it can be—and elevate the bar. I'm all about that. But this is my work. I'm not putting my mental health on the line for this, you know? (Oscar)

Part of the work for Head & Hands, as the organization moved into its new building, involved overcoming this culture of sacrifice and claiming the new facility as rightfully theirs. The organization and its work deserved this space and this investment.

In their study "Space, Place and Identity", Nick Hopkins and John Dixon speak of a moment in which something or someone appears "strongly 'out of place'", when "we become aware of the degree to which spatial behaviour is controlled by particular conceptions of place".[135] Head & Hands and other not-for-profit organizations are conditioned to see themselves in spaces of neglect. Something feels wrong about a small, youth-run organization occupying a fancy building. Hopkins and Dixon suggest that this moment is important; the discomfort is revealing, as it "interrogates common sense assumptions",[136] in this case about how these organizations and their work are valued and characterized. Moving into a valued space into which so much had been invested, both by the

[135] Nick Hopkins and John Dixon, "Space, Place, and Identity: Issues for Political Psychology," *Political Psychology* 27, no.2 (2006): 177.
[136] Ibid.

organization and on its behalf, challenged these unhealthy spatial norms. The expressions of pride in the space and its potential for the organization illustrate the power of a supportive, healthy space, even when the future is unknown. In fact, that unknown future is part of the equation. With a space that was both secure and open, Head & Hands felt safe to be in a state of potential and possibility. Mary speaks about occupying and working in this still-unknown place:

> I really believe that it's given the organization a fresh start and the possibility for growth. We don't really know what that means yet, or who we're reaching out to share this space with. We haven't really figured that out yet. But yeah, it's really been inspiring in a lot of ways, a bit overwhelming. I think we still have stuff to work out. But yeah, really inspiring. (Mary)

The organization is in an unknown place. It's scary, but inspiring. Much of the staff's pride and their excitement in the new space was expressed in terms relating to the organization's ability to serve clients—in effect, to being able to do their jobs. With less time and energy being spent on mitigating the old space's many problems, it freed the staff's imagination towards their programmes and services.

Room for Dreams

The last theme of this research is a difference I noticed between staff attitudes in the new building compared to the old. It was the presence of the organization's future. In the first round of interviews, the focus was on functioning—getting the job done despite the office. Sometimes this was described joyously, but it was a state that remained in the past or present. Because it is difficult to illustrate the absence of something from the first round of interviews, I will focus on moments in which staff explain a link between their new premises and the organization's potential. These descriptions illuminate programme innovation and expansion, community development vis-à-vis the space and organizational cohesion.

Asked whether the building helped or hindered the organization, Amara told me about a programme that had been contemplated in the old space yet never took shape, but which was now possible:

> The counselling program had developed this program for recently out-of-care youth through the youth protection system.[137] Because at 18, they age out and then they're just left to themselves, right? It's sort of a preparedness program, you know: how to cook themselves a meal or how to budget, or things like that. And in the new space, we have a functioning kitchen in YPP. And in the evening, it's not being used, so we could actually start that program—you know, where before we would have needed to rent some other place and have to deal with landlords and all the things. Right, so it's neat to see how things could expand. (Amara)

To run this programme in the old space would have required additional logistics, coordination, time, and funding. With the merger of YPP (a daytime programme) into the main office, the two branches of the organization are able to support each other. In the evening, the large, empty kitchen and the group space become resources that the organization can use for other purposes. Although not originally designed for this new youth programme, Amara looks at the space through a lens of possibility and potential. Similarly, she mentioned how the space can support an additional night of services. While she does not describe how this feels (beyond it being "neat"), having confidence that she can grow her programme and be supported in that journey is clearly meaningful to her.

Another programme affected by the space was the Mia's boot programme. While multiple staff mentioned it, Cora draws a direct link between the new building and the capacity of the organization:

> Just being able to have more space has allowed for Mia, who works at the front desk, to have a boot program. Like we were able to do it in the other space, but it was so cramped that it always ended up being a bit of a bother. And now she has her own place to put the boots and be able to do all the things that she wants to do with her program. It's like when we are also able

[137] In Quebec, youth protection services are provided by youth centres located across the province. These centres operate under the governance of the Quebec Ministry of Health and Social Services.

> to have rooms so that other organizations can come and do a workshop or something. So, we're actually able to serve our community and our clients at the same time. So, it's just nice to be able to do that. (Cora)

In her description, the expansiveness of the building mirrors its ability and malleability for evolving services. Cora mentions Mia's boot programme not as a new programme but as one that feels better in the new space. Having the physical space for the boots has transformed how the programme functions and how staff feel about it. Once "a bit of a bother", now it is something to be proud of.

Similarly, being a resource for the wider community is something the new space has made possible for Head & Hands. Being able to host other organizations, or lend the space for additional uses, broadens their role and enhances their mandate as a community organization. While it is indeed "just nice to be able to do that", this shift is big. These new opportunities highlight a collaboration between the new building and the Head & Hands organization as they explore, together, possible avenues that were previously unavailable. Although some of these changes may seem small, they are not insubstantial. Over time, these micro-adaptations could lead to bigger organizational changes.

Having an office space that provides different options for meetings or independent work helps the staff maintain a fresh perspective. If the space is being used for different purposes, then it will feel different as the atmosphere shifts with each group and task. Tamira illustrates how the space can be used in different ways depending on current needs:

> Just having a space that's movable—like sometimes we will have meetings in the staff kitchen because other things are going on and they need privacy. So, it helps us to be more on our toes, you know, and be able to be more adaptable. And I think that that will transfer to the way we approach clients. (Tamira)

This quality of flexibility is directly connected to how the organization might become more adaptable in serving its clients. If the space can shift to support the organization, it may also be adapted for clients' future needs. In a sense, the versatile relationship that is developing with and through the space is providing tangible experience in emergent ways of working. The space becomes *enabling*, as Duff suggests, by positively affecting the staff's interactions and promoting opportunities for an ongoing relationship.[138]

The office's physical structure and amenities, such as the two kitchens and the large meeting/multipurpose space, enable the organization to have more people in the building. Oscar mentions being able to hold his programme training sessions and workshops in-house. In the old office, staff had the additional task of organizing logistics for offsite events, meetings, training, and so on, whereas the new building makes these activities less arduous. Hosting more people and groups in the Head & Hands office transforms the space into more of a central hub, shifting energy *towards* the space rather than away from it. Using the building and office for major events also allows the community to participate in the space.

For the first time, Head & Hands was able to have their annual general meeting (AGM) in their own space instead of at a community centre. As the community elects new board members, celebrates successes, reviews budgets, and discusses future plans, it does so in the organization's space—a fusion of place, community, and possibility. For Mary, hosting the AGM was just the beginning. It meant the organization is in a position to "start being able to dream a little bit more about what we can do". Mary's thinking on room for dreaming was echoed by Cora, who suggested that the work of setting up the building forced the organization to discuss its future in relation to the space:

> Just knowing that our goal is being better reached with this space kind of brings us closer… . It makes us work together to figure out how to grow more… . And if we all feel like the space is serving us in that way, I feel like it affects the way we work, the way we talk to each other, because there's a different feeling. There's something there where it feels like it's adding onto what we are here to do. It's actually serving us and it's helping us serve people better. (Cora)

Cora's account illustrates the tightly woven threads of the office in how the organization functions. Through their engagement and collaboration

---

[138] Cameron Duff, "Exploring the role of "enabling places" in promoting recovery from mental illness: A qualitative test of a relational model," *Health & Place* 18, no. 6 (2012).

with the space, the staff began to work and to *be* in the space differently. When the space is an actively supportive one, there is freedom to explore and take risks. As Cora mentioned, the new space shifted how the staff spoke to one another and worked together while simultaneously situating their next steps as an organization. When evolving practices and modalities are connected to a malleable space, the entwined nature of the material and social is ongoing. It is no longer about the final design, but the *relationship* embedded in the process of creation and destruction.

Conclusion

In this narrative, the two office spaces themselves were characters—not just accompanying the staff in their lived experiences but contributing to them. Elevating the presence of the physical space in the research shifted the emphasis from purely human-centred to more-than-human. Focusing on the evolving relationship of the staff and their office space during a time of immense change provided a unique snapshot of the moving experience. Everyday moments between the staff and the space told a rich picture of their experience, which emerged through nuanced emotions, tacit knowledge, and aesthetic understanding. Meaning and realization are gleaned from the smell of cookies baking, the reshaping of desks, the sorting of historical documents, graffitied walls, echoes, whispers, and light solitudes.

In taking a relational-materialist approach to organizational space an emplaced and evolving story emerged for the Head & Hands organization. This narrative materialized memories and ghosts, embodied displacement, well-being and light, sterile coldness, echoes, transition, and camaraderie, as well as feelings of support, pride, and hope. Intersubjective and sensory accounts form a foundation, adding depth, radiance, and meaning to spatial experience. These stories do not represent the experiences of Head & Hands as a singular unit, lived and shared equally by all staff; rather, they offer glimpses from those who participated into a myriad of possible relationships and ways of being in the organization's two very different spaces.

The future of Head & Hands as an organization shifted when they moved into the new building. Without the stress of working in an unsupportive and deteriorating building, the organization was freed to hope and dream, sharing heretofore hidden talents and exploring opportunities with their new space. While many of these opportunities took time and were not immediately visible, the seeds were already present in the staff's way of experimenting and collaborating with their new space. In emphasizing the reciprocal and evolving nature between Head & Hands and its space(s), new knowledge and insights emerge. Subtle shifts in atmosphere, created by the sounds of kids, the natural light, and the heightened sound, resulted in changes in how staff members felt and behaved in the space. By framing space as an active participant in organizational development and day-to-day experience, a deeper understanding of experience and potential occurred.

References

Argyris, Chris & Donald A Schön. *Organizational learning: A theory of action.* Jossey-Bass, 1978.

Bachelard, Gaston. *The Poetics of Space.* Beacon Press, 1994.

Barrett, Frank J. "Cultivating an Aesthetics of Unfolding." In *The aesthetics of organization.* 228–245. London: Sage, 2000.

Beyes, Timon, and Christian De Cock. "Adorno's Grey, Taussig's Blue: Colour, Organization and Critical Affect." *Organization* 24, no. 1 (2017): 559–78. https://doi.org/10.1177/1350508416668189.

Beyes, Timon, and Chris Steyaert. "Strangely Familiar: The Uncanny and Unsiting Organizational Analysis. *Organization Studies* 34, no.10 (2013): 1445–1465. https://doi.org/10.1177/0170840613495323.

Bille, Mikkel, and Tim Flohr Sorensen. "An Anthropology of Luminosity." *Journal of Material Culture* 12, no. 3 (2007): 263–284. https://doi.org/10.1177/1359183507081894.

Bjørkeng, Kjersti, Stewart Clegg, and Tyrone Pitsis. "Becoming (a) practice." *Management Learning* 40, no. 2 (2009): 145–159. https://doi.org/10.1177/1350507608101226.

Blesser, Barry and Linda-Ruth Salter. *Spaces Speak, are you Listening?* MIT Press, 2007.

Cairns, George. "Aesthetics, Morality and Power: Design as Espoused Freedom and Implicit control." *Human Relations* 55, no.7 (2002): 799–820. https://doi.org/10.1177/0018726702055007541.

Crang, Mike. "Qualitative Methods: Touchy, Feely, Look-See? *Progress in Human Geography* 27, no.4 (2016): 494–504. https://doi.org/10.1191/0309132503ph445pr.

Curtis, Sarah. *Space, Place and Mental health*. Lund Humphries Publishers, 2012.

de Botton, Alain. *The Architecture of Happiness*. McClelland & Stewart, 2006.

de Certeau, Michel, *The Practice of Everyday Life*. University of California Press, 2011.

De Matteis, Federico, Mikkel Bille, Tonino Griffero, and Andrea Jelić. "Phenomenographies: describing the plurality of atmospheric worlds." *Ambiances. Environnement sensible, architecture et espace urbain* 5 (2019): 1–23. https://doi.org/10.4000/ambiances.2526.

De Molli, Federica. "Participatory Interpretation: a way to Overcome Analytical Challenges in Organizational Aesthetic Research." *Culture and Organization* 27, no. 3 (2021): 1–15. https://doi.org/10.1080/14759551.2020.1806839de.

Degnen, Cathrine. "Socialising Place Attachment: Place, Social Memory and Embodied Affordances." *Ageing & Society* 36, no.8 (2015): 1645–1667. https://doi.org/10.1017/S0144686X15000653.

Dowling, Robyn, Kate Lloyd, and Sandie Suchet-Pearson. "Qualitative Methods 1: Enriching the Interview." *Progress in Human Geography* 40, no. 5 (2016a): 679–686. https://doi.org/10.1177/0309132515596880.

Dowling, Robyn, Kate Lloyd, and Sandie Suchet-Pearson. Qualitative methods II: "More-than-human" methodologies and/in praxis. *Progress in Human Geography 41,* no. 6 (2016b): 823–831. https://doi.org/10.1177/0309132516664439.

Dowling, Robyn, Kate Lloyd, and Sandie Suchet-Pearson. Qualitative methods III: Experimenting, picturing, sensing. *Progress in Human Geography* 42, no. 5 (2017): 779–788. https://doi.org/10.1177/0309132517730941.

Duff, Cameron. "Exploring the role of "enabling places" in promoting recovery from mental illness: A qualitative test of a relational model." *Health & Place* 18, no. 6 (2012): 1388–1395. https://doi.org/10.1016/j.healthplace.2012.07.003.

Emery, Marrelyn. *Participative Design for Participative Democracy*. Centre for Continuing Education, Australian National University, 1989.

Gerdenitsch, Cornelia, Christian Korunka, and Guido Hertel. "Need–Supply fit in an Activity-Based Flexible Office: A longitudinal study during relocation." *Environment and Behavior* 50, no. 3 (2018): 273–297. https://doi.org/10.1080/00140139.2016.1188220.

Hall, Edward T. *The Hidden Dimension*. Anchor Books, 1982.

Harb, Francine, Maria Paz Hidalgo, and Betina Martau. "Lack of Exposure to Natural Light in the Workspace is Associated with Physiological, Sleep and Depressive Symptoms." *Chronobiology International* 32, no. 3 (2015): 368–375. https://doi.org/10.3109/07420528.2014.982757.

Havik, Klaske. "TerriStories: Literary Tools for Capturing Atmosphere in Architectural Pedagogy. *Ambiances. Environnement sensible, architecture et espace urbain* 5 (2019): 1–16. https://doi.org/10.4000/ambiances.2787.

Havik, Klaske, and Kristen Van Haeren. "A Story of Three." *Spool* 3, no. 2, (2016): 5–24. https://doi.org/10.7480/spool.2016.2.1137.

Haynes, Kathryn. "Autoethnography." In *The SAGE handbook of qualitative business and management research methods: Methods and challenges*. 17–31. Routledge, 2017. https://doi.org/10.4135/9781526430236.

Holtham, Clive, Victoria Ward, and Charlotte Rosander. "Designing spaces for knowledge work–can the use of fiction help construct new realities?" In *Managing Knowledge, Conversations and Critiques Conference,* Leicester University, Leicester, UK. 2001.

Hopkins, Nick and John Dixon. "Space, Place, and Identity: Issues for Political Psychology." *Political Psychology* 27, no.2 (2006): 173–185. https://www.jstor.org/stable/3792436.

Howes, David, & Constance Classen. *Ways of Sensing*. Routledge, 2014.

Hultman, Karin, and Hillevi Lenz Taguchi, "Challenging Anthropocentric Analysis of Visual Data: A Relational Materialist Methodological Approach to Educational Research," *International Journal of Qualitative Studies in Education* 23 no. 5 (2010): 524–542. https://doi.org/10.1080/09518398.2010.500628.

Jiménez, Alberto Corsin. "On Space as a Capacity." *Journal of the Royal Anthropological Institute* 9 (2003):137–153. https://doi.org/10.1111/1467-9655.t01-1-00008.

Koenig, John. *Dictionary of Obscure Sorrows*. Simon & Shuster, 2021.

Latham, Alan. "Research, Performance, and Doing Human Geography: Some Reflections on the Diary-Photograph, Diary-Interview Method." *Environment and Planning A*, no. 35 (2003): 1993–2017. https://doi.org/10.1068/a3587.

Leder, Drew. *The Absent Body*. University of Chicago Press, 1990.

Linstead, Stephen & Heather Joy Höpfl, eds. *The Aesthetics of Organization*. Sage Publications, 2000.

Louis, Meryl Reis. "Surprise and Sense Making: What Newcomers Experience in Entering Unfamiliar Organizational Settings." *Administrative Science Quarterly* 25, no. 2 (1980): 226–251. https://doi.org/10.2307/2392453.
Lu, Yichen, and Virpi Roto. "Design for Pride in the Workplace." *Psychology of Well-Being* 6, no.1 (2016): 1–18. https://doi.org/10.1186/s13612-016-0041-7.
Mackrodt, Ulrike. "How Atmospheres Inform Urban Planning Practice: Insights From the Tempelhof Airfield in Berlin." *Ambiances* 5 (2019): 1–19. https://doi.org/10.4000/ambiances.2739.
Nast, Heidi, and Steve Pile. *Places Through the Body*. Psychology Press, 1998.
Nijs, Greg, and Amelie Daems. "And What if the Tangible Were Not, and Vice Versa? On Boundary Works in Everyday Mobility Experience of People Moving into Old Age: For Daisy (1909–2011)." Space and Culture 15, no. 3 (2012): 186–197. https://doi.org/10.1177/1206331212445962.
O'Toole, Paddy, and Prisca Were. "Observing Places: Using Space and Material Culture in Qualitative Research." *Qualitative Research* 8, *no.*5 (2008): 616–634. https://doi.org/10.1177/1468794108093899.
Pallasmaa, Juhani. *The Eyes of the Skin.* John Wiley & Sons, 2012.
Petani, Fabio James. "Space and Process: The Organizational Importance of What we Leave Behind." In unpublished doctoral dissertation. Università della Svizzera Italiana, 2016. https://doc.rero.ch/record/278192
Pink, Sarah. "Engaging the Senses in Ethnographic Practice: Implications and advances." *The Senses and Society* 8, no. 3 (2013): 261–267. https://doi.org/10.2752/174589313X13712175020433.
Pink, Sarah. *Doing Sensory Ethnography*. Sage Publications, 2009.
Pringle, Patricia. "Spatial Pleasures." *Space and Culture 8,* no 2 (2005): 141–159. https://doi.org/10.1177/1206331205274786.
Riach, Kathleen, and Samantha Warren. "Smell Organization: Bodies and Corporeal Porosity in Office Work," *Human Relations* 68, no. 5 (2014): 789–809. https://doi.org/10.1177/0018726714545387.
Ropo, Arja, Erika Sauer, and Perttu Salovaara. "Embodiment of Leadership through Material Place." *Leadership* 9, no. 3 (2013): 378–395. https://doi.org/10.1177/1742715013485858.
Schwartz, Barry. *The Paradox of Choice*. Harper Perennial, 2004.
Shortt, Harriet. "Sounds of the Salon: The Auditory Routines of Hairdressers at Work." *International Journal of Work Organisation and Emotion* 5, no. 4 (2013): 342–356. https://doi.org/10.1504/IJWOE.2013.057400.

Shortt, Harriet. "Scarred Objects and Time Marks as Memory Anchors: The significance of scuffs and stains in organizational life." *Human Relations* 74, no. 10 (2021): 1688–1715.

Sternberg, Esther M. *Healing Spaces: The Science of Place and Well-being*. Harvard University Press, 2009.

Stevenson, Andrew. "We Came Here to Remember: Using Participatory Sensory Ethnography to Explore Memory as Emplaced, Embodied Practice." *Qualitative Research in Psychology* 11, no. 4 (2014): 335–349. https://doi.org/10.1080/14780887.2014.908990.

Stewart, Kathleen. *Ordinary Affects*. Duke University Press, 2007.

Strati, Antonio, "Organizations Viewed through the Lens of Aesthetics," *Organization* 3, no. 2 (1996): 209–218. https://doi.org/10.1177/135050849632004.

Strati, Antonio. "Aesthetic Understanding of Work and Organizational Life: Approaches and Research Developments." *Sociology Compass* 4, no.10 (2010): 880–893. https://doi.org/10.1111/j.1751-9020.2010.00323.x.

Sumara, Dennis J., and Rebecca Luce-Kapler. "Action Research as a Writerly Text: Locating Co-Labouring in Collaboration." *Educational Action Research* 1, no.3 (2006): 387–395. https://doi.org/10.1080/0965079930010305.

Taylor, Steven S. "Overcoming Aesthetic Muteness: Researching organizational members' aesthetic experience." *Human Relations* 55, no.7 (2002): 821–840. https://doi.org/10.1177/0018726702055007542.

Thrift, Nigel, and John-David Dewsbury. "Dead Geographies—And how to Make them Live," *Environment and Planning D: Society and Space* 18 no. 4 (2000): 411–432. https://doi.org/10.1068/d1804ed.

Trigg, Dylan, *The Memory of Place*. Ohio University Press, 2012.

Ulrich, Roger S. "View through a window may influence recovery from surgery." *Science* 224, no. 4647 (1984): 420–421. https://doi.org/10.1126/science.6143402.

Ulrich, Roger S. "Effects of Interior Design on Wellness." *Journal of Healthcare Interior Design* 3, no. 1 (1991): 97–109.

Veitch, Jennifer A. "Lighting for High-Quality Workplaces." In *Creating the Productive Workplace*. 206–222. Taylor & Francis, 2006.

Vischer, Jacqueline C. "Towards a User-Centred Theory of the Built Environment." *Building Research & Information 36*, no. 3 (2008): 231–240. https://doi.org/10.1080/09613210801936472.

Vohs, Kathleen D., Joseph P. Redden, and Ryan Rahinel. "Physical order Produces Healthy Choices, Generosity, and Conventionality, whereas Disorder Produces Creativity." *Psychological Science* 24, no. 9 (2013): 1860–1867. https://doi.org/10.1177/0956797613480186.

Warren, Samantha. "Having an Eye for it: Aesthetics, ethnography and the senses." *Journal of Organizational Ethnography* 1, no. 1 (2012): 107–118.

Warren, Samantha. "Photography and Voice in Critical Qualitative Management Research." *Accounting, Auditing Accountability Journal* 18, no.6 (2005): 861–882. https://doi.org/10.1108/09513570510627748

Warren, Samantha. "Photography in Qualitative Organizational Research: Conceptual, Analytical and Ethical Issues in Photo-Elicitation Inspired Methods." In *The SAGE handbook of qualitative business and management research methods: Methods and challenges.* Sage Publications, 2018. https://doi.org/10.4135/9781526430236.

Wilson, Shawn. *Research is Ceremony: Indigenous Research Methods.* Fernwood, 2008.

Yanow, Dvora. "Space Stories." *Journal of Management Inquiry* 7, no. 3 (1998): 215–239. https://doi.org/10.1177/105649269873004.

7

Conclusion

A few weeks ago, I went to my husband's office for a Halloween party. I had never been there before only knowing a couple things about it: namely that it was fancy (aka recently renovated with all the perks: beverage fridge, snack table, breakout rooms, state-of-the-art technology) and that my husband loved working there. When every post-pandemic news headline lamented the absence of workers returning to the office, my husband was nothing short of eager to get back. With most of my experience and research stemming from not-for-profit workplaces, I was curious how a brand new (and costly) office would feel like to work in. I suspected it would feel cold and mechanical, chalk full of the usual shiny surfaces and impenetrable materials. I assumed it would look like offices in design magazines, the ones we are *supposed* to want to work in, but which do not actually feel good.

When we emerged from the elevators on the sixth floor, we stood facing a wall-sized projection of an old black-and-white film. The moving shapes and images immediately set a whimsical tone as we headed into the office. As we walked into one of the main workspaces, dozens of giant folded paper lights suspended from the ceiling, creating an ocean of warmth above us. It was a beautiful hand-crafted element that balanced

K. Messer, *How to Work with Space*, Palgrave Studies in Business, Arts and Humanities,
https://doi.org/10.1007/978-3-031-46541-3_7

the harder edges inherent in rows of computers and screens. Giant windows filled the far wall with long pillowed seating beneath them. The view—the skyline of Montreal—offered an immediate and intimate connection to what was happening outside. Because I was there at night, we could see the glowing windows in far-off buildings and sparks of light from cars moving through the city. I can imagine what it might look like as the sun arches through the sky or as the rain pours down. Windows in offices are essential for providing natural light, but here it felt more like a connection to the outside landscape and the passing of time.

Being able to witness the orange leaves in October, and the snow-covered roof tops in January, as well as the construction of the new high-rise binds us to the landscape. While it is frustrating to be blinded by the sun or unable to see your computer screen, I always feel a little sad when large blinds cover office windows. I remember being devastated to learn that I had to spend endless hours in a windowless classroom—the only opening to outside being a large overhead skylight permanently covered after the university department moved in because students couldn't see the Power Point presentation.

As we continued the office tour, we walked past a breakout room. I noticed that the couches were askew and large pillows on the floor still carried the imprint of whoever sat there last. Dare I say the room was a little messy. A quality rarely found in perfect, often paperless offices. Wall-sized white boards were covered in layers of marker drawings, lines, and writing under and in-between taped-on paper and various colours of sticky notes. The combination of materials, colours, and layout told a story of how the brainstorm emerged and evolved.

We kept walking, and I noticed half empty shelves along the wall. The other half filled with books, trinkets, and other random objects. As we moved through the space, I saw more and more built-in shelves and other nooks designed for employees to fill with books, nick-nacks, art, or plants. It immediately transformed the space into a collective collage that morphed with each additional object. Over time, older items would become physical records—an embodied history of past projects and people who no longer work there. The space, despite being equipped with state-of-the-art technology (including rooms with touchscreen walls) and expensive desks and chairs, managed to retain and encourage interaction.

I'll admit I was surprised. Too often modern technology and materials end up alienating their inhabitants by shutting out the surrounding landscape and obstructing interactive features.

~~Dis~~Entanglement

As natural environments diminish and small community services cannot afford the rent, larger corporate "monoculture threatens not only biological systems, but neighborhoods, culture, and discourse".[1] The dominance of plastic, glass, steel, and concrete in large-scale projects seems to further entrench the separation and apathy many people feel towards the environment. This modern shift in materials ultimately disrupts the sensations that accompany these places and streets. Over time, our embodiment of this environment can lead to what Nadia Seremetakis describes as a "numbing and erasure of sensory realities".[2] We need to acknowledge this decline as a "crucial" moment in our relationship to and perception of, our surroundings.[3] As buildings and streetscapes are constructed devoid of sensation and wonder, the further and lesser our relationships with them become.

To understand some of how this modern monoculture is affecting us, Colin Ellard, an interdisciplinary researcher from Toronto, invited individual participants to record their experiences of the city. The impetus came from the rise of big-box stores, transforming whole city blocks into identical panels of glass and concrete. While walking around the city, users self-assessed their emotional states and "levels of excitement" at particular locations tracked by the phone's software.[4] Ellard also collected information on the participants through wristbands that measured their "skin conductance—a simple but reliable window into a person's level of automatic arousal".[5] The resulting combination of data showed that

[1] Jenny Odell, *How to do Nothing* (Melville House, 2019), 187.

[2] Nadia C. Seremetakis, "The Memory of the Senses", in *The Senses Still* (The University of Chicago Press,1993), 2.

[3] Ibid.

[4] Colin Ellard, *Places of the Heart,* (Bellevue Literary Press, 2015), 109.

[5] Ibid.

participants experienced increased boredom and fatigue in city blocks with large box stores, as compared to a general happiness and sense of ease in blocks with more visual diversity. While this research was conducted on city streets, it is easy to consider how it might apply to interior settings where dull office environments are almost famously accompanied by boredom and fatigue.

As capitalist pursuits of growth and development continue to dominate our definitions of progress, Jenny Odell believes we need to dismantle this unsustainable view of progress. She writes: "dismantling not only messes with what we consider forward and backward—it also requires a kind of Copernican shift of humans away from the center of things".[6] Reorganizing our focus to include more-than-human perspectives creates an alternative way of living and working that could change how we interact with space. When markers of success incorporate a spatial lens, it is harder to ignore the devastation of our natural and local environments. Current proclivities for efficiency in business and research tend to strip away whatever is deemed non-essential; however, in doing so, we have created a paradigm, "swept clean of all manners of relational dross",[7] coated in plastic and void of whimsy.

This description makes it even more important to understand that we and our organizations are shaped by these places. Yet, collectively, we are losing spatial knowledge and connection the further we get from our sensory, aesthetic, emotional ties to the environment. David Abram considers this detachment a by-product of modern production. He writes:

> Our bodily rhythms, our moods, cycles of creativity and stillness, and even our thoughts are readily engaged and influenced by shifting patterns in the land. Yet our organic attunement to the local earth is thwarted by our ever increasing intercourse with our own signs. Transfixed by our technologies, we short-circuit the sensorial reciprocity between our breathing bodies and the bodily terrain. Human awareness folds in upon itself, and the senses—once crucial site of our engagement with the wild and animate earth—

[6] Odell, *How to do Nothing* (2019), 192.

[7] Nicolas Bourriaud, *Relational Aesthetics,* trans. Simon Pleasance & Fronza Woods (Les presses due réel, 2002), 16.

> become mere adjuncts of an isolate and abstract mind bent on overcoming an organic reality that now seems disturbingly aloof and arbitrary.

The more time we spend perceiving through filtered screens, algorithms of productivity, plastic and concrete, the further away we get from our body's sensory and aesthetic perception. While technological advancements offer a wealth of data through wearable devices and computer monitoring programmes, the quality and usefulness of the results require a more cooperative approach. One question that is important to consider is: How are these tools altering our relationship to ourselves and the environment? Do they enhance our ability to understand our sensory impression, as Lupton and Maslen[8] found with certain instances of self-monitoring, or do they alienate our minds and bodies by overriding intuitive processes with automated feedback and corrective measures, as was found with some employee tracking software?

If a landscape is impenetrable, if it resists and rejects interaction, or, as Abram states, is "aloof and arbitrary", it becomes difficult to find ourselves in it. This can take the form of modern glass buildings, indifferent design, inaccessible spaces, or in an office bound by unmovable, untouchable decor. These spaces are dead spaces. They are covered in "dust" or as though "devoured by overgrown weeds or abandoned" by residents.[9] Nadia Seremetakis describes this lifeless condition as a loss to "otherness" wherein there is a "relation between the accumulation of dust and the displacement of memory".[10] While I think potential is begging to be uncovered in an overgrown garden or a forgotten dusty attic, what Seremetakis is describing are spaces unable to foster relationships. She contrasts dead spaces to ones that act as a "storage site of sensory memory".[11] Here the layers of happenings and interaction are bonded and embedded within the atmospheres, textures, and sensuousness of the room. While not all offices can be blanketed with history, the conditions for interactive relationships can be built in—as was the case at my

[8] Debora Lupton and Sarah Maslen, "The More-Than-Human Sensorium: Sensory Engagements with Digital-Self Tracking Technologies", *The Senses and Society* 13, no. 2 (2018): 190.

[9] Nadia Seremetakis, "The Memory of the Senses", *Visual Anthropology Review* (1993): 12.

[10] Ibid.

[11] Ibid.

husband's office with the unfinished wall shelves. These qualities create the foundation for continued interaction and adaptation that invite the material world into the conversation.

Environments that ignite and stimulate our senses and that provoke curiosity and wonder offer greater engagement and interaction. When rooms flood (or even just tickle) our imagination, there is a sense of potential and possibility. These qualities can be found in artistic installations that are experienced only briefly, or a ramshackle café haphazardly discovered in a small town. They are not completed and aloof in their design; rather, they rouse and respond through their shifting presence. They are collaborative and co-created by the social and material, by the subject and object.

Seeing space as an active participant in an organization fosters a relational and emplaced approach to work that gives organizations, workers, and researchers' greater agency to engage with it—whether it be a dining room table, a community hot desk, or traditional office. When the physical world is seen with greater respect, consideration, and influence, something shifts between organizations and offices. Emphasizing the relationship—the stuff in-between—we get a different picture than when space is valued as an end result or finished design. Seeing space as an unknown part of us makes room for possibilities and emplaced ways of understanding. Atmosphere itself is a repository of "stories yet to be spoken, of ghosts and spirited intelligences—a kind of collective field of meaning from whence individual awareness continually emerged and into which it continually receded, with every inbreath and outbreath".[12] This living dynamic weaves our surroundings into us and winds ourselves into it.

Collective Space

In the Introduction, I spoke about Santropol Roulant, a meals-on-wheels organization that fundraised, designed, and renovated a new space for their office. What struck me at the time about the new space was its influence on the organizations' immediate and long-term evolution.

[12] David Abram, *The spell of the sensuous* (Vintage Books, 1996), 254.

Opportunities related to the space provided new possibilities that would never have been imaginable in the old space. As the organization settled into their new environment, it was like they discovered themselves within the walls. While some of the developments had been realized in the planning and design of the building, such as the ability to grow a rooftop garden, other changes happened more iteratively. Had the majority of employees been working from home during this time, it is hard to say what the impact on the organizational trajectory would have been. Would the space and its potential have been discovered and utilized in the same way? Probably not.

While hybrid and flexible work arrangements are a progressive development for organizations and workers, had employees been working from home, these unknown possibilities may not have been unearthed, individually or collectively. In her work on the attention economy, Jenny Odell speaks to the power of collective attention as she describes visiting the Calabazas creek with a friend:

> It would not have been the same if I had gone to the Calabazas creek alone. The moment that Josh and I combined the fragments of our memories into the same body of water, the creek came not just to individual attention but to collective attention. It became part of a shared reality, a reference point outside each of us. .... Realities are, after all, inhabitable. If we can render a new reality together —with attention—perhaps we can meet each other there.[13]

Odell reveals how a body of water holds their memories together. She signifies the power in collective experience to co-create meaningful places. This is particularly important for organizations as they consider the value and role of the material in day-to-day work and as a shared entity. Being present and interacting alongside co-workers does not require mandatory full-time office work, but *enough* to create and maintain a common experience of the organizational space and each other. There is no point in an employee coming into the office if they are going to be stuck on zoom with their off-site co-workers all day.

---

[13] Odell, *How to do Nothing* (2019), 126.

As space acts upon those who work within it, and vice versa, it creates an informal collaboration that is alive, iterative, and meaningful. It transforms a building from an object that is to something that "acts, … where the shapes and forms being developed [are] constantly tested in their relationality to human use, human scale, and human sensation".[14] Because buildings evolve, their shifting atmospheres and structure continue to impress upon our bodies, our behaviour, our moods, and our abilities. This means that an organization is always in a state of forming at an individual and a collective level. Atmospheres are unique in their ability to appear and transform.[15] They are "taken up and reworked in lived experience – becoming part of feelings and emotions that may themselves become elements within other atmsopheres".[16] In this sense, they may be perceived individually, but belong to the collective.

Shifting the way space is valued and experienced activates it. Making decisions about "colour, materials, and lighting are ways to develop a sense of openness or distance, shaping moods" rather than style.[17] When qualities such as how a space looks, feels, and functions become rooted in values and connection, they are inherently integrated in the organizational structure and culture. After my mum renovated her kitchen, the use of light, materials, and location highlighted her power. The redesign was intended to create an atmosphere of pride, pleasure, and support by enabling her to function with ease and beauty at home. Ultimately, the transformation of the space transformed my mum. Not only from her perspective, but from ours and others as well. Seeing my mum work in and with the space changed how we saw and interacted with her. The kitchen became the central force of the house; how we moved through the house changed, but, more importantly, how we related to each other and kitchen labour changed. Rather than see it as something to be tucked away behind a door, cooking, baking, and eating, was celebrated in our family. This started as a personal project for my parents, but it is

---

[14] Lydia Jørgensen and Robin Holt, "Organization, Atmosphere, and Digital Technologies: Designing Sensory order. *Organization* 26, no.5 (2019): 19.

[15] Anderson, "Affective Atmospheres", *Emotion, Space and Society* 2, no.2 (2009): 79.

[16] Ibid.

[17] Jørgensen and Holt, "Organization, Atmosphere", (2019): 14.

experienced collectively by everyone who enters the house. We saw a similar transformation at Head & Hands with the boot programme, which was a nuisance in the old space but something to be proud of in the new space. While this was a minor detail in the overall narrative of Head & Hands, it emphasizes the impact that appropriate and supportive space can have on the potential of staff and their programmes to succeed. The same can be said for offices and other work environments. Wherever employees are working, it is important to understand how these spaces are actively contributing to their work and well-being at an individual and a collective level.

The Culture of Space

As organizations wanting to connect with their space and researchers of organizations, the work becomes one of attuning—a deepening of aesthetic and sensory perception. We should see sensuous and affective details as moments of potential bound within tangible and intangible qualities between us, others, and our space. Charged moments push and pull at our movements, emotions, and connections as life unfolds. Kathleen Stewart describes the network of affective situations connected to these sparks:

> The chance event might add a layer of conflict or daydream to things. It might unearth old resentments, or set off a search for lessons learned. It might pull the senses into alignment with simple choices or polemics: good luck and bad, laws and liberties, wild rides and common sense. But for now, at least, and in some small way in the future, too, the talk will secretly draw its force from the event itself resonating in bodies, scenes, and forms of sociality.[18]

Stewart insightfully illuminates the connections that exist between layers of affective resonance as they run through our interactions, be they a chance event or a common occurrence. How we perceive the world is

[18] Kathleen Stewart, *Ordinary Affects* (Duke University Press, 2007), 12.

fluid and relational. It is a constant collaboration between us, others, and the environment. Time, of course, is another significant element that contributes to how the world unfurls around us. It is scratched into the wood, embedded into flavours and scents, and woven by hands into fabric and surrounds the forgotten apple core left on the desk. Objects come alive as their threads are pulled into the present moment by memories and sensations. Tuning in to these echoes deepens and enhances our connection by bringing meaning and past lives into the collaboration of the present, which creates a rich collection of influences. Engaging with the material world offers us parts of ourselves and our organizations.

At Head & Hands, the space was entangled with the organization. Their experience and evolution took place at a social level and at a material level. Moving into a new space provided a unique moment to zoom in and reflect on how the staff's spatial relationships—everything from how they interacted and experienced the space to how the space smelled, sounded, and was remembered—evolved over time. These snapshots and fragments cannot tell the whole story, nor can they provide us with a current portrait of the organization. Instead, they highlight the in-between forces and presences that existed for the staff and organization as they interacted and co-created with each other.

We learned that Head & Hands has a culture in which space is malleable, where staff could decorate, arrange, and reshape the physical structures that aided them in their work and how this altered outcomes. We heard how the sounds of the new office overwhelmed the space, originally designed as a church, so much so that staff modified their voices and played music to preserve the organization's values of privacy and confidentiality. We witnessed the disgust and gloom of the old downstairs office—how the smells, noise, and colours seeped into an atmosphere that plagued the staff working there. We experienced memories that had become fused with physical objects and building structure, thus blending the past with the present. We felt the warmth of light as it beamed into the new space providing energy and support to the staff.

We felt and observed all of this—in our bodies, with our spaces, from our memories, and during our work. With a focus on a relational materiality, the emphasis is no longer on the object or the person as separate, but on their sensuous, affective, and entangled relationship, each co-existing in an influential, permeable, and ephemeral dance. To neglect either removes a dancer from the story.

During my own exploration, what I've called my auto-~~ethnography-~~attunement, I actively engaged with my surroundings in an attempt to deepen my connection and ability to notice, listen, feel, hear, smell, and sense my physical space. I regularly touched things in my space, moved them around, and interacted with them. I spent time feeling and sensing the details and energy that surfaced around me. I watched light and shadows flicker and dance along the floors, walls, and objects, taking pleasure in watching their shapes morph before disappearing. I described abstract drawings in words to consider how words themselves act upon space. I danced in a white cotton nightie and listened to the sound of fire crackling (on the TV) to observe changes in how I perceived myself and the space.

All these experiments were personal, embodied, and spatial. They made the theories of space tangible and part of my daily routine while providing insight into the staff's accounts of their office. At times, this mode of attention that I inhabited seemed like doing "nothing at all".[19] But for this exploration, it was some of the "most substantive work" I did.[20] It required letting go of expectations I had around productivity and giving myself permission to attend my spatial relationships. In her graduate address to Harvard's School of Design, Jenny Odell asks: "what could be more productive than giving someone greater access to their own experience, to a world that is richer and makes more sense—and therefore a world in which they have greater agency?"[21] I believe this question illuminates why I have shared so many stories and fragments of spatial relationships. Attending or attuning ourselves to our spaces requires that we slow down and take notice of what surrounds us. The result is a greater sensation, a fuller perception—that includes a more-than-human focus—and a more collaborative way of being.

Hopefully, reading this book has been an exercise in spatial attunement. For me, it has been an emotional awakening to a world previously

---

[19] Odell, *How to do Nothing* (2020), 23.

[20] Ibid.

[21] Ibid.

less present. Being open to and invested in my surroundings ignited a tsunami of previously invisible moments that cascaded into my body as pulses of light, scents, sounds, flavours, and textures. It has caused me to constantly question my ability to sense and feel the environment. Can I learn how to listen, feel, see, smell, and taste more deeply? If we shift ourselves, our organizations, and our research to a more sensuous, aesthetic, and emplaced position, will that begin to affect our relationships?

For organizations, attending to spatial (material and atmospheric) requirements alongside social ones situates and expands our awareness of what is at play and what is possible. Framing work in this way enhances understanding of how ordinary encounters and large-scale change unfold in organizations. It is not about decoding symbolic objects or analysing design but seeing space in action as a participant in the work.

References

Abram, David, *The Spell of the Sensuous.* New York: Vintage Books, 1996.

Anderson, Ben. "Affective Atmospheres," *Emotion, Space and Society* 2, no.2 (2009): 77–81.

Bourriaud, Nicolas. *Relational Aesthetics.* Translated by Simon Pleasance & Fronza Woods. Les presses due réel, 2002.

Ellard, Colin. *Places of the Heart.* Bellevue Literary Press, 2015.

Jørgensen, Lydia and Robin Holt. "Organization, Atmosphere, and Digital Technologies: Designing Sensory order. *Organization* 26, no.5 (2019): 673–695.

Lupton, Debora, and Sarah Maslen. "The More-Than-Human Sensorium: Sensory Engagements with Digital-Self Tracking Technologies," *The Senses and Society* 13, no. 2 (2018): 190–202.

Odell, Jenny. *How to do Nothing.* Melville House, 2019.

Seremetakis, Nadia C. "The Memory of the Senses." In *The Senses Still.* 1–18. The University of Chicago Press, 1993.

Stewart, Kathleen. *Ordinary Affects.* Duke University Press, 2007.

Index[1]

[1] Note: Page numbers followed by 'n' refer to notes.

K. Messer, *How to Work with Space*, Palgrave Studies in Business, Arts and Humanities,
https://doi.org/10.1007/978-3-031-46541-3

Printed by Printforce, the Netherlands